OXFORD CONSTITUTIONAL THEORY

Series Editors:
Martin Loughlin, John P. McCormick, and Neil Walker

The Constitutional State

OXFORD CONSTITUTIONAL THEORY

Series Editors:

Martin Loughlin, John P. McCormick, and Neil Walker

One consequence of the increase in interest in constitutions and constitutional law in recent years is a growing innovative literature in constitutional theory. The aim of *Oxford Constitutional Theory* is to provide a showcase for the best of these theoretical reflections and a forum for further innovation in the field.

The new series will seek to establish itself as the primary point of reference for scholarly work in the subject by commissioning different types of study. The majority of the works published in the series will be monographs that advance new understandings of the subject. Well-conceived edited collections that bring a variety of perspectives and disciplinary approaches to bear on specific themes in constitutional thought will also be included. Further, in recognition of the fact that there is a great deal of pioneering literature originally written in languages other than English and with regard to non-anglophone constitutional traditions, the series will also seek to publish English language translations of leading monographs in constitutional theory.

The Constitutional State

N. W. Barber

OXFORD
UNIVERSITY PRESS

OXFORD
UNIVERSITY PRESS

Great Clarendon Street, Oxford OX2 6DP

Oxford University Press is a department of the University of Oxford.
It furthers the University's objective of excellence in research, scholarship,
and education by publishing worldwide in

Oxford New York

Auckland Cape Town Dar es Salaam Hong Kong Karachi
Kuala Lumpur Madrid Melbourne Mexico City Nairobi
New Delhi Shanghai Taipei Toronto

With offices in

Argentina Austria Brazil Chile Czech Republic France Greece
Guatemala Hungary Italy Japan Poland Portugal Singapore
South Korea Switzerland Thailand Turkey Ukraine Vietnam

Oxford is a registered trade mark of Oxford University Press
in the UK and in certain other countries

Published in the United States
by Oxford University Press Inc., New York

British Library Cataloguing in Publication Data

Data available

Library of Congress Cataloging in Publication Data

Barber, N. W. (Nicholas William)
The constitutional state / N. W. Barber
p. cm.—(Oxford constitutional theory)
Includes bibliographical references and index
ISBN 978-0-19-958501-4 (hardback)
1. State, The.   2. Constitutional law—Philosophy.   3. Social groups.   I. Title.
K3169.B3644 2010
342.001—dc22   2010038620

Typeset by SPI Publisher Services, Pondicherry, India
Printed in Great Britain
on acid-free paper by
CPI Antony Rowe, Chippenham, Wiltshire

ISBN 978-0-19-958501-4

1 3 5 7 9 10 8 6 4 2

This book is dedicated to Jackie, along with my love.

Contents

Acknowledgments

Two of the chapters of this book are revised versions of papers published before. Chapter 9 was previously published as 'Legal Pluralism and the European Union' in the *European Law Journal* and chapter 6 first appeared as 'Laws and Constitutional Conventions' in the *Law Quarterly Review*. Parts of 'The Constitution, The State and the European Union', first published in the *Cambridge Yearbook of European Studies*, are scattered throughout the book. I am grateful to the editors of these volumes for their help with these papers.

A great many people have helped me write this book. Tom Adams, Trevor Allan, Richard Ekins, Jackie Fernholz, Les Green, Adam Tomkins and Alison Young read and commented on all, or almost all, of the chapters. John Bell, Vernon Bogdanor, Rachael Carrick, Timothy Endicott, John Gardner, Joseph Jaconelli, Nico Krisch Janet McLean, Dawn Oliver, Peter Oliver, John Stanton-Ife, Maris Köpcke Tinturé, and Paul Yowell also critiqued parts of the book. I am very grateful to all of them for their help, and apologize for failing to answer all of the doubts they raised.

Nick Barber
JULY 2010

Introduction

Humans are social animals. Even if it is physically possible to live a life in complete isolation, it is certainly not possible to lead a fulfilled and happy life alone. It is natural for us to gather together in groups both in order to undertake activities that we cannot undertake alone and to experience the emotional support that group membership can bring. Balancing, or conflicting with, this need is our need for individuality, for autonomy; just as we are driven to create groups, so too we are driven to distinguish ourselves from others, to want to show ourselves to be unique. This tension between communality and individuality demands the existence of rules: devices which serve to constrain our individualism to allow the existence of groups, but which, in addition, constrain the claims of groups in order to preserve a degree of personal autonomy.

Social groups come in many forms and many sizes: families, villages, companies, and trade unions are all different and distinctive types of social group. One of the most important collections of social groups in modern society—and the type this book will seek to illuminate—is the state. The state is one of the most significant, and perhaps most characteristic, social institutions of the modern world. Practically every person on the planet is, whether they like it or not, a member of a state, and this membership is often a crucial part of their identity and life. Though some have challenged the importance of the state—arguing that its tasks have been superseded by international organizations or that its powers have devolved to smaller social groups—for most of us the state remains the most powerful political entity with which we interact. Our relationship with international bodies is mediated through it, and our membership of other social groups is regulated, and partly constituted, by it. Indeed, even if the state were to wither away, the political entities which replaced it would need, in part, to be understood through the language and concepts that have emerged from the state tradition: citizenship, constitutions, claims of authority, the complex interplay between legal and non-legal rules, and much else besides, would all resurface in some form in these new polities. This book aims to explain and illuminate these constitutional phenomena and the relations amongst them. By so doing, it aims to cast light on the social institution of the state, and to provide a theory of the relations between states and their members.

In writing this book I have approached constitutional theory as a subject that spans the social sciences. In chapter 1, the book begins by reflecting on the methodology of constitutional theory. Constitutional theory—and legal theory too, for that matter—are aspects of the social sciences: the methodology of these disciplines must cohere with the methodology of the social sciences more generally. And it is not only the methodology of constitutional theory that must be understood within a broader context: its subject matter also necessitates engagement with different traditions and different parts of the social sciences. Underpinning this book is the belief that a satisfying account of social institutions such as the state, citizenship, and, indeed, the law, cannot be provided from a narrow legal perspective. In the chapters that follow I frequently draw attention to the hazards of legalistic accounts of such institutions; these accounts are sometimes more misleading than illuminating. Philosophy, social psychology and political science, amongst other disciplines, must be drawn upon to help us understand what is important about these entities. If the book contains an intellectual manifesto, it is this: a commitment to the value of, and need for, interdisciplinary study. Such engagement—though risky—is crucial for the development of both constitutional and legal theory.

At the centre of this book is the state. Chapter 2 begins the project by outlining the nature of the state. The state is presented as a form of social group, consisting of institutions, people, and the territory that they inhabit, all bound together by rules. Two approaches—or sets of approaches—to the state are canvassed. On the one hand, there are those who find the characteristic, defining, feature of the state in the special type of authority claim that it makes over its people. On the other hand, there are those who draw attention to the special type of relationship that members of the state have with the institutions of the state and with other state-members. It is argued that each of these approaches identifies something important about the state, and each is required for the development of a satisfying account of that institution. Having contended that the connection between people and states is central to our understanding of the state, chapter 3 then turns to consider this relationship in more detail. It argues that the paradigmatic form of state membership is citizenship. It is only by instantiating its members as citizens that the state can fully achieve its primary purpose: that is, the advancement of its members' wellbeing. Chapter 3 discusses the nature and implications of citizenship, a discussion to which the book returns in chapters 7 and 8, when the actions and responsibilities of the state, and its citizens, are considered.

As a social group, the state is constituted by rules. Constitutional entities within the state—its institutions, such as legislatures and courts, and its offices, such as those of the judge and the citizen—are also created and shaped by rules. Some of these rules are legal, some are not—and some, it will be cautiously argued, fall between the two. Chapter 4 begins this task by considering the nature of rules and the role they play in the construction of social groups. Chapter 5 then applies this approach to the state: seeking to identify the content of the constitutions of states. Chapter 6 examines the relationship between two collections of constitutional rules—constitutional law and constitutional conventions—and argues that the distinction between these two is less sharp than is often supposed.

Having developed accounts of the state and of the citizen, and having shown how rules serve to constitute these entities, the book turns to consider the actions and character of the state, and the implications these have for the state's members and officers. Chapter 7 develops an account of the capacity of states to undertake actions and form intentions, an account which rests on the discussion of the constitution of states undertaken in previous chapters. This gives flesh to the model of the state advanced in chapter 2, showing how states can develop distinctive characters—for better or for worse. Chapter 8 explains why we should care about these attributions. It considers the capacity of the state to bear responsibility for events, and—more importantly, perhaps—how that responsibility relates back to, and conditions, citizenship and other offices of the state.

The final two chapters use the conundrums presented by the European Union to illustrate some of the possible ambiguities around the model of the state provided in the book. Chapter 9 provides an account of legal pluralism, a phenomenon that commonly—though not invariably—arises as a result of a disagreement about the constitutional ordering within the state or a disagreement over the existence of a state. In chapter 10, legal pluralism is distinguished from constitutional pluralism. Constitutional pluralism arises where there is an overlap of states. It is argued that legal pluralism is a feature of some of the legal orders of the European Union, and constitutional pluralism may—in the future—come to characterize the Union's relationship with its Member States. The discussion of the ambiguous statehood of the European Union demonstrates the value of careful reflection on the types of authority claim characteristically made by the state: the degree to which the European Union resembles a state depends on which account of the authority claims of the state we adopt.

Many of the examples in the book are drawn from the British constitution and—especially in the final sections of the book—from the constitutional structures of the European Union. Some Commonwealth jurisprudence is also discussed, in particular that of Canada and Australia. The book is not, however, an exercise in comparative constitutional law, nor a study of particular constitutions. The arguments it makes should be true of all states and all constitutions; hopefully readers will be able to supplement the examples given with instances from their own experiences. A further, significant, limitation of the book is that it does not provide an explanation of constitutionalism; that is, the principles that should guide those creating and shaping the state. It does aspire to provide the starting point for such an account: any plausible account of constitutionalism must rely on an account of the nature of the state. I hope in future work to show that the model of the state advanced here provides a firm base on which a theory of constitutionalism can be built.

1

The Paths of Constitutional Theory

Constitutional theory suffers from an identity crisis. The subject is taught in universities, enjoys the attention of many academics and has a history that can be traced back hundreds, even thousands, of years, and yet its point and method remain obscure. Most disciplines have aims that can be encapsulated in a handful of words: physics seeks to identify the rules which structure and govern the universe; medical science seeks to illuminate the causes of illness and restore sufferers to health; sociology seeks to explain the functioning of society. There may be disputes about these goals, but they are, normally, sufficiently clear and uncontested to allow practitioners to launch into research without further reflection. Grand debates about the significance of these disciplines are, as was once said in another context, a little like dusty board games brought out of a cupboard on a rainy afternoon.[1] They are entertaining enough but, after a few rounds, the players go back to the serious work they were engaged with before the game commenced. Constitutional theory is different. There is no consensus about what constitutional theory is for or how it should be done; and, as a consequence of this, no agreement about what a good argument within the discipline would look like. Without some sense of what counts as a successful exercise in constitutional theory, a set of criteria against which accounts can be tested, we cannot judge the merits of any particular piece of work. The problem is exacerbated by the barely concealed belief of some constitutional theorists that they have identified the unique path of constitutional theory and those working outside of their school are fundamentally mistaken. Historically-minded constitutional theorists tend to think that critical constitutional theorists are engaged in political agitation. Critical constitutional theorists tend to think that interpretive constitutional theorists are apologists for the existing order. Interpretive constitutional theorists tend to think that political science-oriented constitutional scholars can do little more than helpfully gather in the facts that are to be the subject matter of their interpretation. And so it goes, with each group doubting the value of the others, and each secretly believing that, really, only they are engaged in constitutional theory.

The contention of this chapter is cheerfully ecumenical. There are many different ways of doing constitutional theory: all are valuable, all are compatible, and all play

---

[1] The allusion is to R. Dworkin, 'Model of Rules 1' in R. Dworkin, *Taking Rights Seriously* (London: Duckworth, 1978), 14.

a part in our understanding of the nature and functioning of constitutions. The purpose of this paper is to outline the methodology of interpretive constitutional theory and to locate it amongst other approaches within the discipline. It will be argued that interpretive constitutional theory is prior to these other approaches—in that other approaches presuppose, more or less knowingly, an interpretive account of the phenomena they study—but it does not follow from this priority that interpretive constitutional theory is more sophisticated than other types of explanation, nor more important, nor even that it can be conducted without assistance from other branches of the discipline.

THE PRIORITY OF INTERPRETIVE CONSTITUTIONAL THEORY

There are various apparent rivals to interpretive constitutional theory. This section will focus on one group of explanations, historical explanations, though the argument could equally well be applied to other schools of thought. Historical accounts seek to illuminate constitutional institutions by exploring their origins. A great deal of work has been undertaken which seeks to identify the causes of constitutional institutions, whether these be the causes of their creation or the causes of their flourishing. Perhaps the boldest example is to be found in the work of Walter Bagehot, who, inspired by Darwin, elegantly played with the notion that evolution might explain the emergence of the state and government.[2] Bagehot's tale mixed history, cod-anthropology and a fair sprinkle of speculation, before concluding that the British system of government was the natural winner of history's battles. In warfare, he contended, it is the better organized polity that wins; others either copy its structures or are conquered by it.[3] Thus, 'natural selection' favours some forms of group organization over others. The broad lines of Bagehot's case can still be seen in contemporary accounts of the emergence of the state. Modern anthropologists now place greater weight on the competition between groups within society, fighting for control of scarce resources such as land and water. Once a group has secured these resources, it then creates the structures which develop into the state in order to protect its social position.[4] In contrast to Bagehot's almost Hobbesian account,[5] the state does not emerge to protect its people from external threat but rather is created to protect an elite group from external and internal challenge.

---

[2] W. Bagehot, *Physics and Politics* (2nd edn, London: Henry S. King, 1872); see also H. Spencer, *Principles of Sociology* (London: Williams and Norgate, 1898). For an introduction to contemporary accounts of the emergence of cooperative behaviour, see M. Ridley, *The Origins of Virtue* (London: Penguin, 1996).

[3] Bagehot, note 2 above, 39–48.

[4] M. H. Fried, 'The State, The Chicken, and the Egg; or, What Came First?' in R. Cohen and E. R. Service, *Origins of the State: The Anthropology of Political Evolution* (Philadelphia: Institute for the Study of Human Issues, 1978).

[5] T. Hobbes, *Leviathan*, ed R. Tuck (Cambridge: Cambridge University Press, 1991), ch 17.

These attempted explanations of the origins of constitutional institutions will prove attractive to many working within the social sciences. Historical explanations fall within a style of research energetically defended by a sizeable group of philosophers of social science, a group commonly labelled 'naturalists'.[6] In brief, naturalists argue that social scientists should adopt those methodologies and research agendas which have proved successful in the natural sciences. This leads naturalists to seek to identify the origins of social institutions, just as natural scientists seek to illuminate aspects of nature by tracing the causes of an event; a successful explanation of a social institution is one which shows how it has come to be as it is. And, in addition, some naturalists claim that a good theory of an institution would produce predictions of its development with which it is possible to check the correctness of the causal connections posited. Such accounts would then be open to similar tests of verification and falsification thought to be characteristic of the natural sciences.[7]

The claims made by Bagehot and contemporary anthropologists may be mistaken but they are of the right type—at least according to the naturalists. Their claims are, in principle, subject to falsification. For instance, if it is asserted that the state was developed to protect pre-existing social inequalities, this claim might, one day, be proved or disproved. Perhaps historical evidence will be discovered that shows social stratification to be the consequence of, rather than the cause of, the emergence of the state.[8] If so, the state cannot have been created to protect a pre-existing stratification, and the claims of one group of anthropologists will have been demonstrated to be wrong. Of course, the complexities of history and the vagaries of human nature entail that these disputes may be irresolvable: it is hard to see how the factual claims they make, or the causal connections they assert, could be definitively proved or tested. But, for the naturalist, they at least take the right form, they are explanations which seek to show why the state is as it is, and, which may perhaps point towards what the state may become.

The approach advocated by naturalists towards the social sciences has not gone unchallenged. Perhaps most notably, Charles Taylor has argued that social science must adopt a radically different methodology to that found in the natural sciences if we are to gain an understanding of social institutions. The task of social science, claims Taylor, is interpretive: it aims to bring to light the sense

---

[6] D. Braybrooke, *Philosophy of Social Science* (New Jersey: Prentice Hall, 1987), ch 2. On naturalism in legal philosophy, see B. Leiter, 'Naturalism and Naturalized Jurisprudence' in B. Bix, *Analyzing Law: New Essays in Legal Theory* (Oxford: Oxford Univerisity Press, 1998). See also B. Bix, 'H. L. A. Hart and the Hermeneutic Turn' (1999) 52 SMU L Rev 167, 169–170.

[7] See the discussion in K. Popper, *The Poverty of Historicism* (2nd edn, London: Routledge, 1960), 122–4; C. G. Hempel, *Philosophy of Natural Science* (New Jersey: Prentice Hall, 1966), ch 2.

[8] E. R. Service, 'Classical and Modern Theories of the Origins of Government' in R. Cohen and E. R. Service, *Origins of the State: The Anthropology of Political Evolution* (Philadelphia: Institute for the Study of Human Issues, 1978); G. M. Thomas and J. W. Meyer, 'The Expansion of the State' (1984) 10 Annual Review of Sociology 461, 463–5.

and significance of social phenomena.[9] A good interpretation of a phenomenon is one which illuminates its important features, explaining the part it plays within the life of a community. Those who argue that interpretation is not necessary, that the social scientist should confine herself to reporting factually verifiable 'brute data', are deluding themselves.[10] Even the most apparently straight-forward studies, like simple reports of voting practices, require interpretation.[11] To understand what constitutes a 'vote' we need to ascribe significance to the actions studied, locating them within a broader mesh of institutional rules. Our interpretations may be uncontroversial, but they are interpretations none the less: showing the practice to have meaning, ascribing a unity to it, and drawing out its significance.

At first glance Taylor's work appears to stand in direct opposition to the historical accounts of constitutional institutions we discussed earlier.[12] But Taylor's insistence on the priority of interpretive accounts of constitutional institutions need not exclude such accounts from constitutional theory; his claim is better understood as the more limited assertion that interpretive accounts must, necessarily, precede historical accounts.[13] The point is nicely illustrated by some of the difficulties surrounding questions about the origins of the state. Part of this debate is concerned with the connection between a purported cause and an effect—whether a given factor oper-ated, and, if so, what its consequences were—but occasionally the debate turns on a prior question, that of the nature of the state. The birth of the state has, variously, been traced as far back as recorded history,[14] ascribed confidently to the thirteenth century,[15] and categorized as a distinctive feature of the post-Renaissance age.[16] A debate between these historians as to whether the origins of the state lay in the

---

[9] C. Taylor, 'Interpretation and the Sciences of Man' in C. Taylor, *Philosophy and the Human Sciences: Philosophical Papers Vol 2* (Cambridge: Cambridge University Press, 1985). In addition to Charles Taylor, the methodological framework provided in this chapter draws heavily on the work of John Finnis, but, for reasons explained later, differs from Finnis in some significant respects.

[10] Taylor, note 9 above, 19.

[11] *Ibid*, 28–32; Braybrooke, note 6 above, 57–9.

[12] M. Martin, 'Taylor on Interpretation and the Sciences of Man' in M. Martin and L. McIntyre, *Readings in the Philosophy of Social Science* (London: MIT Press, 1994).

[13] Though a developed interpretive account will, eventually, also be partly shaped by the historical. See J. Finnis, 'Law and What I Truly Should Decide' (2003) 48 Am J Jurisprudence 108, 121.

[14] S. E. Finer, *The History of Government Volume 1: Ancient Monarchies and Empires* (Oxford: Oxford University Press, 1997), 99.

[15] J. B. Morrall, *Political Thought in Medieval Times* (Toronto: University of Toronto Press, 1980), ch 5.

[16] J. Hoffman, *Beyond the State* (Oxford: Polity, 1995), ch 4. For a general discussion of the dating issue, see A. Vincent, *Theories of the State* (Oxford: Blackwell, 1987), 11–16.

binding together of tribes,[17] the growth of trade guilds and other social units,[18] or the emergence of a professional bureaucracy,[19] would obviously be futile. It is plain that each writer has a slightly different interpretation of the 'state': the unaddressed interpretive question would cause the historical debate to misfire.

The priority of interpretive explanations does not entail that such explanations should be thought of as harder, or more important, than their causal counterparts. Our historians, reflecting on the origins of the state, might resolve their interpretive disagreements quite quickly. They could, perhaps, agree to differ: they might recognize that each holds a different conception of the state, concede that the conception adopted will partly determine the correctness of the causal claim, and leave it at that. Such a truce would have the whiff of failure about it: after all, our three historians are part of a wider academic community, and we expect this community to aspire to use terms like 'state' in a consistent fashion. More profitably, perhaps, they might start to talk of three different, but related phenomena: the classical state, the medieval state, and the modern state.[20] Once they were sure that they had sufficient agreement about the nature of the phenomena being investigated, they could then return to debate the causal question.[21] This would not require them to reach complete agreement on every nuance of the nature of the state. All that matters is that the historians reach a level of agreement at which the causal question ceases to be undermined by interpretive disagreement.

THE CENTRAL CASE

When trying to refine their understanding of the state, the historians would be faced with a bewildering range of possible accounts. When Charles Titus set himself the task of counting and delineating the various definitions of 'state' in 1931, he found 145 different usages.[22] If we tried to extract the common elements from these definitions we would probably end up with a uselessly thin account of the state—or, worse still, no account at all.[23] The answer, as many have realized, is to formulate a concept which captures the important features of the phenomena under consideration, but does not attempt to encompass all the many and various concepts of the phenomena that exist within our community; we must pick and choose, including some elements

---

[17]   P. Crone, 'The Tribe and the State' in J. Hall, *States in History* (Oxford: Blackwell, 1986).

[18]   Morrall, note 15 above, 60–61.

[19]   M. Weber, *From Max Weber: Essays in Sociology*, trans and ed H. H. Gerth and C. Wright Mills, (Abingdon: Routledge, 1991), 82; C. Pierson, *The Modern State* (2nd edn, Abingdon: Routledge, 2004), 16–17.

[20]   Pierson, note 19 above, ch 2.

[21]   Taylor, note 9 above, 38.

[22]   C. H. Titus, 'A Nomenclature in Political Science' (1931) 25 Am Polit Sci Rev 45; L. Green, *The Authority of the State* (Oxford: Oxford University Press, 1990), 64.

[23]   J. Finnis, *Natural Law and Natural Rights* (Oxford: Oxford University Press, 1980), 4–6.

and discarding others. H. L. A. Hart wrote of identifying the 'standard case',[24] Max Weber spoke of identifying an 'ideal-type', and John Finnis discussed the process of deducing the 'central case' of a state of affairs.[25] Though each advocated different methods by which this abstraction could be determined, all agreed that an abstraction was needed, and that it could not slavishly accommodate every prevailing understanding of the phenomena.

A consequence of this process of abstraction is that the theorist's account of a constitutional institution will not mirror or incorporate the accounts of everyone else in her community. Sometimes there will be disagreements. Occasionally these disagreements will be profound, reflecting differences in methodology or in the application of a methodology. On other occasions, though, these disagreements will be comparatively superficial. Theorists may disagree about the significance that should be attributed to elements of an account, and then disagree about whether a given state of affairs falls within the reach of the concept. So, for example, there is a lively and interesting debate about whether the European Union is a state. This issue will be discussed later, but, in short, most sensible folk would acknowledge that the European Union is a borderline instance of this institution. It is like a state in some ways, and unlike a state in others. The obvious question—whether the Union is sufficiently like a state to be included within the group of things meriting the application of the label 'state'—is uninteresting; it is a matter of degree. But borderline cases can help sharpen our understanding of the central case of the phenomena, leading us to reflect on the relative significance of the elements within our account. Such reflection can also help us understand the entity under discussion, clarifying its nature. Contrasting the Union with a state understood in its focal sense is, hopefully, a revealing exercise, illuminating some of its core features, its self-perception, and its possible futures.

Given that it is necessary for a theorist to depart from the common understanding of constitutional institutions—lest, like Titus, she be cast adrift in a sea of contradictory and confused accounts—it might be asked what significance the popular understanding should possess for us, the extent to which it constrains our interpretation. The answer to this question partly turns on whether the theorist is part of the community whose institutions she is theorizing about, or is—like an anthropologist studying a tribe—outside of that community.

A theorist is constrained to speak and think in the language of a community. If she is seeking to provide an account of a state of affairs to those within the community, their understanding of the phenomena limits her interpretive latitude in two respects. First, it is the popular understanding of phenomena that provides the starting point for theoretical reflection. If we are trying to provide an account of the state or of citizenship, we need a collection of phenomena to analyse, and it is the popular understanding that points us towards this basic material. A theorist who commenced her interpretation of citizenship by looking at the group of people who sought to heal the sick would have fallen at this

---

[24] H. Hart, *The Concept of Law* (2nd edn, Oxford: Clarendon Press, 1994), 4.

[25] Finnis, note 23 above, 9–11.

first hurdle. Secondly, and relatedly, if the account produced by the theorist is to be given back to the community that has been the subject of the study it must be intelligible to members of that community. As the theorist hopes to communicate her understanding of constitutional institutions back to the community, she is, to an extent, limited by their common criteria for usage. It is an essential aspect of being part of a language community that members accept that the correct meaning of a term is set by common criteria.[26] And the theorist is part of such a community. A successful account of the state could not conclude that, for example, France was not 'really' a state, or that Germany lacked a constitution, though such an assertion might be made for rhetorical effect.[27] Sometimes, of course, writers provide radical interpretations of social phenomena, interpretations which purport to bring out important features of the practice of which members of their community were unaware. For instance, Lenin claimed that an important feature of the state is that it acts as a mechanism for class oppression; this is part of its true nature.[28] People within his community, he asserted, did not realize this because the powerful cunningly hid the truth from them. Even radical interpretations, like Lenin's, must be sufficiently close to the popular understanding of the phenomena to be intelligible. They may amount to a campaign for a shift in popular usage: the popular understanding needs to be modified to capture the significant features of the phenomenon to which it refers.

Constitutional theorists generally address their theories to folk within the community being studied. Sometimes, though, they may be more like anthropologists, who provide accounts of the practices of one community to another community. Such an anthropologist need not express her interpretation of these practices in language and concepts that the studied community could understand.[29] She might, for instance, interpret the community's ritual practices as a form of proto-science, even if such a claim would be meaningless to the practitioners of the ritual. Nevertheless, even anthropologists are limited by the popular understandings of the community to which their accounts are addressed: the two considerations discussed above still apply to her, but in the context of the recipients of her theory, not in the context of the community studied.

---

[26] J. Raz, 'Two Views About the Nature of the Theory of Law: A Partial Comparison' in J. Coleman (ed), *Hart's Postscript: Essays on the Postscript to* The Concept of Law (Oxford: Oxford University Press, 2001), 16–19.

[27] See further, T. Endicott, 'Herbert Hart and the Semantic Sting' in J. Coleman (ed), *Hart's Postscript: Essays on the Postscript to* The Concept of Law (Oxford: Oxford University Press, 2001), 51–5.

[28] V. Lenin, *The State and Revolution*, trans R. Service (London: Penguin, 1992), 7–9. See further, K. Dyson, *The State Tradition in Western Europe: A Study of an Idea and Institution* (Oxford: Oxford University Press, 1979), 104–7.

[29] C. Taylor, 'Understanding and Ethnocentricity' in C. Taylor, *Philosophy and the Human Sciences: Philosophical Papers Volume 2* (Cambridge: Cambridge University Press, 1985).

Finally, social institutions are partly constructed by their participants' understandings of them.[30] If, for instance, people generally believed that states should, or do, have a connection with a unique national group, this belief will affect the nature of the state. Citizenship would be defined in nationalistic ways: a good citizen would be a member of the national group, one who maintained and advanced the nationalist story. The conduct of state institutions would also be affected: one of their most basic duties would be to foster national cohesion. The preservation of the national group's identity would shape education and immigration policy, and might also influence the criteria for membership of those institutions. Nationalist beliefs about the state may be wrong, but, if widely held, an account of the state that ignored them would fail to capture an important feature of the practice, a feature that made a significant impact on the lives of people touched by the state. Any account must be sensitive to the participants' beliefs about institutions studied, even if it is ultimately concluded that some of these beliefs are mistaken.

DESCRIPTION AND EVALUATION

If the task of the theorist is to articulate the central case of constitutional institutions, we will need criteria by which the features of this central case can be identified; we cannot just describe what we see. Partly, this is because we need to choose between the conflicting and unclear popular understandings of phenomena before we begin our description; what we see before us is already shaped by these unarticulated criteria. But, in addition, we need to choose between the features of the phenomena studied, in order to prevent the description collapsing into a dull, arbitrary, and unconnected list of features possessed by the phenomena. Some mechanism of selection is required if we are to provide an interesting and illuminating account of constitutional institutions. The process of selection must, of necessity, be evaluative, assessing the claims of possible features of institutions to be included in the account, but what criteria should be used to conduct this exercise? In particular, to what extent should the theorist avoid basing the selection on controversial ethical judgements?[31]

Those worried by the vagaries of ethical theory have argued that it is possible to provide a good account of social phenomena without resort to full-blown moral evaluation. They point to expository principles which are 'neutral', in that they do not require us to pass judgement on the potential goodness or badness of features of the practice.[32] So, for example, a theorist should strive to provide an account of the state

---

[30] C. Taylor, 'Social Theory as Practice' in C. Taylor, *Philosophy and the Human Sciences: Philosophical Papers Volume 2* (Cambridge: Cambridge University Press, 1985), 98–104. See also J. R. Searle, *The Construction of Social Reality* (London: Penguin, 1996).

[31] The importance of this question was brought home to legal philosophers by the work of John Finnis, see the seminal first chapter of his *Natural Law and Natural Rights* (Oxford: Oxford University Press, 1980).

[32] See the discussion in B. Leiter, 'Beyond the Hart/Dworkin Debate: The Methodology Problem in Jurisprudence' (2003) 48 Am J Jurisprudence 17, 34–38; J. Dickson, *Evaluation and Legal Theory* (Oxford: Hart, 2000), 32–35.

that is as clear and as straightforward as it can be. These demands flow from a writer's broad duty of courtesy, or compassion, to her readers: she should, as far as she can, avoid confusion, perplexity, and tedium. But expository principles do not shape the interpretation as such; they instead shape the way in which the interpretation is communicated. We still need guidance about the features of the state that should be placed in our account, some criteria by which we can assess what features of the practice should be included and the degree of significance we should attribute to them. In addition to these expository principles there also needs to be a test of importance. Brian Leiter[33] and Julie Dickson,[34] both drawn by the charms of 'descriptive' jurisprudence, concede that the theorist must apply a test of importance but contend that the theorist need not resort to ethical evaluation in the application of this test.

Brian Leiter seeks to confine 'importance' to what people involved in the practice consider important; it is, after all, *their* practice we are trying to illuminate.[35] We can then describe the concept as it exists within that community simply by reporting back the beliefs of the participants, without evaluating its worth. The attractions of this strategy are plain, but its execution would swiftly prove problematic.[36] A theorist who followed Leiter's strictures would quickly run up against the same problems that beset Charles Titus' lexicographical strategy. Leiter does not explain how we are to pick between various explanations of the practice's importance, and without some process of selection we will be faced with a wide range of conflicting beliefs. The participants may well believe a great many confused and inconsistent things about the significance and importance of the practice they are engaged in. A further difficulty with this methodology is that it precludes an interpretation that brings out features of which the participants were unaware: Lenin's account of the state, for instance, would immediately be ruled out of consideration. This concern points us towards a final, and deeper, worry raised by Leiter's approach. There is a difference between an account of the popular conception of the state and an account of the state.[37] The former is an account of the way in which folk perceive and understand the state; an exercise in political psychology. The latter is an account of the state itself; the social institution referred to by the concept. The former task is interesting and worthwhile, but it is the latter task that is normally the goal of constitutional theorists.[38]

---

[33] Leiter, note 32 above.

[34] Dickson, note 32 above. Dickson's approach may also be shared by Raz: see J. Raz, 'The Problem About the Nature of Law' in J. Raz, *Ethics in the Public Domain* (rev edn, Oxford: Clarendon Press, 1995), 209.

[35] Leiter, note 32 above, 42–43; Dickson, note 32 above, 64.

[36] J. Dickson, 'Methodology in Jurisprudence' (2004) 10 Legal Theory 117, 138–9.

[37] A point Leiter recognizes in another context: B. Leiter, 'Legal Realism, Hard Positivism and the Limits of Conceptual Analysis' in J. Coleman, *Hart's Postscript: Essays on the Postscript to* The Concept of Law (Oxford: Oxford University Press, 2001), 358.

[38] On the ambiguities between the analysis of a concept and social phenomena, see Finnis' discussion of H. L. A. Hart's methodology in J. Finnis 'H. L. A. Hart: A Twentieth Century Oxford Political Philosopher' available at <http://ssrn.com/abstract=1477276>.

Julie Dickson has mooted two further criteria beyond those identified by Leiter. First, she argues that a feature is important when it reveals something distinctive or characteristic about the practice.[39] Secondly, a feature is important when it is one which we would consider when assessing the goodness or the badness of the practice.[40] In contrast to Leiter, Dickson opens the possibility that the features to be identified are those which are *actually* important, and does not confine the test to factors identified as important by the participants. As Charles Taylor and John Finnis have demonstrated, it is only through application of an evaluative framework that we are then able to bring out the important features of a practice.[41] Dickson accepts this: 'importance' can only be assessed from within a value-loaded theoretical structure. Once the subjective sense of importance is put to one side, having been identified as of secondary—but real—interest, there is no other content that could be given to the notion. Any assertion of importance is, then, a statement about the actual or potential impact of a given phenomenon on people's lives. We are compelled to assess what is potentially valuable—or potentially harmful—about a social phenomenon in order to describe it. Dickson hopes to stop short of full-blown moral evaluation, though, as the features identified need not be pre-determined as good or bad; they are relevant to this assessment, but the assessment could go either way. Her contention is that it is enough that we conclude the feature is of significance to ethical evaluation, but we can stop short of undertaking this evaluation. For instance, both an anarchist and a communitarian might agree that the action-guiding function of law is an important feature of the institution, but the anarchist might regard this as an ethically bad thing, whilst the communitarian might regard it as an ethically good thing. So, Dickson might argue, action-guiding is an important feature of law, but whether it constitutes a positive or a negative feature of the practice will depend on whether you are an anarchist or a communitarian.

It is, however, difficult to see how we can stop the slide from the descriptive towards the evaluative at the point suggested by Dickson. The trouble with her line of reasoning is that it runs the wrong way: we cannot identify the important features of a practice and then assess whether these are good or bad, we must begin with an ethical framework which gives content to the good and the bad, and then use this to identify features of importance. To conclude that action-guiding is an important feature of law we must first either be an anarchist or a communitarian, or hold some other ethical schema that picks out this element as significant. Without being committed to a prior ethical framework, we have no reason to suppose that the feature is of importance. This is, after all, supposed to be a test of actual, genuine, importance to people: it cannot just report back what folk, the anarchist and the communitarian, *think* is of importance, otherwise it will collapse back into Leiter's position.

---

[39] Dickson, note 32 above, 58.

[40] Dickson, note 32 above, 60–1; 137.

[41] C. Taylor, 'Neutrality in Political Science' in C. Taylor, *Philosophy and the Human Sciences: Philosophical Papers Vol 2* (Cambridge: Cambridge University Press 1985); Finnis, note 23 above, ch 1.

It is too late for the theoretical restraint advocated by Dickson: any theorist who believes that the action-guiding feature of law is important must also already be committed to a view about the positive or negative aspects of this feature.

A good account of a constitutional institution will identify those features which enable it to advance, or to threaten, the well-being of people. An unhappy consequence of this is that a theorist's account will be conditioned by her ethical beliefs. For instance, those whose ethical beliefs focus tightly on the individual will highlight the state's coercive power, whilst those who place weight on the individual's role within a community will tend to emphasize its collective aspects. So, to take an extreme example, a nationalist might argue that individuals can only flourish within a community that is characterized by a high degree of social solidarity, and that such solidarity can only be found within a national grouping. A nationalist account of the state might then present it as a political forum through which a national group can exercise political power, and within which the national group can flourish. A connection between the formal institutions of the state and a national group would be central to the interpretation; states which lacked this connection would be deviant cases; identifiable as states only because of their relationship to, and aspiration to move towards, this ideal. A libertarian, on the other hand, would place great emphasis on the state's coercive power, but would have little or no interest in the possible connections between the state and national groups. These differing understandings of the state are caused by differing understandings of human flourishing, and their attractiveness will depend on the attractions of the rival political ideologies that lie behind them.

Our criteria of importance can be refined a little further still. Not only should the theorist pick out those features that are of ethical significance, she should also, within this group, consider which of these features are of importance to the recipients of her theory. What is important depends, in part, on the constituency to which the account is addressed. An account of citizenship published in a journal of psychiatry would properly differ from that published in a journal of public law. An academic asked to provide an account of the state to a meeting of cartographers should not simply recycle the account she presented a few months before to a group of religious leaders. Provided that these accounts are compatible, that they are capable of being combined into a bigger and more general account of the phenomena, these differences should not alarm us.

THE SIGNIFICANCE OF THE ETHICAL FRAMEWORK

Given that different political ideologies will generate different accounts of social phenomena, a successful interpretation will turn, in part, on the ability of the interpreter to correctly identify and appreciate the content of human well-being.[42] To a considerable extent, of course, theorists holding different ideological positions will find they agree about many of the significant features of constitutional institutions,

---

[42] Taylor, note 29 above, 120; J. Finnis, Aquinas (Oxford: Oxford University Press, 1998), 50.

disagreeing over the relative emphasis attributed to them. This may permit us to provide partial accounts of constitutional institutions which will prove attractive to people holding a number of different ethical perspectives.

Although ethical evaluation is needed if we are to identify features of importance, this need not cause us to provide an idealized interpretation of constitutional institutions. A line can be drawn between the methodology that underpins this book and the similar, but more controversial, methodology that can be traced back to Aristotle and has found its clearest modern expression in the work of John Finnis.

Aristotle contended that to understand institutions as they exist in the world it is necessary to understand them in their ideal form.[43] A division should be drawn between the healthy, mature, manifestation of the institution and its deviant, or immature, manifestations.[44] Turning to the state, Aristotle identified six different groups of constitutions: monarchies, aristocracies, constitutional governments (that is, government by the citizenry), tyrannies, oligarchies and democracies.[45] Democracy, in this context, should be understood as a form of unconstrained majoritarianism, a type of mob-rule. The first group of three constitutions are potential models of healthy polities; the second group of three are models of unhealthy polities. Though all six are potential forms of the state, Aristotle's methodology allowed him to refine his account still further, picking out constitutional government as the central case of the state.

A healthy state, according to Aristotle, is one which pursues the proper end of the state, that is, it advances the well-being of its members.[46] Perverted cases of the state—tyrannies, oligarchies and democracies—can only be understood as forms of the state by reason of their deviation from the ideal. But what of the variety of healthy forms of the state? Monarchy and aristocracy have the potential to be good forms of government: if there is a select group of people or a person in the state who would do a better job of government than the citizenry itself, their right to rule should be acknowledged, and political power passed to them.[47] These are not deviant forms of the state, yet Aristotle distinguishes them from his central case. The answer to this conundrum turns on a further divide, a divide between the theoretical ideal and the obtainable ideal.[48] This distinction can clearly be seen in Aristotle's

---

[43] C. Johnson, *Aristotle's Theory of the State* (London: Macmillan, 1990), ch 2. J. Finnis, Natural Law and Natural Rights (Oxford: Oxford University Press, 1980), ch 1.

[44] Johnson, note 43 above, 6–7; see, for instance, Aristotle, *The Politics and Constitution of Athens*, ed S. Everson, (Cambridge: Cambridge University Press, 1996), I.V, 1254a36; Aristotle, *Nicomachean Ethics*, trans J. A. K. Thomson (London, Penguin, 1976), VIII.IV, 1157a30–3.

[45] Aristotle, *The Politics*, III.VII, 1279b4–6.

[46] See the discussion in S. Everson's introduction in Aristotle, *The Politics and Constitution of Athens*, ed S. Everson, (Cambridge: Cambridge University Press, 1996), xxiv–xxxii. The attractions of this claim are discussed in chapter 3 of this book.

[47] Aristotle, note 46 above, III.XIII,1284b33–34; III.XVII, 1288a27.

[48] On the distinction in Plato, see C. H. McIlwain, *Constitutionalism: Ancient and Modern* (rev edn, New York: Cornell University Press, 1947), 27–35.

reflection on the institution of monarchy. In theory, monarchy could provide the best form of government for a state; perhaps there is one person in the state whose excellences are so great it would be unjust to deny him the powers of the king. Aristotle compares such a person to a god, a being beyond normal human capacities.[49] If a person who possessed the qualities of the divine were found, it would indeed make sense to hand them absolute power. Their perfect good nature combined with an omniscient knowledge of human affairs would ensure the very best of governments. Unfortunately, such a person has yet to be discovered—and on those occasions when people believe they have found such a leader the consequences have nearly always proved disastrous. Aristotle realized this: though monarchy and aristocracy are ideal forms of government, they are impossible ideals. To see manifestations of these states we have to look back into the semi-mythical past.[50] The ideal state is, therefore, that which is ideal for us, that which we can hope to achieve: this is the state characterized by constitutional government and citizenship.

John Finnis provides a contemporary, and perhaps more sophisticated, defence of Aristotle's methodological conclusions. To understand a social institution, like law or the state, Finnis argues, we must start by asking *why* we have the institution.[51] This question is answered by considering the reasons that people have for creating it. According to Finnis, true reasons for action are those that point towards the good, reasons which tell us what we ought to do. Consequently, the central case, for Finnis, will present an institution in its healthiest and most mature form, the product of rational people correctly acting on valid reasons.[52] Other states of affairs can be understood as instances of the institution by virtue of their relationship with this central case. This approach is successful when the phenomenon studied is of value to us. It enables us to pick out the important features of the practice—those which are necessary within the practice to advance our well-being—and facilitates our comprehension of unhealthy manifestations of the practice, where it fails to achieve its potential. The approach struggles, though, when faced with a harmful practice, or a practice that has both harmful and valuable elements. In a recent work on Aquinas, Finnis wrestles with the problem of providing an account of slavery. He contends that the best way of understanding a bad practice, like slavery, is by interpreting it as a deviant version of good practices, like penal servitude and inheritance.[53] Doubtless a similar move could be made with other entirely bad practices like, for instance, torture, genocide, and apartheid; perhaps if we reflect for long enough we could identify virtuous practices of which these are deviant forms.

This approach, the use of virtue-full central cases to illuminate vicious practices, is an intuitively odd way of proceeding. If a person asked for an explanation of slavery

---

[49] Aristotle, note 46 above, III.XIII, 1284b28–35.

[50] Johnson, note 43 above, 163–166.

[51] J. Finnis, 'Law and What I Truly Should Decide' (2003) 48 Am J Jurisprudence 108, 115.

[52] Finnis, note 42 above, 11.

[53] *Ibid.*, 49–50.

she would be surprised, and perhaps her patience tested, if we commenced with an account of inheritance. And some practices—like genocide or torture—have no obvious virtuous counterpart. Such an account would risk obscuring rather than illuminating the important features of the practice by diverting attention from the phenomenon studied. These practices are instances of unredeemed irrationality, but such irrationality is far from uncommon in our world. The more frequently people act irrationally, the greater the gap between the practices and institutions identified by Finnis' methodology and the practices and institutions of our own world. We will find ourselves trying to illuminate social institutions indirectly, through comparison with the ideal, rather than directly, by examining the actual institutions that are before us.

Finnis', and Aristotle's, methodology correctly recognizes that any test of importance must relate back to ethical theory, but it is a mistake to think that we must search for an idealized version of the practice. Our ethically informed test of importance can pick out bad features of a practice as well as the good; it can show a practice to be potentially harmful as well as potentially valuable.

A final distinction that needs to be drawn is between those questions of ethical importance that relate to the practice studied, and those questions raised by the consequences of the resulting theory.[54] These questions are frequently confused. Lon Fuller notoriously attacked the positivist account of law for giving succour to fascism by encouraging people to pay unquestioning allegiance to the law.[55] Those responding to Fuller have tended to dwell on the substance of this claim, objecting that it turns on an erroneous understanding of legal positivism[56] or that it overestimates the interest of Nazis, and others, in legal theory.[57] Fuller's challenge is a wider one, though, and raises the interesting question of how attentive a theorist should be to the probable consequences of her theory. If a legal theorist writing in Weimar knew her work might assist or encourage the Nazis, would this consideration affect the success of her interpretation of law?

There is certainly some merit in Fuller's case. He was right to contend that the way participants understand law can affect their conduct within the legal system. Interpretations of social practices can, occasionally, alter the phenomena they purport to describe.[58] Sometimes this may draw the phenomena closer to the interpretation: participants accept the theorist's account of their practice and change the practice to make it more like the account. Sometimes the opposite may happen: an accurate account may cause practitioners to alter their conduct. Accounts of the

---

[54] On this distinction, see generally Dickson, note 32 above, ch 5.

[55] L. Fuller, 'Positivism and Fidelity to Law—A Reply to Professor Hart' (1958) 71 Harvard L Rev 630. For a broader reflection on the responsibilities of the theorist, see Braybrooke, note 6 above, ch 4.

[56] M. Kramer, *In Defense of Legal Positivism* (Oxford: Oxford University Press, 1999), 114–115.

[57] See generally, S. Paulson, 'On the Background and Significance of Gustav Radbruch's Post-War Papers' (2006) 26 Oxford J Legal Studies 17, 32–35.

[58] Taylor, note 30 above.

state that claim to expose its inherently repressive nature often hope to inspire people to end or mitigate this repression, and thus render the interpretation obsolete.[59] Fuller was also correct to claim that a theorist should be concerned with the reception of her interpretation. If it could be shown that an otherwise brilliant interpretation of the constitution might aid fascism—even if only because the account was likely to be misconstrued—this would be a very good reason not to publish the interpretation.

Fuller's error lies in the conclusion he draws from these two considerations: that the beneficial consequences of adopting an interpretation provide a test for the success of an interpretation of a phenomenon. Instead, in these extreme cases there are good reasons to advance a bad interpretation of the practice or to refrain from publishing. The point of an interpretation of a contemporary social practice is to explain and illuminate the important features of the practice as it currently exists. Fuller, in contrast, argued that the theorist should advocate the adoption of a particular conception of the practice in order to influence people's behaviour in the future.[60] There is nothing inherently objectionable in advancing an interpretation of a phenomenon with the aim of persuading folk to change their behaviour; Lenin's account of the state aspired to change popular behaviour, but, crucially, Lenin hoped to do this by revealing the state's true nature. Fuller's methodology, on the other hand, pushes the practice studied to one side. We cannot reason from the claim that it would be good if people believed certain things about an institution, to the claim that these things are, consequently, features of that institution. A theorist who followed Fuller's strictures could end up with an account of a practice that radically diverged from the phenomenon which it purported to illuminate.

THE MANY PATHS OF CONSTITUTIONAL THEORY

This chapter has argued that constitutional theory requires an interpretative account of constitutional institutions. This account can only be conducted within an ethical framework, a framework which enables us to pick out and illuminate important features of the practice studied. Other parts of constitutional theory—historically-oriented accounts, critical accounts and so forth—presuppose an interpretive account. But the relationship goes both ways: historical and critical accounts also inform interpretive accounts. A historical account of the state, for instance, may cast light on the factors that lead the state to flourish or which threaten its existence. Given the state is of importance, these factors are also shown to be of significance—and may therefore form part of a good interpretive account of the state. A critical account of the state, one which points to the moral inadequacies of the state as an institution, or to the dangers inherent in its operation, also highlights features

---

[59] See, for instance, R. Miliband, *The State in Capitalist Society* (London: Quartet, 1969).

[60] This motivation is made more explicit in the work of contemporaries who have been inspired by Fuller: see F. Schauer, 'The Social Construction of the Concept of Law: A Reply to Julie Dickson' (2005) 25 Oxford J Legal Studies 493, and the other papers cited in that article.

of ethical importance. These are also factors to which a good interpretative account would give attention. The happy conclusion to be drawn is that the various branches of constitutional theory are engaged in compatible exercises, the difference between them is a matter of focus, not of subject matter or conflicting methodologies. The identity crisis of constitutional theory can be ended: there is no single way of undertaking constitutional theory, but a variety of complementary methods which can help to enhance our understanding of constitutional institutions.

2

Approaching the State

This chapter introduces many of the ideas that will run through this book. The state is presented as a complex social group: a creature of territory, institutions, rules, and—crucially—people.

Most accounts of the state pick out, with more or less clarity, three elements for our attention: the state possesses a territory, a people, and a set of governing institutions.[1] Merely listing these three elements will not provide us with a satisfying account of the state. Partly, the list is unsatisfying because it is disconnected and, apparently, arbitrary; there are lots of other features that might be included on it. We could, perhaps, add the building of roads, the maintenance of an army and a fire-service; these are activities and institutions which are also commonly found within states. More importantly, these three elements do not distinguish the state from other, similar, social institutions. Lots of other bodies possess these features: some churches, most trade unions, and many other collective associations have a defined membership, a territorial reach, and a set of governing institutions. From time to time, these similarities have caused scholars to doubt the importance of the state as a social institution. In the early part of the twentieth century pluralists tried to shake the hegemony of the state over political science by emphasizing the importance of other social groups within and outside the state.[2] Much was made of the ways in which the Roman Catholic Church influenced state policy,[3] and of the occasional failure of the state to maintain its rule against powerful groups in times of crisis.[4] The

[1] See, for instance: J. A. Hall and G. J. Ikenberry, *The State* (Buckingham: Open University Press, 1989), 2; A. Vincent, *Theories of the State* (Oxford: Blackwell, 1987), 19–21; H. Kelsen, *Pure Theory of Law*, trans M. Knight, (Berkeley: University of California Press, 1967), 279–319.

[2] A. Vincent, note 1 above, ch 6; P. Craig, *Public Law and Democracy in the United Kingdom and the United States of America* (Oxford: Oxford University Press, 1990), 140–8; E. Barker, 'The Discredited State' in E. Barker, *Church, State and Study* (London: Methuen & Co, 1930), 166–70; H. Laski, *Authority in the Modern State* (New Haven: Yale University Press, 1919); H. Laski, *Foundations of Sovereignty* (London: George Allan & Unwin, 1921).

[3] H. Laski, *Foundations of Sovereignty* (London: George Allan & Unwin, 1921), 238.

[4] Vincent, note 1 above, 184; H. Laski, *Authority in the Modern State* (New Haven: Yale University Press, 1919), 45–6.

suggestion of the pluralists was that, when push came to shove, the state either complied with the demands of these potent groups, or collapsed under their pressure. In recent years this challenge has taken a new form, with international organizations and multi-national companies replacing churches and trade unions. Writers on globalization point to the control exercised over the state by such organizations.[5] International courts judge and punish states, attempting, with more or less success, to impose the constraints of international law upon them. Powerful companies are able to dictate the content of states' legal orders by threatening to withdraw investment in the face of unfavourable legal structures. In this context pluralists and globalization scholars advance two, intermeshed, challenges to the significance and autonomy of the state. First, they claim that the state lacks the freedom of action commonly ascribed to it by state theorists; that it is the puppet of other powerful bodies. Secondly, they claim that the state is not, analytically, distinguishable from these other institutions. Like states, these other bodies possess controlling institutions, have a territorial reach and constituencies which they control and regulate.

These critiques seek to cut the state down to size: they demonstrate that there are many other institutions that affect people's lives just as profoundly, perhaps even more profoundly, than those of the state. But whilst providing a valuable counterbalance to old-fashioned state-centred political theory, they also, perhaps unintentionally, acknowledge the distinctiveness of the state. To claim that the state is under the sway of other groups presupposes that the state can be identified separately from these groups.[6] It may be that the state is dependent on contesting associations, is the creature of the powerful, or is under the control of international forces, but for this to be shown to be true, the state must be distinct from these entities. Similarly, the claim that the state is not analytically distinguishable from these bodies is misguided. It is certainly true that the state lies within the same broad genus as churches, trade unions, international associations, and so forth, but it would be a mistake to conclude from this that the state is the same thing as these other entities. To assert, correctly, that these other institutions have state-like features requires us to have a distinct account of the state against which they can be contrasted, even if we end by concluding the state as an institution has withered away. One task of this chapter is to illuminate the difference between the state and these other, similar, social entities.

What is it that sets the state apart from other social institutions? Many writers on the state point to a special, distinctive, connection between the institutions of the state and its people and territory. This connection has been glossed in many ways, but the varied accounts can be collected into two broad groups. On the one hand, there are those who see the distinctive character of the state in the claim made by the state over its people. The state claims authority over its people: it is entitled to

[5] B. de Santos, *Toward a New Common Sense: Law, Science and Politics in Paradigmatic Transition* (2nd edn, London: Butterworths, 2002), ch 5; G. Anderson, *Constitutional Rights after Globalisation* (Oxford: Hart Publishing, 2005), 20–33.

[6] As Barker and Laski eventually recognized: D. Nicholls, *The Pluralist State* (Basingstoke: St. Martin's Press, 1994), 10.

command, and they are obliged to obey. On the other hand, there are those who present the state as a social group: the state is also, in some sense, constituted by its nationals. The relationship of people to the institutions of the state and the relationships between members of the state are therefore necessary features of a successful account of the state. Accounts of the state as a social group are wider than those focused on the claims of the state. Whilst it will be argued that it is necessary to adopt this wider understanding if we are to adequately explain the nature of the state, this does not require us to abandon the insights of those who have written, more narrowly, about the claims of the state. They have succeeded in identifying some of the important and characteristic elements of the state.

THE CLAIMS OF THE STATE

It is undoubtedly the case that states—all states—issue commands directed towards people, that these commands are intended to be obeyed, and that, in general, these commands enjoy a certain degree of success. This observation underpins one of the most famous, and briefest, definitions of the state: that provided by Max Weber. Weber wrote that the state was 'a human community that (successfully) claims the *monopoly of the legitimate use of force* within a given territory'.[7] Discussion of this definition has often dwelt on the exertion of force as an aspect of the state, but, as Weber recognized, force is not the only, or even the normal, means of state action.[8] Of at least equal importance in the definition is the qualification that the state's exertion of force purports to be legitimate; it is this that distinguishes the claim of the state from the claim of the gunman.[9] Both the gunman and the state issue commands that are backed by a threat of force. The state, however, claims that its commands ought to be obeyed irrespective of the threat; it claims that it is entitled to be obeyed. Whilst the definition talks of 'legitimate force' the relationship could then also be characterized, as Weber acknowledged, in terms of authority.[10] The state issues commands which, it claims, are authoritative. Read in this way, force becomes a secondary element within the definition. Force is exerted when the state's authority is challenged;[11] if the state's authority were universally accepted, force would become unnecessary.

In recent years Leslie Green has developed a similar account of the state which provides a closer examination of its authority claims.[12] Authority is, says Green, 'a triadic social relation among a superior, a subject, and a range of action'.[13] Within

---

[7] M. Weber 'Politics as a Vocation' in H. H. Gerth and C. Wright Mills (eds), *From Max Weber: Essays in Sociology* (Abingdon: Routledge, 1991), 78.

[8] *Ibid.*, 78.

[9] H. L. A. Hart, *The Concept of Law* (2nd edn, Oxford: Clarendon Press, 1994), 18–20.

[10] M. Weber, *Economy and Society*, G. Roth and C. Wittich (eds) (California: California University Press, 1978), 263. Weber, note 7 above, 78–9.

[11] Weber, note 10 above, 903–4.

[12] L. Green, *The Authority of the State* (Oxford: Clarendon Press, 1990).

[13] *Ibid.*, 42.

this range of action the superior claims to issue commands to the subject that provide, in Joseph Raz's terminology, pre-emptive content-independent reasons for action. A command constitutes a pre-emptive reason for action when, rather than adding to the balance of reasons considered by the subject, it excludes and takes the place of some of those reasons.[14] The state having spoken, the subject should act on the command, not on her own assessment of the balance of reasons. These commands are also content-independent reasons for action: the command provides a reason to act that does not directly relate to the action specified by the command.[15] As Weber wrote, in less precise terms, the subject of the authority makes 'the content of the command the maxim of their conduct for its very own sake'.[16]

Most authorities claim authority only within a narrow jurisdiction. The doctor claims authority to prescribe the medicines we should take, but not over the way we wire our houses, or the places we can go on holiday. The captain claims the authority to direct his men in battle, but not the authority to determine whom they marry or how they invest their salaries. The state, in contrast, makes a wide assertion of authority: every area of its subjects' lives falls, potentially, within its reach.[17] Green presents the state as claiming *supreme* authority,[18] whilst Weber wrote of the state claiming the *monopoly* of legitimate force—an assertion which, as we have seen, can also be couched in terms of an authority relation. The fine distinction between these two formulations becomes of interest when we reflect on the relationship between the state and other authorities. There will be many other bodies within the state's territory that exercise authority over people, and whose authority is backed by a form of coercive power. The list might include religious courts which determine property disputes, trade unions that command and regulate their members—even parents who set the bedtime for their children. On Green's version of the authority claim of the state, whilst the state claims to be entitled to remove or fetter other authorities, it does not claim that these bodies find the source of their authority in the express or tacit permission of the state. The state may tolerate, or ignore, such bodies. Indeed, this point could be developed further.[19] The state must, by its very nature, claim the right to determine the limits of its own jurisdiction. And it must, in addition, exercise its power within the jurisdiction of the authority that it claims for

---

[14] J. Raz, *The Morality of Freedom* (Oxford: Clarendon Press, 1986), 46–7. Green, note 12 above, 38–9.

[15] Green, note 12 above, 40–1; See also Raz, note 14 above, 35–7, and H. L. A. Hart 'Commands and Authoritative Reasons' in H. L. A. Hart *Essays on Bentham* (Oxford: Oxford University Press, 1982).

[16] Weber, note 10 above, 946.

[17] Though see T. Endicott, 'Interpretation, Jurisdiction and the Authority of Law' (2007) 6(2) American Philosophical Association Newsletter on Law and Philosophy 14.

[18] Green, note 12 above, 78–83.

[19] I am grateful to Timothy Endicott for drawing my attention to this point. See further, Endicott, note 17 above.

itself. But it need not claim that all exertions of authority, even those backed with coercion, fall within its proper jurisdiction. Though the state claims to be entitled to determine the limits of its authority, it need not claim that it can legitimately draw these limits anywhere it pleases. Potentially, the state could accept that other bodies enjoy legitimate, non-derivative, authority which the state is not entitled to encroach upon.

Weber, in contrast, makes a far grander claim on behalf of the state. According to Weber's account, toleration of other authorities amounts to either tacit empowerment by the state, or a failure by the state to make good on its monopolistic claims.[20] An example may help clarify this rather convoluted point. Many religious groups within states claim to exercise, and succeed in exercising, authority over the lives of their members. Religious courts make decisions about marriage, divorce, and even inheritance. These institutions are often able to function because those whom they address would face social sanctions if they disregarded the institutions' commands. If we follow Weber's monopolist account of the state we would either conclude that the state gave these bodies tacit permission to exercise authority, or that these bodies were challengers to the state—and that widespread acceptance of their authority would eventually point towards the collapse of the state. Green's more sophisticated account of the state, in contrast, can tolerate—or simply recognize—the existence of such authorities. The supremacy claim advanced by the state only implies that it asserts the right to set the boundaries between its authority and the authority of these institutions, but it need not claim to tacitly empower them, nor need it be threatened by their existence.

Though Green's account is preferable, the divide between Green and Weber remains a narrow one and, it might be thought, nothing of interest turns on it. However, as we shall see in chapter 10, the claims made by the European Union over its citizens accord with Green's account of the characteristic claims made by a state, but not with Weber's. The line between these theorists, in this matter, is a very fine one, but our interpretation of the self-understanding of the European Union depends on it: a small part, at least, of our uncertainty about the nature of the European Union might, perhaps, be traced back to our uncertainty about the nature of the state.

Anyone can claim authority over others. A fantasist might purport to found a state by inventing a set of institutions which issue commands over a people within a territory. Many of the features of an actual state—institutions, territory, people, commands which claim authority—would be present, but the fantasist's imaginings would not amount to a state. States are features of the real world, and for a state to exist its commands must, to an extent, be successful. This requires that the commands it issues must alter the way people behave, and must, additionally, lead them to behave in the manner specified by the command. To make use of Raz's terminology once more, the state must be, at the very least, a *de facto* authority.[21]

---

[20] J. Hoffman, *Beyond the State* (Oxford: Polity Press, 1995), 35–7.

[21] Raz, note 14 above, 26–8, 46; Green, note 12 above, 25–8, 65–6.

The state's commands must generally be effective, but this effectiveness need not rest on endorsement of the state's claim to exercise authority.[22] The state's subjects may obey its orders for many other reasons: perhaps because of their fear of sanctions or because of bribery.

Weber went further than this, contending that the state must, by and large, also succeed in persuading its subjects that it is entitled to govern them.[23] It is not enough that they treat the state as an authority, they must also endorse its claim to legitimacy. Weber probably intended this proposition to stand as an empirical assertion: a claim that a state cannot survive for a significant period of time if its ability to command rests entirely on fear and bribery.[24] Of course, much will turn on strength of the contention. States can survive for a time without widespread belief in their legitimacy, and all states depend, to an extent, on punishments and inducements to supplement, or complement, popular belief in their legitimacy. It is, though, at least plausible to argue that states rarely last for long periods—in particular surviving that tricky moment when governmental power passes from one generation to the next—without convincing a significant proportion of their population that they are entitled to rule.

So far, we have only considered two of our three elements of the state. The state's people and its institutions have been shown to be connected through a claim of authority, advanced by the institutions towards the people and embodied in its commands. The third element of the state, its territory, has been left to one side.[25] Weber regarded territory as crucial to his account,[26] but Green treats it as dispensable.[27] Whilst acknowledging that a state must have a spatial existence generated by its connection with its subjects, Green questions the requirement for a defined territory, with borders and associated land-rights. On Green's analysis, nomadic tribes could constitute states, or, more speculatively still, states could become 'overlapping, co-territorial (or non-territorial) global villages'[28] with people of different allegiances living in the same area. The apparent failure of the authority claim to embrace territory makes this argument attractive: the institutions of the state, its people, and the relationship that ties them together form a unity. Territory seems an extra element. Perhaps, like flags, anthems, and armies, territory is something that states commonly possess, but is not an essential aspect of their nature?

---

[22] Green, note 12 above, 73–5, 86–8; Raz, note 14 above, 65.

[23] Weber, note 10 above, 18–19.

[24] See further, T. R. Tyler, *Why People Obey the Law* (Princeton: Princeton University Press, 2006), especially chs 12 and 13.

[25] See generally, T Baldwin 'The Territorial State' in H Gross and R Harrison eds., *Jurisprudence: Cambridge Essays* (Oxford: Clarendon Press, 1992).

[26] Weber, note 10 above, 901–40.

[27] Green, note 12 above, 83–4. Though see also Green, note 12 above, 228.

[28] *Ibid.*, 84.

Though tempting, the argument against territory as an essential feature of the state is mistaken.[29] Territory interacts with the state's claim to authority and with the identity of those subject to these claims, adding to the complexity of each element. Weber and Green speak in relatively undiscriminating terms about the people of the state, the subjects of the state's commands. Most constitutional lawyers would seek to distinguish a number of relationships a person might have with a state—or, to put it another way, a number of constitutional identities a person might possess. These identities can be divided into two very rough groups. There are the constitutional identities held by the nationals[30] of the state: primarily those of the citizen and the subject. And then there are the constitutional identities that can be held by non-nationals: primarily those of the friendly alien and the enemy alien. These four are not exhaustive, and states have created many variations on them.[31] They do capture, though, the four most common, basic, relationships a person can have with a modern state.

Both nationals and non-nationals can find themselves the recipients of the state's commands, but the nature of the claim made against them differs. Nationals are expected to obey the state's institutions simply because they are nationals; they are members of the state, and, as such, should accept its authority. In older constitutional thought, this duty was understood as, or at least presented as, a natural and unshakable tie between king and subject.[32] Because this is a personal obligation, it can reach beyond the territory of the state: nationals may be prohibited from travelling to certain countries, or have restrictions placed on the trade they conduct with non-nationals. In English constitutional law, the breadth of the subject's duty is mirrored by that of the state: the state is under a (non-enforceable) legal obligation to protect its nationals whilst they are out of the territory.[33] Unless they present a challenge to the state's security, non-nationals, in contrast, ordinarily only come within the scope of the state's claimed authority whilst they are within its territory. Their allegiance to the state is temporary and geographically bounded; once beyond the boundaries of the state non-nationals are normally left to their own devices, free to travel and to act as they choose. The basis of the authority claim therefore appears to differ between nationals and non-nationals. With nationals, the authority claim rests on their constitutional identity as state-members; it is a personal obligation.

[29] On the centrality of the requirement of territory in the international law understanding of the state, see J. Crawford, *The Creation of States in International Law* (2nd edn, Oxford: Oxford University Press, 2006), 46–52.

[30] By national I mean a state member, a person who need not also be a member of a nation. The contrast between a member of a national group and a member of the state is discussed further in chapter 8.

[31] A. Dummett and A. Nicol, *Subjects, Citizens, Aliens and Others* (London: Weidenfeld and Nicholson, 1990).

[32] E. Morgan, *Inventing the People: The Rise of Popular Sovereignty in England and America* (London: Norton & Co, 1988), ch 1.

[33] *China Navigation v AG* [1932] 2 KB 197.

With non-nationals, the state's authority claim rests on their presence in the state's territory; it is an obligation that is generated by occupation of space.

It is not just the nature of the state's claim that is affected by territorial boundaries. As was discussed a little earlier, the state must, in some sense and to some extent, be successful in the authority claims that it makes. This requirement of efficacy is confined to the territory of the state. On those rare occasions in which a country seeks to exert its will in another's territory, its failure in no way challenges its identity as a state. So, for example, the United States has often sought to determine the behaviour of people in other states. From the banning of trade with Cuba to the invasion of Iraq, its efforts have met with varying degrees of success. But even if these projects failed completely, this lack of success would not, in any sense, affect the identification of the United States as a state. In contrast, the collapse of law in New Orleans which followed Hurricane Katrina in 2005 was so comprehensive and profound it could plausibly be said that the state had ceased to exist within that area.

Finally, the state also levels a set of authority-claims against people that are mediated through their occupation or ownership of the state's land. Ultimately, people own land within the territory at the mercy of the state: the state regulates the acquisition, sale, and use of property. In exceptional cases the state may confiscate land, taking ownership of property itself, or passing it on to another private party. Once again, the boundaries of the state make a difference to the state's relationship with land. All land within the territory of the state comes within the scope of the state's authority claim. This includes land owned by nationals, non-nationals, and land without an owner. In contrast, land outside of the territory is beyond the state's reach, unless it is controlled by a national or annexed by the state. There is, then, an interesting contrast between the state's relationship with land in its territory and its relationship with land out of its territory. Within its territory, the state has a direct relationship with land and claims a set of rights with people consequent on this relationship. This is especially clear in the state's jurisdiction over unowned land, where its claim to determine use of the land arises entirely from the presence of the land within its territory and not because this land is owned or possessed by a person who owes allegiance to the state. Outside its territory the state only purports to have authority over land which is owned, or possessed, by its nationals: its relationship with the land is mediated through its relationship with its people.

Despite Green's scepticism, territory is an important element of authority-based accounts of the state, one which is intertwined with, and helps shape, the other elements. It adds nuance to the blunt authority claims of the state, permitting us to distinguish between the claims levelled against nationals and non-nationals. In so doing, it also begins to draw attention to the divisions between the different relationships a person can have with a state—divisions which will become increasingly important as this book progresses.

Accounts of the state that focus tightly on its authority claims are vertical and one-directional. They highlight the claims that the institutions of the state make over its people: the state commands, and commands in a characteristic way. These models are vertical, in that they present the institutions of the state addressing nationals and non-nationals. They are one-directional, in that there is no necessary connection made, within the model of the state, between the addressees of the command and the manner of the production of these commands. Of course, many would argue that there should be such a connection—that the commands ought to be produced democratically, for example—but this is not a necessary feature of the state, but instead part of a distinguishable, if connected, account of how the state should be structured and function.

If, in contrast, we interpret the state as a social group things become more complex. Treating the state as a social group puts the people of the state, the members of that social group, at the very heart of the model. As well as recognizing the importance of the distinctive claims of the state, the account would also consider the position of the members of the state. It would consequently possess a horizontal dimension: the relationship between members of the state would become an issue of interest. Furthermore, the model would be bilateral, directing our attention to the ways in which the members of the state interact with, and constitute, state institutions.

THE STATE AS A SOCIAL GROUP

The central thesis of this book is that the state should be understood as a social group. In order to demonstrate this it is necessary to consider the nature of a social group and some of the forms that social groups take. It will be argued that the state should be considered a complex, formalized, social group which exists to benefit its members. Both of these issues—the nature of social groups in general, and the state in particular—are explored further in subsequent chapters. It will then be argued that this model of the state is far from novel: that it is found in Aristotle's writing on the state, and in the work of those who follow in the Aristotelian tradition.

(i) The nature of social groups

Sometimes when people talk of a group they merely mean a collection of things that share a common attribute. A collection of old pianos is a 'group' in this sense. Such a 'group' could also consist of people: the 'group' of red-headed men consists of those men who have red hair. A social group, in contrast, consist of people who are connected in a special way.[34] Membership of a social group alters the rights and obligations that people owe each other. So:

1. A social group consists of people;
2. Who are bound together by rules.

Proposition two, the inclusion of rules as a key aspect of the social group, is required for the existence of those rights and obligations which are characteristic of social groups. Being subject to a common rule is not, in itself, sufficient to create a

[34] T. Honoré, 'Groups, Laws and Obedience' in T. Honoré, *Making Law Bind* (Oxford: Clarendon Press, 1987), 33–4; D. Forsyth, *Group Dynamics* (4th edn, Belmont: Thomson, 2006), 2–5; R. Brown, *Group Processes*, 2nd edn (Oxford: Blackwell, 2002), 2–4.

social group. A resident of London and a resident of Liverpool are subject to many common rules, but these two people, by themselves, need not constitute a social group. Members of a social group are *bound* together; that is, they are identified as belonging to the group by a rule of the group. The other rules which shape their rights and duties are consequent on this rule governing membership. So, we could render proposition 2 with more precision:

2a Who are identified as members of the group by a rule of the group;
2b And whose rights and obligations are altered by virtue of their identification by this rule.

These propositions are inextricably bound together. The rules which determine the rights and duties of group membership presuppose a rule which determines group membership. Reflexively, the rule which determines group membership presupposes rules which determine rights and duties within the group. Not everyone within the group need be bound by the same set of rights and duties. A large collection of rules may constitute the group, with different people playing different roles in the group and possessing different statuses. A number of further features of social groups can be derived from these two features. A social group must, for instance, possess a purpose or purposes.[35] It exists in order to *do* something. What this 'something' is may be quite limited. The purpose of the group may merely be to act together, to undertake a task collectively, where that action has yet to be decided upon. Or the purpose of the group may be to work for the benefit of its members; families, for example, have this very nebulous purpose. The objectives of the group are derived from its rules; these rules require a certain course of conduct from the members of the group, and, consequently, set the group's purpose. Furthermore, given the significance of rules to the existence of social groups, members of the group must normally be aware, or be capable of becoming aware, of their membership of the group.[36] This does not mean that they must choose to be a member of the group, or even that they must accept their group membership. The rules may be imposed upon them by other group members: people can be coerced and bullied into following the obligations of group membership.

It has sometimes been asserted that social groups require a further feature: the recognition of other social groups.[37] This assertion can serve as a healthy corrective to over-attention on the internal aspects of group life, and there is a great deal of interest and importance to be said about the ways in which social groups interact.[38]

---

[35] J. Finnis, *Natural Law and Natural Rights* (Oxford: Oxford University Press, 1980), 150–3; against this view, see M. Gilbert, *On Social Facts* (New York: Princeton University Press, 1989), 171–2.

[36] See the discussion in T. Honoré, 'Groups, Laws and Obedience' in T. Honoré, *Making Law Bind* (Oxford: Clarendon Press, 1988), 34–5.

[37] T. Honoré, 'What is a Group?' in T. Honoré, *Making Law Bind* (Oxford: Clarendon Press, 1988), 58; Brown, note 34 above, 3.

[38] Brown, note 34 above, ch 6.

Indeed, a successful account of particular brands of social groups, especially the state, would include an account of the interaction between that group and other groups. However, it is less clear that recognition by other groups should be taken as a necessary condition of the existence of a group. It is easily conceivable that some groups could exist in secret, or in isolated places, without the recognition of other groups.

(ii) Social groups: simple and complex

The simplest type of social group consists of a collection of people who possess a common intention to act in a certain way—for example, a group of people who meet by chance in the street and decide to go for a coffee together.[39] There is a rule which determines membership of this group: individuals are members of this group when they intend to be part of the group, and are accepted as such by other members of the group. Various rights and duties then arise consequent to this rule: for instance, group members must work towards buying a drink and they must not act in a way which stops the group from achieving this objective.

Michael Bratman argues that this type of simple group, one which he styles as embodying a form of shared cooperative activity, is constructed through a complicated mesh of interacting intentions.[40] In Bratman's account shared cooperative activity arises when each of the participants intends to act in a certain way, and intends to act in this way in accordance with and because of the meshing sub-plans generated by the parallel intentions of other members of the group. Allied to this definition, Bratman insists that the meshing of intentions not be obtained through coercion, or at least that coercion not be present beyond a certain minimal point,[41] if the group is to be said to be engaged in *cooperative* activity. The coffee-seeking group fits Bratman's model. Each of our coffee-seekers intends to buy coffee, and intends to buy coffee along with and because of the others' intentions to seek a collective cup.

John Searle analyses the same situation slightly differently.[42] Searle contends that people are capable of 'we intentions' that cannot be reduced to sets of 'I intentions'. In our group of coffee-goers, each intends that 'we' seek coffee, and their individual intentionality is derived from the collective intentionality that they share; the collective intentionality comes first, the individual intentionality comes second. One way of understanding Searle's claim is as the conclusion of a piece of speculative evolutionary psychology. It has been argued that our social and (individual) technical

[39] See further the discussion in R. Ekins, *The Nature of Legislative Intent*, D.Phil submitted to Oxford University, 2009, ch 3.

[40] M. Bratman, 'Shared Cooperative Activity' in M. Bratman, *Faces of Intention* (Cambridge: Cambridge University Press, 1999). See also P. Pettit and D. Schweikard, 'Joint Actions and Group Agents' (2006) 36 Philosophy of the Social Sciences 18, 21–4.

[41] Bratman, note 40 above, 104.

[42] J. Searle, *The Construction of Social Reality* (London: Penguin, 1996), 23–6; J. Searle, 'Collective Intentions and Actions' in P. R. Cohen, J. Morgan and M. E. Pollack (eds), *Intentions in Communication* (Cambridge: MIT Press, 1990).

intelligences have different origins.[43] Perhaps our ancestors could not have reduced 'we intentions' into 'I intentions'. Like dogs and ants, they could act together, but they could not re-conceptualize these collective intentions in terms of a mesh of interlocking individual intentions. This might explain why, as Searle notes, something seems to be lost when we translate collective intentions into individual intentions; we are shifting from one mode of thought into another.

Simple social groups have a 'natural' quality to them. We do not need to reflect on the rules which construct such simple social groups. Whether these rules are learned in early childhood or are the refined product of complex evolutionary forces, for most of us obedience to them is unconscious and instinctive.[44] It seems that simple social groups speak to, and rely upon, an innate psychological need to be included within collectivities, a need that has been likened to hunger or thirst.[45]

It might be objected that simple groups—in contrast to complex groups, discussed later—are not constituted by rules. Bratman argues that people involved in shared cooperative activity need not, for this reason alone, owe obligations to each other.[46] It is enough that there are a number of people with shared, or interlocking, intentions. It will, he concedes, often be the case that obligations arise—through promises or agreements prior to the activity—but it is possible to imagine instances of shared cooperative activity which were not accompanied by such obligations. Here, the abandonment by one party of the joint task might upset others' expectations and might, even, be unreasonable, but would not violate any obligation. Under the account of social groups developed in this chapter, some of the very weakest forms of Bratman's shared cooperative activity might not count as groups at all. Two people who, by chance, happen to be walking in the same direction and exchange a few words would not constitute a social group even if, in some very thin sense, their conversation met Bratman's test.[47] But most of the examples that Bratman gives of shared cooperative activity should be understood as rule-based, and are underpinned by duties and entitlements. Bratman correctly notes that even the simplest forms of shared cooperative activity are buttressed by social pressure towards stability:[48] people are required to demonstrate some level of consistency when engaged in collective actions. In the language of social rules, discussed later, people are subject to social criticism when they abandon collective activities without good reason. When a group member unreasonably abandons the simple group, she breaks a rule of that group, a rule set by the wider community of which she is a part. The annoyance felt by other group members is not merely the irritation experienced when something

[43] S. Mithen, *The Prehistory of the Mind* (London: Thames and Hudson, 1996), esp chs 4, 7.

[44] See generally, M. Ridley, *The Origins of Virtue* (London: Penguin, 1996).

[45] Forsyth, note 34 above, 73–4.

[46] M. Bratman, 'Shared Intention' in M. Bratman, *Faces of Intention* (Cambridge: Cambridge University Press, 1999), 125–9. See the contrary view of Gilbert: Gilbert, note 35 above, 410–16.

[47] See further, Pettit and Schweikard, note 40 above, 31–2.

[48] Bratman, note 46 above, 126.

we expect to happen fails to happen (as when, for example, a friend who is often in the coffee shop at noon fails to show) but is an annoyance caused by the frustration of an expectation we were entitled to expect would be satisfied—even if this entitlement was not engendered by a promise or agreement. This observation is reinforced by Bratman's developed example of an instance of shared cooperative activity that is not, he argues, accompanied by the creation of obligations. Bratman hypothesizes a pair of singers who decide to sing a duet together but have a clear understanding that either can abandon the project at any point. Here, the singers have decided to adopt a new rule which alters the basic set of rules which constitute simple social groups: they have included in the constitution of the group a rule empowering either to dissolve the group at will. Contrary to Bratman's analysis of the example, it demonstrates both that the basic social template of a simple group includes a rule that would ordinarily limit the freedom with which a member can (without criticism) abandon the project of the group, and, also, that people within a simple social group have some latitude to depart from that template through agreement.

There are limitations on the tasks that can be accomplished by simple social groups and the problems that such groups can overcome. Simple groups lack significant capacity to divide up tasks between their members.[49] Neither Bratman's nor Searle's model allows much latitude for the group to decide in advance that some of its members will execute one part of a task whilst others undertake another function. These accounts require that, in Bratman's words, 'each agent attempts to be responsive to the intentions and actions of the other, knowing that the other is attempting to be similarly responsive'.[50] What division of labour that can arise within simple groups arises spontaneously or through express agreement: one member sees another member acting towards their common objective and shapes her conduct to fit in with this, or the two agree to divide elements of the task between them.[51] Simple groups also lack sophisticated mechanisms to end disagreement about their objectives or membership. Any dispute that cannot be resolved unanimously leads to the collapse of the group—though the pressures towards unanimity in such disputes can be considerable. Joining a simple group is correspondingly difficult. A person who wishes to join must gain the acceptance of all existing group members. Leaving a simple group is, in contrast, startlingly easy. A person who decides she has had enough of the group at once ceases to be a group member; she no longer has the common intention which is the part of a test of group membership. Simple groups are effective at pursuing easy, straightforward objectives over a short period of time. They are not effective at pursuing complicated objectives over a long period of time, which require planning and during which the membership of the group may need to change.

This discussion takes us to a second collection of social groups: complex social groups. In a complex social group not all members need be aware of the intentions,

---

[49] Though simple social groups can arise within more complicated structures.

[50] Bratman, note 40 above, 94.

[51] Bratman, note 46 above, 110–11.

the tasks performed, or even the existence of all the other members. Complex groups may include members who disagree about the overall objective of the group, and may use coercion to secure obedience to group rules. Complex groups are constituted, at least in part, by rules that have been consciously chosen. These rules may have been chosen by some or all members of the group, or members of the group may have chosen to act within a template of rules created by others. Complex groups have the capacity to include rules in their constitutions which allow for the division of tasks, the resolution of disputes and the regulation of membership. Some aspects of the rules of complex social groups, and the functions these rules can have, are investigated further in following chapters.

The state is, obviously, a complex social group. But the phenomenon of the simple social group lurks behind our understanding of complex groups, shaping the ways we interpret group activity. For instance, there is a standing temptation to assume that when a complex group undertakes an action or adopts an intention, all members of that group undertake that action or adopt that intention. Such attribution is also common in the context of states: we are tempted to assume that all members of a war-like state are war-like, or all members of a prejudiced state are prejudiced. This type of derivation makes sense in the context of simple social groups, where the intentions ascribed to the group are a function of the intentions of the totality of the group's members. It does not make sense in complex groups, where the intentions ascribed to the group can be unknown to, or rejected by, some group members.[52]

(iii) The purposes of social groups

Social groups do lots of things. A rough divide can be drawn, though, between those groups which exist primarily for the benefit of their members, and those which exist primarily to accomplish some task which is not of direct benefit to their members. Families and trade unions exist to benefit their members. These groups undertake tasks which directly benefit their members (negotiating a pay rise) or which their members benefit from participating in (an employer against employee football match). When such groups undertake tasks with the direct aim of benefiting someone else (the trade union campaigns on environmental issues), these tasks are a secondary activity of the group. Charities and businesses, in contrast, exist to achieve goals which are not to the direct benefit of the members of the group. Charities aim to provide a benefit to people who are outside of the group: caring for the sick or giving resources to the poor. Businesses operate to benefit a specific sub-section of the group, the owners of the business. Of course, this division must not be overstated. Families can, and should, undertake tasks to benefit needy people outside the family group; businesses ought to care for the welfare of their employees. But a group which loses focus on the broad category of which group it belongs to will quickly get into trouble. A trade union which spends all of its time campaigning on

---

[52] See chapter 7.

environmental issues or a business that is preoccupied with the well-being of its workforce are groups which are fundamentally dysfunctional. Almost certainly, they will not succeed in their pursuit of these aims—because the tasks pursued run against their structures—and, almost certainly, the existence of the group will become precarious.

Some of the literature on group dynamics draws a similar distinction between relationship interaction and task interaction within social groups.[53] Task interaction occurs when the group works together in order to achieve a plan or goal. Relationship interaction occurs when group members provide support and help for each other. Invariably, both of these types of interaction will occur within all social groups. A healthy business, for instance, will primarily contain instances of task interaction, but must also contain a significant amount of relationship interaction as well. The personal bonds between workers, and between workers and managers, are important to the successful functioning of the business. However, different types of groups are characterized by varying levels of these types of behaviour. Dealings within successful charities and businesses will be predominantly characterized by task-related interaction, whereas dealings within successful families and trade unions will tend to be predominantly characterized by relationship interaction.

(iv) The state as a social group

We are now at a point where we can step back and consider whether it is correct to characterize the state as a social group and, if so, what form it takes. The state clearly has the key attributes of a social group. It has members, in its citizens and subjects, amongst others, and it has rules which bind the group together, in its constitution. It is a complex group, and many of its constitutive rules will exhibit a considerable degree of formalization. The purposes of the state will be considered at length in a later chapter, but it will be argued that its primary objective is to advance the well-being of its members. It falls into the same broad category of groups as families, trade unions, and friendly societies.

There is nothing novel about conceptualizing the state as a social group. Indeed, one of the very first accounts of the state emphasized this aspect of the state's nature: that of Aristotle, in *The Politics*.

The types of governing unit that Aristotle was writing about were very different from our modern states. These were city-states, far smaller in territory and in population than most of our contemporary equivalents. When Aristotle discussed the duties and entitlements of citizenship, the confined nature of these polities shaped his account. His account of citizenship included a number of assertions that are only plausible within a very confined citizenry. Aristotle claimed, for example, that

---

[53] Forsyth, note 34 above, 10–12, ch 2; Brown, note 34 above, 40–44. For similar observations made from a very different tradition, see W. Halton, 'Some Unconscious Aspects of Organizational Life: Contributions from Psychoanalysis' and J. Stokes, 'The Unconscious at Work in Groups and Teams: Contributions from the Work of Wilfred Bion' both in A. Obholzer and V. Z. Roberts (eds), *The Unconscious at Work* (London: Routledge, 1994).

citizenship can only function where it is possible to possess knowledge of the character of your fellow citizens; only then can citizens know each other sufficiently well to pick the best people for government office and to adjudicate in law-suits.[54] Furthermore, it is a central aspect of Aristotle's citizen that he—and it was, of course, only a he—held an office of state.[55] In modern states, often containing many millions of people, all members of the state cannot possibly know each other, even at a superficial level. And it is difficult to argue that each citizen must occupy an office of state in addition to the office of citizen: there are not enough state offices to go around. When we talk of modern citizens, and modern states, then, we are reflecting on institutions which have changed significantly since Aristotle's time. Nevertheless, Aristotle's city-state is an ancestor of our modern state, and it is relatively easy to imagine how his understanding of the state might have evolved in response to growth in territory and population.[56]

In *The Politics* Aristotle identified six different groups of constitutions: monarchies, aristocracies, constitutional governments (that is, government by the citizenry), tyrannies, oligarchies, and democracies,[57] with democracy here implying a type of mob-rule. Aristotle argued that the central case of the state was to be found in constitutional government, thus drawing a tight connection between citizenship and the state. To properly understand the state it is necessary, in Aristotle's analysis, to understand citizenship. Citizenship is the state institution which instantiates the proper relationship between state members and the state. Members can have other types of relationship with the state—subjects and monarchs, for instance—but these are deviant forms to be understood by their connection to citizenship. For Aristotle then, citizenship and the state are inseparable.

The insistence on the significance of citizenship for an account of the state raises two issues which are discussed elsewhere in this book. Aristotle's methodological commitment, his invocation of the virtuous central case as a way of illuminating other manifestations of social phenomena was critiqued in chapter 1. The nature of citizenship, and the further question of whether an understanding of citizenship is essential for an understanding of the state, will be considered in the following chapter. What is of present interest is the extent to which Aristotle's account of the state squares with our model of a social group.

Aristotle's state is not just a set of institutions that addresses the people, it is also partly constituted by those people occupying offices of the constitution. Insisting on the inclusion of the citizenry as an element of the state gives Aristotle's account a horizontal dimension. Not only is his account concerned with the types of demands which states levy over their people, and the proper reaction of those people to these demands, it also includes an account of how those people should interact with each

---

[54] Aristotle, *The Politics and Constitution of Athens*, ed S. Everson (Cambridge: Cambridge University Press, 1996), VII.IV, 1326b10–26.

[55] Aristotle, note 54 above, III.II, 1276a4–7.

[56] C. Johnson, *Aristotle's Theory of the State* (London: Macmillan, 1990), 2–3.

[57] Aristotle, note 54 above, III.VII, 1279b4–6.

other within the state. Aristotle insists on the 'natural equality' of the citizens, that they must share in the government of the state;[58] the salvation of the community is the common business of them all.[59] The good citizen, the good state member, owes, at the very least, two duties to his fellow citizens. The first is to play a part in the governing of the state. The second is to execute that task in the interests of all the citizenry; the state's aim is to promote the well-being of all citizens, not just a portion of them. The institution of citizenship also gives Aristotle's account of the state a bilateral quality. Citizens interact with the institutions of the state, these institutions are under the control of the citizenry. Whilst the state produces commands which it expects its citizens to obey, these commands are the indirect product of the citizens themselves. Consequently, there is a sense in which Aristotle's citizens own their state; it is their state, they are responsible for it, and their lives are—in part, at least—coloured by its successes and failures. The citizen shares in the honours, and the dishonours, of the state.[60]

The deviant models of state in Aristotle's work—tyrannies, oligarchies, and democracies—are also social groups, but are presented as failing social groups. A tyranny, for example, is a state which is run as if it were a business. The tyrant compels those within the state to work for him; taking the profits of their labour. Here, the group has a purpose—the enrichment of the tyrant at the expense of the people—which is at odds, on Aristotle's account at least, with the basic purpose of the state.

CHOOSING AN ACCOUNT OF THE STATE

We now have two accounts—or two groups of accounts—of the state before us. The first, set out by Weber and Green, focused on the institutions of the state and the type of claims those institutions made over individuals. The second, set out by Aristotle and forming the basis of much of the rest of this book, presented the state as a particular type of social group. The gap between these models is not as great as it seems. Those who conceptualize the state as a social group need not—indeed, it will be argued, should not—reject the broad thrust of the work of those who have focused on the particular types of claims made by the state. After all, there are many social groups which seek to advance the well-being of their members. At least part of what is distinctive about the state is the manner in which it pursues this goal, the demands it makes of its people in the course of its activities. The second group of accounts of the state must include, in some form, the insights developed by Weber and Green.

In reply to this, supporters of the narrower accounts of the state could argue that they are happy for constitutional theory to discuss the nature of citizenship and the

---

[58] *Ibid.*, II.II 1261b1–5.

[59] *Ibid.*, III.IV, 1276b28–31.

[60] *Ibid.*, III.V, 1278a35–36. Citizens' responsibility for the state is discussed further in chapter 8.

relationship of people with the state, but would reject the claim that reflection on these issues is a necessary part of a satisfying account of the state. There are, however, two arguments, or groups of arguments, that require us to move from the first set of accounts of the state to the second. The first set of arguments contends that a satisfying account of the state would present it as a social group. The second, more ambitious, set of arguments contends that Aristotle was correct: not only should the state be considered a social group, it should be considered a social group of which citizenship is an essential aspect.

First, returning to our discussion of methodology in chapter one, a successful account of the state will bring out the features of the state which are of importance to us. The authority-based accounts of the state certainly bring forward some of its important features. States do issue commands, these commands do take the form of authoritative directives—and these directives are of enormous importance to the people of the state. The ability to produce directives of this type creates the possibility that the state can coordinate action. The possibility of coordination brings with it the possibility of great benefits to people—facilitating collective action and solving coordination problems—and the possibility of great harm. Models of the state as a social group point to other important features of the state. They emphasize the interaction between the people of the state in the context of the state—that is, their interaction as state members rather than as private individuals—and the connection between the people of the state and the institutions of the state.

It might be objected that whilst these features of states are often of interest they are not necessary features of the state. It is conceivable, it might be argued, that a state could exist in which there was no interaction between its people in the context of the state, and in which its people had no connections with the state. Setting aside the troublesome question of whether it is helpful to ask for the 'necessary' or 'essential' features of a social phenomenon,[61] it can be contended that the features of the state which characterize it as a social group are, indeed, necessary features of an account of the state, features that all states must possess to some degree. Every state contains people, and in every state those people will have a relationship with the state, even if it is merely the reaction of a recipient of a command to the commander. The bilaterality of the state is a necessary feature of the state. Further questions about the proper attitude of the members of the state towards these commands relate, therefore, to a central feature of the state. Additionally, at a minimum the people of the state are bound together as the addressees of these commands. How they respond, how they should respond, to these commands will depend on the actions of their fellows. The horizontal aspect of the state is, consequently, also a necessary feature of the phenomenon.

The discussion so far has attempted to show that the inclusion of people within the state requires that accounts of the state treat it as a social group, leaving space for reflection on the bilaterality and horizontality inherent in group membership. But a broader response could be given to supporters of narrow accounts of the state. There

---

[61] On this issue, see B. Bix, 'Conceptual Questions and Jurisprudence' (1995) 1 Legal Theory 465.

are other important features of the state which these accounts fail to accommodate. For instance, functioning states are invariably constituted by a mix of social and legal rules. The nature of social rules will be discussed later, but such rules are only comprehensible in the context of a social group. An understanding of the role of social rules within the constitution is necessary for an understanding of the functioning and continuity of state institutions.

A second, more ambitious, defence of the state as a social group would follow Aristotle's lead, and present citizenship as a central feature of the state: the paradigmatic instance of state membership against which other forms of state membership should be contrasted. An understanding of the state would consequently require an understanding of citizenship. Furthermore, if correct, this aspect of the state's nature would condition and shape the authority claims identified by Weber and Green. This argument requires a fuller account of citizenship than has been provided here, and must wait until the next chapter.

༄ 3 ༄

The Members of the State

This chapter discusses the relationships people can have with states and the ways in which these relationships interact with, and are conditioned by, the purposes and claims of the state. At the heart of it is an account of citizenship. Here we will reflect on the nature of citizenship as it is manifested in the connection between the citizen and the state, and—equally importantly—in the interaction of citizens. It is argued that citizenship is the paradigmatic form of state membership; an institution which must be established if the state is to maximally achieve its primary purpose. To lay the foundations for this argument, the chapter starts by identifying this purpose, and then demonstrates how this illuminates the claims of the state, discussed in the previous chapter.

THE PURPOSES OF THE STATE

All social groups possess purposes. These are the aims of the group which are determined by the rules which constitute the group. The success of the group will then be judged by the worth of its aims and its achievement of these goals. A group fails either where its objectives are morally flawed—a group established to persecute a minority, for instance—or where its objectives are valuable, but it fails to achieve them. Sometimes the group sets its own purposes. A charity has a wide range of objectives it can pursue, from caring for the sick to educating the young. On other occasions, these purposes are determined for the group, either by limiting the group's options—a charity cannot exist to make the rich richer—or by setting a purpose for the group which cannot be altered or disregarded. An understanding of the purposes of a group has significance for membership of the group. It establishes whether the group is one which a person should wish to join and support, and, moreover, for a person who belongs to the group, it partly determines whether she is a member of a successful or a failing group.

Before we turn to consider the purposes of the state it is necessary to distinguish the needs of the state; that is, those features which the state must enjoy if it is to retain its identity as a state. Not all of the essential needs of an institution are also objectives of that institution. The objective of a doctor is to treat the sick, but, to accomplish this purpose, the doctor needs to keep herself fed. A doctor who fails to treat the sick has failed to succeed in her role as a doctor—she has failed to achieve one of the goals set for that role by the social rules which constitute it. A doctor who fails to eat, in contrast, has not failed as a doctor until she fails to heal the sick as a result. There is a distinction to be drawn between failing to satisfy the necessary prerequisites of a role and failing to meet the requirements of the rules which define that role.

(i) The necessary prerequisites of the state

There are a few prerequisites which the state must meet, to some extent, if it is to retain its identity as a state. For instance, even the very narrowest accounts of the nature of the state require that it possess a functioning legal order. If the state is to issue authoritative directives to its people it will require institutions to produce these directives, to adjudicate upon disputes, and to coerce backsliders into obedience. This is a consequence of the size and complexity of the state. In contrast to some tribes or small communes, the state requires a legal order through which it can address its people. Furthermore, given the type of authority claim that the state makes, this legal order must be controlled by the state. A body which relied on an outside legal order to validate and enforce its commands would not be presenting itself as a supreme authority, or asserting a monopoly of legitimate force. Whilst a functioning legal order does not require a state, states do require at least one functioning domestic legal order. In short, knowingly or unknowingly, states need to maintain the rule of law, at least on some understandings of that much disputed term.[1]

Maintenance of the rule of law is not the only prerequisite which a state must meet. There are a number of other qualities which it must possess, some of which intermesh with the rule of law. The state must also maintain, to an extent, the separation of powers, at least in a thin sense.[2] The state must preserve its capacity to issue commands, adjudicate disputes, and enforce its decisions. To be effective, people must, generally, know the content of the law and be reasonably confident that it will be upheld by the courts and enforced by the executive. It is hard to see how a polity which completely lacked these characteristics could function for very long.

A further question might be asked about the relationship of the rule of law and separation of powers to the state. Given the state *needs* to maintain these features, is it also the case that their maintenance is a necessary *purpose* of the state? Or is it like the need of the doctor to eat: a prerequisite to the successful execution of her role as doctor, but not an objective set by that role? Many constitutions explicitly identify the health of the legal order as one of the objectives of the state. Injunctions to comply with the rule of law and separation of powers are commonly found in the first few paragraphs of constitutions.[3] Even where this is not the case, the importance of these principles is often recognized in the decisions of courts or by the social rules

---

[1] On the nature of the rule of law see: J. Raz, 'The Rule of Law and its Virtue' in J. Raz, *The Authority of Law* (Oxford, Oxford University Press: 1979) and N. W. Barber 'Must Legalistic Conceptions of the Rule of Law Have a Social Dimension?' (2004) Ratio Juris 474.

[2] On which see N. W. Barber, 'Prelude to the Separation of Powers' (2001) 60 Cambridge LJ 59.

[3] See, for example, the Spanish Constitution, Art 1(1).

that constitute the state. For many states, then, the rule of law and the separation of powers are both needs that the state must meet and purposes set for the state by its constitution. It does not follow, though, that their maintenance is a necessary purpose of the state, a purpose that all states ought to pursue by reason of their identity as a state. It is conceivable that a state could exist which did not appreciate the significance of the rule of law or separation of powers, and this failure of appreciation would not challenge its identity as a state. Provided that it had the good fortune to possess a functioning legal order, providing this need was met, it would not matter that the state did not regard its maintenance as one of its objectives.

(ii) The purposes of the state

All of the tasks discussed above are objectives which the state must, to some degree, achieve, but none are purposes which the state must pursue. The state could achieve them unthinkingly, or in the process of pursuing some other objective. Aristotle contended that there was a further task which the state must pursue, and pursue directly; an objective of the state which gave direction and moral force to its other tasks. Aristotle contended that it is a necessary feature of the state that it is obliged to operate for the advancement of the well-being of its members.[4] His claim embodies two sub-claims. He asserted that, first, the state ought to promote the well-being of its members (as a doctor ought to treat the sick). And, second, that this is a necessary aspect of the nature of the state: it is this purpose that partly defines an institution as a state (just as treating the sick is a purpose which partly defines being a doctor). We might also add a third possible claim to these two: the state must, of necessity, endorse this purpose. Not only should the state promote the well-being of its members, not only is the existence of this obligation on the state an aspect of its nature, it must, furthermore, also acknowledge that this is its primary purpose. An entity which rejected the duty to promote its members' well-being would not amount to a state—or would, at the very least, be a fundamentally deviant form of the state. These three claims are of increasing ambition. To claim that the state ought to promote the well-being of its people is, or should be, fairly uncontroversial. To claim that this obligation is an aspect of the nature of the state is harder to demonstrate. And to show that it is an aspect of the nature of the state that it recognizes this obligation is more ambitious still.

(a) The state's obligation to promote the well-being of its members

Not all social groups exist to promote their members' well-being. Some exist to promote the well-being of others, or to promote the well-being of a sub-section of their members. A charity, for instance, may operate to benefit the poor; a

---

[4] See, for instance, Aristotle, *The Politics and Constitution of Athens*, ed S. Everson, (Cambridge: Cambridge University Press, 1996), I.II 1252b28–30; III.IX 1280b39–40.
C. Johnson, *Aristotle's Theory of the State* (London: Macmillan, 1989), ch 4. Aquinas advanced similar arguments: J. Finnis, *Aquinas* (Oxford: Oxford University Press, 1998), ch 7. See also T. Endicott, 'The Logic of Freedom and Power' in J. Tasioulas and S. Besson (eds), *Philosophy of International Law* (Oxford: Oxford University Press, 2010).

business may operate to benefit its shareholders. Frequently members of these groups use the group to advance their well-being indirectly: charity workers often adopt the goals of the group as one of their life-projects; employees are paid for their efforts by the business. The state, in contrast, belongs to a collection of social groups which exist in order to advance their members' interests directly. It stands alongside families, trade unions, and social clubs. Aristotle's functionalist account of the emergence of the state draws attention to this aspect of the state's identity. States come into existence, wrote Aristotle, because of their capacity to advance members' well-being. At the start of this process was the family, a form of association which provides for the needs of those who share a biological connection.[5] Whilst family groups might be sufficient to provide for the bare subsistence of their members, as time progressed families bonded together into villages in order to better their minimal existence.[6] The village, like the family, exists for the well-being of the villagers; it has an overriding purpose similar to that of the family, but lacks its biological base. And then, villages, in their turn, united into large communities: the city-states, in which people could achieve their fullest flourishing.[7] The historical accuracy of this story is open to question, but it brings forward the similarities between the state and these other groups. In some respects, at least, the state is the family writ large.

As well as pointing to the similarities of the state with other groups which advance the well-being of their members, Aristotle also defended this assertion by drawing attention to the structure of the state. A satisfying understanding of a social phenomenon, contended Aristotle, would present it in its healthiest form.[8] A 'healthy' manifestation of a social institution is one which we have reason to create, and we only have reason to create institutions that advance our well-being. The state must be understood as an institution which advances our well-being, and it is the task of the theorist to illuminate the distinctive ways it acquits, or fails to acquit, this task. Reflection on the wide powers of the state show that it possesses a broad and distinctive capacity to advance the well-being of its members. Aristotle's methodology was discussed in chapter 1, but it is not necessary to accept his strong thesis that a good explanation of a social institution invariably shows it in its best light in order to accept the more limited thesis that the purpose of the state is the advancement of the well-being of its members. A more conservative version of Aristotle's argument would couch it in terms of importance. Looking at the state, reflecting on the powers it asserts and, to an extent, possesses, its capacity to advance the well-being of its members is one of its defining features. At the very least we can say with some confidence that the state *ought* to seek to achieve this objective.

[5] Aristotle, *The Politics and Constitution of Athens*, ed S. Everson (Cambridge: Cambridge University Press, 1996), I.II 1252b12–14.

[6] *Ibid.*, I.II 1252b16–18.

[7] *Ibid.*, I.II 1252b28–32.

[8] *Ibid.*, I.II 1253a23–26; Johnson, note 4 above, 5–7.

(b) This obligation as an objective of the state

The preceding arguments have not taken us quite as far as we need to go in order to show that the promotion of the well-being of the state's members is a necessary purpose of the state. It may be the case that the state ought to promote the well-being of its members, but it may not be the case that it is invariably an objective of the state to promote their well-being. The torturer, for instance, ought not to torture, but this moral obligation does not set her objectives as a torturer. To show that it is invariably an objective of the state to promote the well-being of its members it must be shown that there is invariably a constitutive rule of this type of social institution which sets this as that institution's goal. Once again, the institution of a doctor provides an example of this. It is invariably a constitutive rule of the institution of a doctor that the doctor heal the sick. In all societies, at all times, if a person is a doctor she will only have succeeded in this role to the extent to which she achieves this end.

The obligation to promote members' well-being is an obligation of this type. It is an external rule which we impose on the state. The nature and scope of external rules will be discussed further in the next chapter, but, for now, they may be understood as the rules which set the templates within which social groups are constituted. A charity, for instance, may not adopt as its primary purpose the benefit of its donors. A group which specified this as its primary purpose would not be a charity—even if it considered itself to be charitable. This is an external rule which is imposed upon charities. In the context of the state, it is invariably the case that there is a rule of the state's constitution which sets the well-being of its members as its primary purpose. A state which fails to advance the well-being of its members has not just failed to acquit a moral obligation which applies to it (as an active torturer fails to meet the moral obligation not to torture) it has also failed as a state (whilst the active torturer may have succeeded in her role). It is, perhaps, worth noting that a state which fails to pursue the well-being of its members, or pursues this goal ineptly, is not less of a state for this reason: it is a clear instance of a state, but is a failing state.

The plausibility of this claim turns on the plausibility of the methodological assertions advanced in chapter 1. The account of the state being provided is our account of the state; that is, it is an account of the state developed out of our community's understanding of the institution and paying attention to those aspects of that phenomenon which are of particular importance to us. It is an aspect of our community's understanding of the state that it is partly constituted by a rule requiring that it act in the interests of its people.

A common reaction to an argument of this type is to postulate an example of the institution under discussion which does not include the feature contended, and then to argue that this hypothetical shows the feature is not a 'necessary' element of the institution. Depending on the imagination of the interlocutor, these examples can expand to include angels, gaseous Martians, and bloody-minded drafters of laws whose sole aim is to prove one school or other of legal philosophy mistaken. So, it might be objected, what of a state constitution that explicitly asserts that the purpose of the state is not the advancement of the well-being of its members? What of a constitution which specified the goal of the state was the retardation of their well-being?

Would not the bare possibility of such a state show that the argument of this chapter is mistaken? Three things could be said in reply to such an example. First, we might exclude the masochistic 'state' from the set of phenomena to be studied as the base material for an account of the state. A band of robbers who controlled a territory with the explicit and unashamed aim of enriching themselves would not count as a state, even in a borderline or deviant sense. Were we to criticize this group, we would not claim that they had failed as a state—though we could properly criticize them for many other things. Secondly, we might accept that this polity is a form of state, but present it as an odd one; a borderline or deviant form of the institution. It resembles the central case of the state in some respects, but differs from it in others. Such a polity is not just a failing state, it also falls outside the central case of the state. Thirdly, we could insist that our rule did apply to the polity, even if people within it denied the operation of the rule. The drafters of the constitution have made a mistake: they have tried to include a rule in the constitution of the state which the nature of the state does not permit to be included. Such a 'state' would be like a 'charity' which set the enrichment of its donors as its primary goal: it is either not really a charity or its purported primary goal is not, in reality, its primary goal.

(c) The recognition of this obligation as an aspect of the nature of the state
The previous section argued that it is a constitutive rule of all states that their primary purpose is the advancement of the well-being of their members. This section makes a more ambitious argument: not only is this a constitutive rule of all states, it is, furthermore, part of the nature of the state that it acknowledges this as its primary goal. These two claims are distinct. There could be social institutions or social roles which are defined by rules of which the people within those institutions or roles are not aware. It is a constitutive rule of the institution of a prison, and a constitutive rule of the role of prison guard, that the welfare of prisoners in their care should be protected. Those responsible for the atrocities at the Abu Ghraib prison in Iraq appeared to be unaware of this rule. Not only did they mistreat the prisoners, they also appeared to think that this mistreatment was a proper way of acting within their prison system.[9] They were mistaken. Not only had they acted immorally by torturing prisoners, they also failed to acquit the obligations which fell on them as prison officers. They had not just failed as humans, but as officials as well. In contrast, the social role of doctor requires that the person occupying it acknowledge that her objective is to heal sick patients. A person who worked in the medical sciences but rejected this as one of her objectives would not be a doctor, she would be something else—perhaps a medical researcher.

The state is an institution of this type. Not only is it an aspect of the nature of the state that its primary purpose is the well-being of its members, it is also part of the nature of the state that it acknowledge this as its primary purpose. An organization which denied this would not be a state at all. A violent criminal gang, in which the strongest member took all the spoils, would not be a state for this reason. The acknowl-

---

[9] For an examination of the institutional psychology of Abu Ghraib, see P. Zimbardo, *The Lucifer Effect: How Good People Turn Evil* (London: Random House, 2007).

edgment of the primary purpose of the state can be seen in the constitutions of states and in the rhetoric of leaders and commentators. Sometimes, admittedly, the claim appears contrived and implausible. No matter how bad the tyrant, or oppressive the regime, rulers and their supporters invariably present the government as acting in the best interests of the people.[10] A number of ingenious justifications are invoked. Monarchy and dictatorship, for example, are often explained in terms of parental benevolence. Robert Filmer, the grand defender of monarchy, depicted the king as a father, whose duty was to protect and aid his people.[11] Another justification that is sometimes given is that a dictatorship is needed to cope with a period of crisis and to facilitate a return to democratic government.[12] The people are temporarily stripped of their liberties, but only in order to preserve these liberties in the long run. A combination of these arguments, often used by colonial powers, is that a native population has yet to reach the stage at which it can govern itself. Their domination is, then, in their own best interests; a subjugation which they should be grateful for, if only they could fully appreciate its rationale.[13] Finally, some states carve up their membership to exclude certain groups. A persecuted minority ceases to count as members of the state, and the state, therefore, need not consider their well-being when acting.[14]

It is an invariable rule of state constitutions that the state's primary purpose is the promotion of the well-being of its members. A state which failed to satisfy this duty, or which did not even attempt the task, would still be a state, but would be a failing state. Its identity as a state would not be in dispute, but it would be a bad and an inadequate state, a state of which it would be a misfortune to be a member. But a political entity which disavowed this rule would either not be a state or would be a radically deviant form of state—like a 'state' which lacked governing institutions or a territory.

Before moving on to discuss the ways in which the primary purpose of the state shapes and conditions the claims of the state, it is necessary to calm a worry which might have been raised by the previous paragraphs. The account of the state presented here does not argue that the state is entirely defined by its function; it is not, on at least some understandings of the term, a 'functional kind'.[15]

---

[10] See generally C. Travis and E. Aronson, *Mistakes Were Made (But Not By Me)* (London: Pinter & Martin, 2007), especially chapter 7. For a revealing set of interviews with dictators see R. Orizio, *Talk of the Devil: Encounters with Seven Dictators* (New York: Walker & Co, 2003).

[11] R. Filmer, *Patriarcha*, ed J. Sommerville (Cambridge: Cambridge University Press, 1991), 12. See also D. Oliver, *Common Values and the Public-Private Divide* (London: Butterworths, 1999), 124–6, and M. Loughlin, *The Idea of Public Law* (Oxford: Oxford University Press, 2003), 13–19.

[12] See generally, C. Rossiter, *Constitutional Dictatorship* (New Jersey: Princeton University Press, 1948), chs 1 and 2. See also D. Dyzenhaus, *The Constitution of Law: Legality in a Time of Emergency* (Cambridge: Cambridge University Press, 2006).

[13] H. Arendt, *The Origins of Totalitarianism* (London: Harcourt, 1968), 128–9.

[14] T. Janoski, *Citizenship and Civil Society* (Cambridge: Cambridge University Press, 1998), 46–50.

[15] See the discussion in M. Moore, 'Law as a Functional Kind' in R. P. George, *Natural Law Theory: Contemporary Issues* (Oxford University Press, Oxford, 1992), and the criticisms made by Green in L. Green, 'The Functions of Law' (1998) 12 Cogito 117.

Some parts of our world can be understood wholly by reference to their function. A weapon, for example, is a 'functional kind' of this type: anything which is given the function of a weapon is a weapon. In contrast to this, an understanding of the 'function' of the state, that is, the primary purpose of the state as discussed above, is a necessary element of a satisfying understanding of the nature of the state, but it is far from sufficient. The state is also characterized by other features. It has a people, and a territory, a set of governing institutions, to name but three. Furthermore, other social groups—families and trade unions, for instance—have the same function as the state, but do not become 'states' for this reason. For both of these reasons, it would be a mistake to claim that the state was a functional kind.

(iii) The interaction of the primary purpose of the state and its authority claims: the nature of those claims[16]

The authority claims identified by Weber and Green as characteristic of the state are very similar, to say the least, to those claims identified by Joseph Raz, and others, as characteristic of law.[17] Much has been written about the nature of the supposed claims made by the law, with discussion coalescing around two issues: first, how can law 'claim' anything, and, second, if law does advance a claim, what is the content of that claim? Though these issues have been canvassed in the context of law, they are also of interest to those working on the state. The first question, the question of the ability of the state to advance claims, will be discussed later in this book, alongside the parallel problem of the ascription of actions and intentions to the state. The second question, the nature of the authority claim levelled by the state, can now be reconsidered following the identification of the primary purpose of the state.

Joseph Raz contends that law claims moral authority over those it addresses: through its language and its officials, law asserts that its subjects ought to obey the law 'as it requires to be obeyed'.[18] Similar assertions have been made by many other scholars.[19] A question can be raised about how this claim to moral authority should be interpreted. It could be that law simply, blankly, tells us that we ought to behave in a certain way, and we should behave in this way because it tells us to. It could be that the law tells us we ought to behave in a certain way and, implicit in so doing, also claims that there are good, if undefined, (moral) reasons for the demand. It

---

[16] I am grateful to Maris Köpcke Tinturé for leading me to reflect on the points made in this section.

[17] See generally, M. Köpcke Tinturé, *Some Main Questions Concerning Legal Validity,* D.Phil submitted to Oxford University (2009), ch 6; J. Gardner, 'How Law Claims, What Law Claims' (2008) Oxford Legal Studies Research Paper No 44/2008.

[18] J. Raz, 'Authority, Law and Morality' in J. Raz, *Ethics in the Public Domain* (rev edn, Oxford: Clarendon Press, 1995), 216.

[19] Gardner, note 17 above, 1–3.

could be that the law tells us we ought to behave in a certain way, and then indicates the good (moral) reasons it relies upon, expressing them through the reasoning of its officials.[20] It is not necessary to resolve these conundrums about the nature of law here. When the state exercises its purported authority—often, but not invariably, using the medium of law—its claim must be understood in the context of its primary purpose.

The primary purpose of the state requires that all of its exercises of power are undertaken to advance, directly or indirectly, the well-being of its members. When it issues purportedly authoritative directives it therefore claims not only that its people ought to act in conformity with these commands, but, addition-ally, it implies some further explanation of the basis of this obligation. The state implies that there are good moral reasons which apply to the subjects of the directive which render their obedience mandatory. There is a wide range of dif-ferent reasons which might lurk behind the directive. It could rest on reasons which concern the subject's immediate welfare: she will be healthier, or her projects will meet with greater success if she complies with the directive. The directive might duplicate existing moral obligations the subject owes to others, or provide a mechanism through which she can partially acquit the obligations she owes them. There are a large variety of possible reasons which might under-pin the directive. Frequently, the state will not explain what these reasons are, but it will nonetheless represent that they exist. If these reasons are not present, the state has acted wrongly: it has represented something that is not the case.

(iv) The interaction of the primary purpose of the state and its authority claims: the integrative function of the state

States are, of course, not the only form of social group which exists to advance the well-being of their members. The family is also a social group of this type. Like the state, the primary purpose of the family is the promotion of the well-being of family members. Like the state, this primary purpose can be pursued in a wide range of different ways. The difference between the family and the state lies, in part, in the reach of the authority which the state claims to exert over its people. This authority claim, considered in some detail in the previous chapter, interacts with the primary purpose of the state in a distinc-tive fashion. In Leslie Green's account of the state, the state claims to possess supreme authority over its people,[21] whilst Weber wrote of the state claiming the monopoly of legitimate force, a claim that can also be understood as an assertion of authority. In each of these versions, the state asserts that it is entitled to have the final say about its mem-bers' connections with other social groups and the ways in which these groups conduct themselves. When the state functions well, this interplay between the state and other

---

[20] Perhaps this is one way of interpreting Dworkin's position: see R. M. Dworkin, *Law's Empire* (Cambridge Mass: Harvard University Press, 1986).

[21] L. Green, *The Authority of the State* (Oxford: Clarendon Press, 1990), 78–83.

collective associations is mutually beneficial.[22] A healthy state will exercise this authority to facilitate, limit, and integrate social groups which come within its sphere of authority. The state facilitates social groups in a number of ways, principally by protecting weaker groups from stronger groups and by protecting the right of individuals to form groups. Companies, for instance, may be compelled to give recognition to trade unions, and unions are limited in the types of pressure they may place on companies. Human rights law can protect the right of individuals to create groups, guaranteeing the right to form trade unions, businesses and partnerships. Furthermore, a healthy state places limits on social groups to prevent them from abusing their power. The flip side of protecting weaker groups from the strong is that stronger groups are restricted in the ways they can interact with the weak. The state may limit the types and extent of pressure which can be exerted within a group to maintain group cohesion, regulating the relationship between members and the group as a whole. Finally, and most importantly, a healthy state exercises an integrative function. Members of the state are also members of many other groups but, according to the state, their membership of these groups must be placed in the broader context of their membership of the state. The breadth of concern which characterizes state membership may permit a narrowness of concern within particular social groups.[23] Trade unions, for instance, need not consider the wider public interest when campaigning on their members' behalf; they need not settle for a small pay increase simply because of a fear that a larger raise may stoke inflation, or that other workers in other industries may feel jealous of their members' success. Similarly, a business—ordinarily—need not consider the ability of the poor to buy its goods when setting its prices, or the financial well-being of its rivals when making decisions about promoting its product. But these limitations on the types of consideration that bear on unions and businesses are only justifiable within the context of a broader political framework which does provide a mechanism which accommodates them. In a healthy state, the trade union and business operate within structures which ensure that, overall, the common good will be promoted even as they pursue their particular goals. It is at the level of the state that inflation is tackled—and, if it is thought helpful, pay restraint imposed—and it is at the level of the state that the possible harshness of the market is mitigated, through regulation and welfare support. If the state does not undertake this integrative role it becomes harder to justify the narrow concern of other social groups. A company that knew, for instance, that promoting its product would lead to its rivals starving, and not merely being put out of business, would not be justified in ignoring this consideration.

The integrative function of the state has implications for the role of political parties within the political system.[24] Whilst political parties have recently had a bad

[22] M. Walzer, 'The Civil Society Argument' in R. Beiner (ed), *Theorising Citizenship* (Albany: State University of New York Press, 1995), 168–74. See the related discussion of the integrative function of the state in N. Walker, 'European Constitutionalism in the State Constitutional Tradition' (2006) 59 Current Legal Problems 51, 63–6.

[23] Against this view, see M. Seidenfeld, 'A Civic Republican Justification for the Bureaucratic State' (1992) 105 *Harvard Law Review* 1511, 1531.

[24] On the nature of political parties, see N. L. Rosenblum, *On the Side of the Angels: An Appreciation of Parties and Partisanship* (New Jersey: Princeton University Press, 2008), 18–21.

press in constitutional scholarship,[25] political scientists have long recognized that they are an essential feature of a functioning democracy.[26] Most writing on political parties treats them as representing sectional or class interests, elevating group struggle into the political arena.[27] This is, of course, often a depressingly accurate depiction of party politics. But surprisingly little has been written about how parties *ought* to behave, and the role they should play in the government of the state.[28] The answer is that political parties are fighting over the proper direction of state policy and, consequently, when politics is functioning properly, they fight within the bounds set by the state's primary purpose. Parties ought to be advocating measures which will benefit all of the members of the state—not just the members of their party, nor a particular subsection of the community.[29] A political party which claims to seek power to secure the unfair benefit of one group over another has misunderstood the nature of the state, the party members' status as citizens, and the task which falls to political parties in the democratic process.

To say that political parties ought to be disputing over the content of the common good raises a great many further questions which will not be answered in this chapter. In particular, it raises the question of whether the justification of a party's policies must be provided in terms of reasons which others in the state could accept, or whether it is enough that those making the claims sincerely believe that they should be accepted. Political parties with a religious affiliation commonly claim—often sincerely—that they are acting in the best interest of the whole community, justifying their claims on the basis of religious texts or divine revelation, but such faith-based explanations could never persuade those outside of their religion. Furthermore, the extent of the sacrifices one section of the population should bear for the common good is often unclear. We all have an interest in the well-being of others. The obligations of justice require us to ensure that we do not possess more than our due, and, moreover, to some ill-defined extent, we ought to help the needy, even once the demands of distributive justice have been satisfied. The obligations of distributive justice extend beyond the boundaries of the state. Our shared humanity with those outside of the state may mean that we are bound to alleviate their poverty, and the state may advance the well-being of its people by acquitting their obligations in

---

[25] See, for instance, A. Tomkins, *Our Republican Constitution* (Oxford: Hart, 2005), 136–9. For a different view from a similar tradition, see R. Bellamy, *Political Constitutionalism*, (Oxford: Oxford University Press, 2007), 230–9.

[26] S. M. Lipset, 'The Indispensability of Political Parties' (2000) 11 Journal of Democracy 48 and Rosenblum, note 24 above.

[27] For a survey see, S. C. Stokes, 'Political Parties and Democracy' (1999) *Annual Review of Political Science* 243.

[28] Though see B. Manin, *The Principles of Representative Government* (Cambridge: Cambridge University Press, 1997), chs 5 and 6.

[29] See generally, M. S. Williams, 'The Uneasy Alliance of Group Representation and Deliberative Democracy' in W. Kymlicka and W. Norman (eds), *Citizenship in Diverse Societies* (Oxford: Oxford University Press, 2000) and the discussion in S. Macedo, *Liberal Virtues* (Oxford: Oxford University Press, 1990), 116–27.

this respect. Even if distributive justice does not require the state to provide such support, if the state nevertheless provides aid to non-members it exhibits the virtue of charity and is, for this reason, a better and more valuable institution, again enhancing, indirectly, the well-being of its members. Finally, sometimes people ought to accept the burden of a particular area of policy because of the benefits they receive elsewhere. A childless couple may chafe at the money spent on education, but should consider the compensations provided by the provision of a national healthcare service. Citizens cannot win in every policy area, but ordinarily—hopefully—the overall benefits they receive outweigh the costs they pay. The upshot of these reflections is that political parties will often be arguing for specific policies which benefit one group above another, even those outside of the state, but will do so in the wider context of the common good. The conferment of a benefit to a section of the citizenry, or to non-citizens, may be fair, even if it is not shared by all.

There are occasions in which political parties do not even come close to the model set out above. In consociational democracies the constitution is premised upon—indeed, relies upon—the parties representing sectional interests.[30] Consociational constitutions structure government so that rival ethnic or religious groups must share the power of the state. In Northern Ireland, for example, the constitution establishing the devolved assembly requires that members elected to it register a designation of identity (nationalist, unionist, or other).[31] Executive power must also be shared between these groups, with ministerial posts shared between nationalists and unionists.[32] In some areas legislation can only be enacted with cross-community consent—this may require a majority of those voting in both the nationalist and unionist groups, or a weighted majority (60 per cent) of those voting, including at least 40 per cent of those voting in the nationalist and unionist groups.[33] Whilst it is possible for non-aligned candidates to stand for election and to sit in the Assembly, they are plainly at a disadvantage: they are less likely to secure senior executive posts and, in some circumstances, their vote will count for less in the legislative process. Consociational settlements present a number of problems, but perhaps their central disadvantage is that they discourage the emergence of the type of citizenship described later in this chapter.[34] Inside the constitutional structure of the

---

[30] See generally, A. Lipjhart, *Democracy in Plural Societies* (New Haven: Yale University Press, 1977), ch 2.

[31] C. McCrudden, 'Northern Ireland and the British Constitution' in J. Jowell and D. Oliver (eds), *The Changing Constitution* (6th edn, Oxford: Oxford University Press, 2007) and C. J. Harvey, 'The New Beginning: Reconstructing Constitutional Law and Democracy in Northern Ireland' in C. J. Harvey (ed), *Human Rights, Equality and Democratic Renewal in Northern Ireland* (Oxford: Hart Publishing, 2001).

[32] Northern Ireland Act 1998, ss 16–19.

[33] Northern Ireland Act 1998, s 4(5).

[34] For wider criticism, see B. Barry, 'Political Accommodation and Consociational Democracy' (1975) *British J Political Science* 477 and B. Barry, 'The Consociational Model and its Dangers' (1975) *European J Political Research* 393.

consociational institution, politics is conducted as a negotiation between two distinct political communities. Within each of these communities there is, or may be, deliberation about the general good of the group, but the settlement discourages members of these groups from considering the collective good. Given that the constitutional structure is premised on concessions by one group being bought by concessions from the other, a group member who tries to include the well-being of rival group members in her political action risks unsettling the constitutional balance and (unfairly) disadvantaging her group. Many areas of political life resemble versions of the prisoners' dilemma,[35] but in a consociational settlement the dilemma can ultimately only be solved by re-writing the rules which frame the problem. Consociational settlements are a necessary evil, a political structure which, hopefully, will prove transitional rather than long-lasting.

The discussion so far has focused on the interaction between the authority claims of the state and the primary purpose of the state. It has sought to demonstrate the ways in which the special type of authority claim levied by the state can make a distinctive contribution to the achievement of that purpose. But the discussion has also touched on a further pair of issues: the proper relationship of the individual to the state, and the proper relationship between members of the state. The previous paragraphs assumed that not only was it the purpose of the state as a whole to promote the well-being of its members, it was also, as a consequence of this, the task of each of its members. This assumption requires further explanation.

THE NATURE OF CITIZENSHIP

There are many relationships a person can have with a state. Nationals of the state are members of the state; part of the social group which makes up that body. Non-nationals are not members of the group, but they may still have a relationship with the state. Friendly aliens can trade with nationals and receive the protection of the state whilst within its territory. Enemy aliens are considered threats to the state, they may not trade with nationals and are often interned or deported if found within the state's territory. Setting aside unusual forms of state membership—such as monarchs, princes, and tyrants—members of the state can be divided into two broad categories: citizens and subjects. These two forms of state membership should be thought of as poles on a spectrum rather than as hermetically sealed categories. The subject is the passive recipient of the state's commands. Obedience to these commands should promote the subject's well-being—the state remains under this obligation—but the subject is not the author of these commands, even indirectly. As Filmer explained, the relationship of the subject to the state is like that of a child to her parents.[36] The parents issue commands to the child which ought to be in the child's best interests to obey, but the child has no control over these commands, nor need she understand why they are in her best interests. The citizen, in contrast, has

---

[35] On which, see Green, note 21 above, ch 5.

[36] Filmer, note 11 above.

a stake in the state's commands. As Aristotle argued, the citizen shares in the government of the state, she rules and is ruled in turn.[37] Furthermore, this participation leads to a particular form of responsibility: the citizen shares in the honours, and the dishonours, of the state.[38]

Any good account of citizenship will be, in part, derived from an account of the state. Even when citizenship is applied outside this context—as with discussion of 'world' citizenship, or European citizenship—it is still an institution shaped by its origins as a particular type of membership that a person can have with her state. Though there are many instantiations of citizenship in the world, many different models of citizenship to be found in various polities, common features can be identified. For our purposes, one of the most important of these is that citizenship has an aspirational quality: it is, in part, to be understood as the best type of relationship the mass of the people of a state can enter into with that state. Part of a good account of citizenship will therefore present it in its ideal form; as the kind of state membership other real-world instances of citizenship seek to imitate. This aspirational aspect of citizenship does not confer unrestricted licence. A good account of citizenship will accommodate other features of the institution, such as the way citizenship is constituted, the special connection between citizenship and government, and the practical limitations on mass participation in the state, amongst other elements. These serve to constrain what citizenship can aspire to be.

(i) The institution of the citizen

Citizenship is an institution of the state. As such, it is defined by a sub-set of the rules of the constitution, those rules that constitute the state. It is an institution which particular individuals can enter into; an office of the state. It therefore endows individuals with a particular status. They are no longer merely group members of the state, they are members of a particular sort: citizens. This account of the nature of citizenship has, from time to time, been challenged. Margaret Somers, alongside other writers, has argued that rather than understanding citizenship as a status, it should be conceptualized as an 'instituted process'.[39] Her re-characterization seeks to emphasize the social character of citizenship, that is, the interaction of legal rules and social practices in the construction of citizenship. Somers' move is a reaction against those interpretations of citizenship which present it as a simple set of legal rights conferred by the state on the individual.[40] Such accounts are inadequate in two

---

[37] Aristotle, note 5 above, III.IV, 1277b13–22.

[38] *Ibid*, III.V, 1278a35–36.

[39] M. R. Somers, 'Citizenship and the Place of the Public Sphere: Law, Community and Political Culture in the Transition to Democracy' (1993) 58 Am Soc Rev 587. See also Janoski, note 14 above, 11.

[40] See, for instance Janoski, note 14 above, ch 2; J. Carens, *Culture, Citizenship and Community* (Oxford: Oxford University Press, 2000), ch 7; and, of course, H. Kelsen, *General Theory of Law and State*, trans A. Wedberg (New York: Russell and Russell, 1961), 233–42.

respects. First, they fail to recognize the significance of social rules in the construction of citizenship: citizenship is not simply concerned with the relation of the state
to the individual, it is also concerned with the interaction of the citizenry. As will be
argued below, citizens treat each other in a distinctive fashion. This type of interaction can be partly instantiated by law, but is more commonly constructed through
social rules backed by social pressure.[41] Second, citizenship can be rejected—to a
degree. A person may be defined as a citizen, regarded by their fellows as a citizen,
and yet may refuse to act as a citizen. Such a person would not be a citizen in the
fullest sense. Institutions of the state, including citizenship, are constituted by rules
but cannot be reduced to those rules. Without people acting within the structures
created by rules, institutions exist only in a desiccated state. A person who declined
to act as a citizen would leave her potential citizenship in this desiccated form: only
if and when she starts to act as a citizen would she take on this office. Once these two
qualifications are admitted, it is possible to see citizenship both as a process, as
Somers claimed, with a social and an active element, but also as an institution and a
status, constituted by rules.

(ii) Citizens and states

The core of citizenship lies in participation in the government of the state. The citizen shares in the government of the state, and, partly as a function of this, is responsible for the actions of the state. It is from this simple idea of participation that the
rights and duties which are characteristic of citizenship are derived. However, this
model of citizenship is not beyond challenge. In his classic and widely discussed
account of citizenship, T. H. Marshall proffered a three-part account of this institution, only one of which matches our account.[42] Marshall's first model of citizenship
is purportedly tied to the eighteenth century form of the institution, a brand of state
membership defined by civil rights such as freedom of the person, speech, thought
and property rights. His second model is rooted in the nineteenth century, when,
according to Marshall, citizenship developed a 'political element', expanding to
include rights related to participation in political power. Finally, in the twentieth
century, a social element emerged to complement these two: citizenship became
characterized by a right to a certain level of welfare and security. One way of interpreting Marshall's account is as a piece of intellectual history, charting the development of state membership from a broadly monarchical model, already well in decline
in the eighteenth century, to our contemporary states which, to varying extents,
shoulder responsibility for the economic and physical well-being of their people.
Marshall's effort to illuminate citizenship as a distinctive constitutional institution
was of secondary importance to the telling of this story, and, for this purpose, it
might be acceptable to use 'citizenship' as a synonym for 'rights accruing by virtue

---

[41] Social rules can also shape the interaction of the state and the citizen.

[42] T. H. Marshall and T. Bottomore, *Citizenship and Social Class* (London: Pluto Press,
1992), 8.

of state membership'.[43] The account of citizenship developed in this chapter needs to be more precise, and, in the context of the relationship between the citizen and the state, differs from that of Marshall in two respects: first, in the centrality it accords to participation, and, secondly, in its insistence on the significance of duties as well as rights.[44]

It is only in the second of his three models that Marshall emphasizes the importance of participation in citizenship. The first model is not, according to the interpretation advanced in this chapter, a form of citizenship at all. It is better understood as a form of another, related, constitutional institution: that of the subject. In Marshall's account she is a subject accorded certain protections by a sovereign, but it is still a form of state membership which is characterized by a divide between the people who are ruled, and those who do the ruling. Marshall's third model is closer to our account of citizenship. It includes participation rights, but also insists on social and economic rights to complement these. However, it is hard to see that it is a necessary feature of citizenship that individuals within that institution possess particular rights against the state for social benefits. Social justice may require this, but citizenship does not. There may be societies in which it is not necessary for the state to provide healthcare or education to its people because other institutions exist—charities and businesses, perhaps—which meet these needs. Having said that, a certain level of social well-being is necessary in order for the creation of citizenship. Full citizenship requires a certain level of education: a citizen needs to possess some knowledge of the mechanisms of her state, and have the ability to express opinions and communicate with others. It also requires a certain level of material well-being: a person who is starving or desperately unwell will not be able to participate in political discussion. Consequently, it will often be the case, perhaps it will ordinarily be the case, that the state needs to provide for the education, health and general well-being of its people in order for citizenship to be instantiated within the community. And in these territories these social rights may indeed be part of that state's model of citizenship. But it is conceivable that citizenship could flourish without the state intervening in some or all of these areas. It is inconceivable, in contrast, that citizenship could flourish in the absence of the participation rights identified by Marshall in his second model: these are at the heart of the institution.

A further deficiency in Marshall's account of citizenship is the absence of a sustained discussion of the obligations that a citizen owes to the state.[45] The assertions of authority advanced by the state create a relationship of sorts: the state commands, and expects its nationals to obey. In a state characterized by citizenship this relationship is more complex. The mesh of duties that the citizen owes to the state and to her fellow citizens, discussed further below, creates a complex relationship between the citizen and state. This relationship demands more of the citizen than her bare

---

[43] Which may have been his meaning: *ibid.*, 6.

[44] It also differs in respect of the relationship between citizens, discussed later.

[45] Though he recognizes citizenship is partly constituted by duties: Marshall, note 42 above, 18, 41. See also Janoski, note 14 above, ch 3.

acquiescence in the demands of the state, but it can also demand rather less. The relationship between the citizen and the other institutions of the state is best described as one of loyalty: a relationship comparable to that which exists between friends.[46] Like a loyal friend, the citizen does not merely react to the state's commands—or, in the context of friendship, her friend's requests—she also acts positively to provide support to the state, even when this support is not expressly required or requested. Citizens not only enjoy a right to participate in the running of the state, they are also under a duty to shoulder a portion of this task. Some aspects of this duty are virtually mandatory: a good citizen ought to vote, ought to reflect on politics and governance, and ought to assist the police and other state officials—at least, when called upon to do so and when these officials are acting for the public good. A further, larger, part of citizenship is optional, with the individual presented with a large range of opportunities to choose from. A person may join a political party, may participate in political debates, may help run after-school sessions for local children, or might choose to help out at her local hospital. A good citizen will choose to undertake some activities of this type, but could not—and should not—attempt them all.[47]

Loyalty does not demand blind obedience.[48] Friendship does not require, indeed, it may even proscribe, assistance in projects that are contrary to the interests of the person who wishes to pursue them. Similarly, whilst the state demands obedience to its commands, there may be occasions in which the citizen, because she is a citizen, should refuse to obey the commands of the state, even if those commands are the product of an impeccable process of participation and deliberation. Just as a good friend will refuse to help her comrade undertake actions which will be harmful, so too the good citizen should sometimes refuse to help the state undertake actions which run contrary to its basic purpose. In these situations, loyalty to the state may require that the citizen disobey the state's commands, refuse to support its activities, or even take steps to frustrate its actions. A citizen who withholds a portion of her taxes because of her opposition to the purchase of nuclear weapons, for instance, may be refusing to pay because of, rather than in spite of, her obligations as a citizen.

(iii) Citizens and citizenry

The primary purpose of the state is to promote the well-being of its members. The citizen, an officer of the state, is also bound by this primary purpose.[49] Consequently,

---

[46] This type of relationship may be what Raz had in mind when he wrote of people adopting an attitude of respect for law in reasonably just societies: J. Raz, *The Morality of Freedom* (Oxford: Clarendon Press, 1986), 94–9.

[47] Janoski, note 14 above, 54–66.

[48] Janoski, note 14 above, 70–3; M. Janowitz, *The Reconstruction of Patriotism: Education for Civic Consciousness* (Chicago: University of Chicago Press, 1983).

[49] See generally, A. Tomkins, *Our Republican Constitution* (Oxford: Hart, 2005), 62–3.

in addition to the duties that the citizen owes to the state, she also owes duties to her fellow citizens. These obligations condition the ways in which citizens should treat each other; they are the flip side of the entitlements that characterize citizenship. A person can only participate in the governance of the state if other citizens are willing to let her participate and value her interests. Being entitled to express your views about the governance of the state is virtually worthless if others ignore you: citizens listen to other citizens and consider what they have to say.[50] The obligations which exist between citizens entail that the institution cannot be a purely legal construction. The law cannot compel people to listen to each other, to respect the views and interests of their fellows. Laws can help instil, or undermine, mutual respect, but an important dimension of citizenship is manifested in the attitudes that citizens adopt towards each other. Some people may find that whilst they are legally defined as citizens they are not, in the fullest sense, citizens of the state. Members of a minority group that is consistently ignored—or which chooses to set itself apart from the polity—may be legally defined as citizens but may lack the ability to participate in the governance of the state that is crucial to citizenship. This need not be an all or nothing affair. Citizenship is not a binary concept:[51] the constitutional institution available to a particular person may be more or less like our ideal of citizenship. Some people within the state may be able to participate more fully than others.

The law can play an important role in facilitating the participation of minority groups. On occasion, political equality requires legal inequalities. Legally required or permitted positive discrimination can help alleviate social discrimination. Minority groups might be given special access to government posts, or have seats in the legislature reserved for them. They might be given special protection from discrimination—the law might, for example, prohibit discrimination against homosexuals, but not against heterosexuals. In these situations the state is not seeking to give members of the disadvantaged group an unfair benefit, rather it is seeking to ensure that all members of the community can enter into the institution of citizenship to the greatest extent possible. The law is seeking to create a political environment in which all voices can be heard, and in which all of the members of the state are treated with respect.

THE CENTRALITY OF CITIZENSHIP

Not every state contains citizens. Some states—historically, perhaps, even the majority—neither pretend to constitute, nor aspire to turn, their nationals into citizens. Nevertheless, an understanding of citizenship is central to an understanding of the state. It is the paradigmatic relationship a national can have with her state, a model which provides a contrast against which other types of state membership may be understood.

[50] S. Macedo, *Liberal Virtues* (Oxford: Oxford University Press, 1990), ch 2.

[51] I once thought otherwise, but I was wrong: see N. W. Barber, 'Citizenship, Nationalism and the European Union' (2002) 27 European L Rev 241, 243.

It is possible to argue for the centrality of citizenship to the state through a reflection on the nature and purpose of the state. Given that the nature of the state is as it was argued in chapter 2, and given that it has the primary purpose argued for it in the first part of this chapter, citizenship will have been shown to be a central feature of the state if the creation of citizenship is necessary for the state to achieve this purpose.

This all boils down to the most basic question of all: what is so good about being a citizen?[52] There are lots of arguments that can be made for citizenship. Some of these, probably some of the most important ones, are instrumental and contingent. These point to features of citizenship which may facilitate the achievement of other desirable objectives under certain circumstances. It is, for example, highly likely that the existence of citizenship within a state leads to good government—or, at least, to better government than would have been the case in the absence of citizenship. The deliberative aspect of citizenship probably encourages the adoption of sensible policies by the state. It facilitates the expression of different views and allows people to articulate their needs and wants. It also provides a forum in which policies can be challenged and scrutinized, and state officials can be held to account. Citizenship may reduce corruption in state office, both through scrutiny but also through the instillation of a sense of pride in the state, a belief that success in state office is something of which the holder should be proud. A consequence of these considerations is that the economy may function better in such a state, people's freedoms may be better protected and many other good things may also be secured. These are all strong, sensible, arguments for citizenship, and they are, probably, ordinarily valid. But they remain contingent: there may be some states at some points in time for which they are not true. There may be states in which the views of the people have been perverted by a demagogue, or are just a bit silly.[53] There may be people who regard corruption as ordinary, and who would look on an honest state official as a fool. In such states, turning the nationals of the state into citizens might lead to the state adopting foolish policies or encouraging corruption.

However, citizenship may also be intrinsically valuable, that is, there may be aspects of the institution which render being a citizen worthwhile in itself, and not merely desirable because of the other attractive things citizenship may help achieve. An argument that citizenship is intrinsically valuable takes the following form:

First, it is important to have control over your life, to be able to choose the projects and relationships you wish to pursue, and to make decisions about how these will be pursued. This is not just because a person who possess such a power is likely to exercise it to protect her interests, nor merely because of the psychological benefits such

---

[52] See the discussion in R. Dworkin, 'What is Equality? Part 4: Political Equality' (1987) 22 University of San Francisco L Rev 1.

[53] Indeed, Surowiecki demonstrates that there are certain types of question which groups are *less* likely to answer correctly if they deliberate before voting: J. Surowiecki, *The Wisdom of Crowds* (London: Abacus, 2004), ch 1. See also C. Sunstein, *Why Societies Need Dissent* (Cambridge Mass.: Harvard, 2003).

empowerment brings, but rather because it is an essential part of making your life your own. Control brings with it ownership of one's character; the activities that the person pursues are truly hers, an instantiation of who she is. Someone who is compelled to pursue particular projects, no matter how attractive or valuable these are, has been denied the opportunity of self-authorship, denied an essential aspect of a good life. This simple point has been recognized and elaborated by many different authors from many different traditions: Joseph Raz frames the claim in terms of autonomy,[54] Philip Pettit talks of the significance of non-domination.[55] Though the elaborations of this insight differ widely, the essential point is the same: the successful life is, at least in part, a chosen and self-controlled life.

Secondly, people must belong to various social groups if they are to flourish. People need groups to pursue projects and schemes and to provide them with support and comfort. They also need such groups to allow them to exhibit those social virtues which can only be expressed within a group setting—the virtues of friendship, loyalty and teamwork. A person who was denied the chance to belong to any group would not only be miserable—though she would certainly be that—she would also be denied the chance of leading a life of value.

Thirdly, there is, in a very basic sense, a moral equality shared by humans: each person is morally important, and no person is of greater moral importance than another. This moral equality conditions the nature of moral reasons, requiring that they are universalizable. If there is a moral reason to treat a given person in a certain way then that moral reason must apply just as strongly to another person in the identical situation. If it is wrong for you to torture me, for example, it must, all else being equal, also be wrong for me to torture you. This claim of moral equality is so basic, so obvious and intuitive, that it is often overlooked. But when it is absent from politics the consequences are grotesque. People excluded from the reach of this principle are treated as sub-human; they no longer count as moral agents.

Fourthly, in a society like ours the state is necessary for the regulation and integration of these social groups. This point was discussed earlier in the chapter, when the interaction of the authority claims of the state and the primary purpose of the state was considered. The state can, and should, provide an environment in which many different groups can flourish and safely conflict; by standing above all other groups it permits the myopia of interest which is essential to the success of certain types of group.

These four propositions—the importance of control, the importance of groups, the principle of moral equality, and the need for the state—combine to found an argument for the intrinsic value of citizenship. Citizenship is the brand of state membership which combines, in societies like ours, the need for the existence of social groups with the maximum possible control over action at the state level which is compatible with the general principle of the equal moral worth of people. Every

---

[54] Raz, note 46 above, ch 14.

[55] P. Pettit, *Republicanism: A Theory of Freedom and Government* (Oxford: Oxford University Press, 1997), ch 3.

citizen has as great a say in the government of the state as is compatible with permitting the same level of participation to every other citizen. There will, of course, be citizens who acquire governmental power within the state: the Prime Minister has greater control over the state than you or I, but the extra power is accrued by virtue of her exercise of her rights as a citizen—and the exercise of others' citizenship rights through the electoral process—and not by virtue of a special right accorded to her in her capacity as a citizen.

The argument for the intrinsic value of citizenship is confined to societies like ours. Not all societies should create a state, and so not all societies need or should strive towards citizenship. Tribal communities and small religious communes might flourish without an institution which functions like the state. These societies may not need an authoritative institution to integrate smaller groups within their communities: the social groups within their borders may co-exist without conflict, or may be able to sort out their differences consensually. It would be a mistake to think that such people would necessarily benefit from the imposition of state-like structures. They may be able to lead happy and fulfilled lives without a state and without the possibility of citizenship. Indeed, on some occasions the attempt to impose state-like structures on such people may prove profoundly damaging. It may weaken existing social groups within the community, strip away the structures which regulate inter-group relations, and deprive some social roles within these groups of their meaning and value.

A converse challenge to the intrinsic value of citizenship could come from those interested in the globalization of politics and governmental structures. If the state has been overtaken by these higher bodies, perhaps the integrative function of the state has been passed upwards, they could argue, taking with it the value of citizenship. Two replies could be made to this point. First, it could be that on some occasions it will be appropriate to think of international bodies in terms of the state. When this occurs, the arguments made in this chapter about the purposes and membership of the state could be applied to these bodies. A world-state would differ in some respects from the state as we know it, but might still be a recognisable development of this institution; a world-state would require world-citizenship to complement it. To an extent, developments within the European Union can be understood as a shift of constitutional ideas and institutions from the national to the supranational level. In a later chapter the nature of the European Union will be considered, in particular its similarity to the classical model of the state and its claim to constitute its people as citizens. Secondly, reports of the death of the state are still premature. Whilst global organizations play an important role in many people's lives, the state's role is, generally, more important still. The state remains the broadest and most powerful political institution with which most people engage, and, for most, their contact with international organizations is mediated through it.

CONCLUSION

The argument made in this chapter for the intrinsic value of citizenship seeks to show that all states ought to be moving towards constituting their people as citizens. For some states this will require a great deal of work over a long period of time.

States which are emerging from dictatorship or oligarchy often need time to develop a citizenry. It is a hard task to facilitate the growth of a political community in which people are willing to express their opinions and needs, and—equally crucially—are willing to respect and consider the opinions and needs of others. For other states that have developed the institution of citizenship there is an on-going need to foster and maintain the institution. Even in a state with a healthy citizenry, there are areas of imperfection. Sometimes certain groups will suffer some level of exclusion from the political process. They may find it difficult to access state institutions, or find that others fail to give proper consideration to their views. Sometimes certain political decisions lack satisfactory public input. States should be innovative in creating forums and mechanisms for citizens to engage in deliberation about those issues which affect them, even where those issues are of local or sectional interest, and not suitable for discussion on the national stage.

4

The Constitution of Social Groups

It is easy to underestimate the importance of rules. Those of us who are interested in the law have a special appreciation of their value: we spend our time reflecting on those rules which guide conduct, regulate behaviour, and prevent wrong-doing. But even lawyers often fail to recognize the full significance of rules in the construction of our world. Rules do not merely regulate and prevent, they also create and empower. And the kingdom of rules is not exhausted by the genus of law: indeed, the quantity and importance of legal rules is dwarfed in comparison to the work done by non-legal rules. That part of our world identified by John Searle as consisting of social facts is constructed by these rules.[1] Social facts are those things which exist because they have been ascribed social significance. These include objects, like coins and houses, people who occupy roles, like mothers and soldiers, and institutions, such as churches and states. Social groups are one type of social fact, a particular form of social institution. To understand social groups—and, eventually, to understand the state—it is necessary to understand the essential role rules play in their construction.

This chapter will reflect on the nature and types of rules which constitute social groups. It will have little to say about the state directly, but it will establish a framework for understanding rules and groups which will be applied to the state in the remainder of the book. In the following two chapters this account will be applied to state constitutions, permitting us to delineate the content of constitutions and casting light on their complex mix of legal and non-legal rules.

SOCIAL RULES

A rule is a directive which purports to provide a person with a reason to act in a certain way.[2] For a social rule to be operative, at least some of the subjects of the directive must act in accordance with the rule, and the rule must play a part in the causal explanation of their behaviour. There are many different types of rules and a number of different models which illuminate varying features of their nature. For

---

[1] J. Searle, *The Construction of Social Reality* (London: Penguin, 1996).

[2] On social rules see especially: J. Raz, *Practical Reason and Norms* (2nd edn, New Jersey: Princeton University Press, 1990) and D. Galligan, *Law in Modern Society* (Oxford: Clarendon Press, 2007), ch 3.

our purposes, the two most important types of rules are mandatory rules and power-conferring rules.[3] Joseph Raz provides a careful and thorough account of the nature of these rules, demonstrating the ways in which they claim to affect people's decisions and conduct.

A mandatory rule obliges a person to act, or forbids a person from acting, in a certain way. The rule purports to provide a reason to act (a primary reason) coupled with an exclusionary reason (a second-order reason) not to consider the reasons that would ordinarily apply in the situation.[4] A rule forbidding the parking of cars on double-yellow lines combines a primary reason not to stop on the lines with a second-order reason not to consider the desirability of parking in that spot.

A power-conferring rule enables a person to alter the obligations, rights and, indeed, powers of other people.[5] When a person satisfies the conditions of the power-conferring rule, she alters the normative position of others. The rules which speak to those people have been changed. When a person meets the formality requirements specified for creation of a contract, she alters her rights and duties towards the other party to the contract. New mandatory rules come into existence which require action by the participants: a car must be provided to one, cash must be provided to the other. The contract might also confer a new power-conferring rule: perhaps the buyer is now empowered to set the date for delivery.

Each of these types of rules will be explored more fully in the following paragraphs. Three elements of our brief definition of a rule need further elucidation: that the rule is a directive; that the rule purports to provide a reason; and that this reason relates to an action. This third element brings forward the 'internal aspect' of rules, the difference that an operative rule makes to the reasoning of those acting in conformity to it.

(i) Rules as directives

The depiction of rules as directives is not intended to imply that rules are invariably issued by one person or institution over another, that there must be, in some sort of Austinian[6] sense, a rule-maker speaking to a rule-receiver. Rules can emerge over time through practice and through developing social attitudes without the intervention of a distinct author. But there is an element of truth in the crude picture of a rule-maker addressing a rule-receiver. Rules operate to curtail or shape a person's reasoning process; the individual would have reasoned in a different fashion but for the rule. There must, then, be a gap between the production of the rule and the application of that rule in a particular instance.[7] At the very least, there is invariably

---

[3] Raz also discusses permissions: Raz, note 2 above, 85–97.

[4] Raz, note 2 above, 97–107. F. Schauer, *Playing by the Rules* (Oxford: Clarendon Press, 1991), 3–6.

[5] Raz, note 2 above, 104–6.

[6] J. Austin, *The Province of Jurisprudence Determined* ed H. L. A. Hart (London: Weidenfeld and Nicolson, 1954).

[7] Schauer, note 4 above, 112–18.

a period of time between the formulation of the rule and its application. A person faced with a decision cannot apply a rule which has yet to be formulated—though she might formulate a rule, then apply it. In the case of social rules it may be very difficult to determine the point at which a mere habit has shifted into rule-governed behaviour, but the shift occurs within a time-period, nonetheless. Moreover, there must also be a gap of sorts between the individual applying the rule and the instigators of the rule. Commonly this gap will exist between the social group whose rule it is, and the person who is subject to the application of that rule—who may or may not also be a member of the group.

One complication with this understanding of rules as directives arises with personal rules, that is, rules that an individual adopts to govern her own behaviour. Such 'rules' are a common feature of our experience of the world. For instance, a person may resolve never to send emails after drinking alcohol, however sober she feels and however pressing the need to respond to an annoying friend. Here, a rule embodying a primary reason not to send the email is coupled with a second-order reason not to consider the various reasons for and against emailing. Does such a resolution have the directive quality which is characteristic of a rule? The answer is that it does. It is possible for an individual to impose rules upon herself, dividing herself between different periods of time.[8] The sensible—sober—self has issued a directive to the less sensible—tipsy—self. The agent predicts that her future self might be under the sway of some intoxicant that would affect her reasoning process in a fashion she believes to be undesirable, and she would be better served by following the rule.

(ii) Rules as reasons

Rules purport to provide a reason, or reasons, for action to people. This is plainly the case for mandatory rules, which claim to oblige people to act or not to act in certain ways, but it is also true, in a less direct fashion, of power-conferring rules. Power-conferring rules, in contrast to mandatory rules, are, to an extent, optional.[9] When the option is exercised, a new set of rules is produced which purport to alter the normative position of people. These new rules are generally either mandatory—requiring or forbidding action—or establish new power-conferring rules in their turn. Power-conferring rules are therefore intimately connected to mandatory rules.

Sometimes a person may incur criticism for failing to make use of a power-conferring rule when circumstances would seem to require its exercise. A person who steadfastly refuses to enter into an advantageous contract might be acting foolishly by refusing to contract. In this instance she has a reason to make use of the rule. When she refuses to agree the contract she has not broken any rule (that is, acted against the reason any rule purported to supply) but has acted contrary to a (non-rule

---

[8] See generally, T. Schelling, 'The Intimate Contest for Self Command' in T. Schelling, *Choice and Consequence* (Cambridge Mass: Harvard University Press, 1984); D. Ariely, *Predictably Irrational* (London: HarperCollins, 2008), chs 5 and 6; Schauer, note 4 above, 160–1.

[9] H. L. A. Hart, *The Concept of Law* (2nd edn, Oxford: Oxford University Press, 1994), 28.

derived) reason. Similarly, power-conferring rules invariably have conditions which must be satisfied before the power is activated. A person may then have reason to comply with these conditions—to sign her will, for instance—but, again, does not necessarily break a rule by failing to follow this reason.

(iii) The internal aspect of rules

Operative non-systematic social rules exist where there is a regularity of behaviour which has been caused[10] by subjects' acceptance of a rule. This acceptance is manifested in both the following of the rule and in criticism of those who depart from the rule. As H. L. A. Hart demonstrated, in his discussion of the internal aspect of rules, it is inherent in the nature of a non-systematic social rule that breach of the rule grounds social criticism of the rule-breaker.[11] To put it another way, the community within which this rule exists accepts the rule as setting a valid standard for the subject of the rule; the subject *ought* to behave in conformity with the rule.

The internal aspect of non-systematic social rules should be distinguished from that of systematic social rules. Systematic rules exist within a mesh of rules. Crucially, part of this mesh includes rules which determine the inclusion of rules within the system: Hart's rules of recognition. Where rules are systematic it is not necessary that folk regard each of these rules as constituting valid reasons for action. The most obvious instance of systematic rules—the law—frequently contains rules which the community does not regard as setting a valid standard for behaviour. Sometimes this is because the legal rule is just plain silly—like some of the odder parts of copyright law. On other occasions, the rule made sense once, but times have changed and the rule has not. The sadly apocryphal rule requiring that London taxi drivers keep a bail of hay in their cab to feed their horse would be an example of such a rule. Here, few if any people, including judges and the police, would contend that a person who breached the rule should be criticized for disregarding *that* rule. Everyone would recognize that the continued existence of the legal rule is a mistake, and that the rule does not, as it purported to do, provide a valid reason to the taxi drivers. The rule-breaker might be criticized, though, for weakening the system by picking and choosing those laws she was willing to obey—and a judge faced with a misguided prosecution of a bale-less taxi-driver would still be legally required to apply the rule. These rules, whose merits no one believes in, retain their identity as rules because they are part of a system, a system which renders them legally binding. As Hart demonstrated, in the context of systems of rules it is (minimally) enough that a significant part of the community accepts the rules which identify these other rules; that is, they accept the rules of recognition.[12]

---

[10] The causal part of this account is not found, or is not emphasized, in Hart: Raz, note 2 above, ch 3. But see Hart, note 9 above, 90–1 where Hart draws attention to the significance of people *using* the rule.

[11] Hart, note 9 above, 56–9.

[12] *Ibid*, 109–10.

Hart described the attitude that people manifest towards rules as one of 'accept-ance'.[13] He was attracted to the word by its breadth: people might 'accept' the rule for lots of reasons.[14] In the context of a legal system, Hart thought that the attitude of officials was crucial: they, at least, must 'accept' the rule of recognition. The basis of this acceptance might vary widely. One judge might believe herself to be bound by her oath of office, a second has a conformist turn of mind, a third just wants to keep her job—and so forth.[15] As an empirical matter this is doubtless true, but, as John Finnis argues, a good account of law would identify the central case of the internal attitude as one in which the agent regards the law, or, at least, the rules of recognition, as morally justified.[16] It is this attitude that other officials in the system mimic when they engage in legal reasoning. When we turn to non-systematic social rules, Finnis' characterization of the internal attitude is even more compelling. Whilst it is plausible to imagine that there are some within the community who obey through fear or hope of advantage, for a non-systematic social rule to exist a significant portion of the community must believe that the rule is justified; that peo-ple ought to behave as the rule specifies. If this is lacking, the apparent rule is not a rule at all: it is a threat or a bribe.

It is perhaps worth noting that we now have two 'internal aspects' necessary for the identification of rules.[17] First, there is the disposition of those who accept the rule as a valid standard for conduct. This is manifested in exhortations to follow the rule and criticism of those who fail to follow the rule. Secondly, there is the disposition of those who follow the rule, those for whom the rule plays at least a part in the causal explanation of their conduct. For a non-systematic social rule to operate within a community both of these must be present. If the first is present without the second we have a situation in which some folk are advocating that other folk *ought* to adopt the rule as a standard for conduct. The potential social rule is not yet operative. In contrast, the second cannot exist without the first simultaneously being in place. Frequently, these two dispositions are combined within individuals: people believe that the rule sets a valid standard for conduct, and follow the rule as a result. But sometimes there will be a division: some people will follow rules they do not believe in because of social pressure. On very rare occasions there may a complete split. One section of the community may believe a rule is a valid standard for another group, and, by enforcing the rule, cajole that group into following the rule even though no members of the subject group believe in its validity. Social rules regulating the con-duct of minorities in deeply prejudiced societies may sometimes be of this type.

Unsurprisingly, determining whether a social rule exists is a tricky business. Identifying a regularity of behaviour is—comparatively—easy. What is harder is to

---

[13] *Ibid*, 257.

[14] *Ibid*, 257.

[15] Raz, note 2 above, 148.

[16] J. Finnis, *Natural Law and Natural Rights* (Oxford: Oxford University Press, 1980), 12–16.

[17] On the ambiguities of Hart's discussion of the 'internal attitude', see B. Bix, 'H. L. A. Hart and the Hermeneutic Turn in Legal Theory' (1999) 52 SMU L Rev 167, 183–6.

show that this regularity of behaviour has been *caused* by people following a rule. Often there will be no clear answer to this question: even if we desired to, it is hard to make windows into men's souls. And sometimes, even once the window is made, what can be seen through it will be confused and ambiguous. Such worries have led some to define rules as mere regularities of behaviour. John Griffith's quip about the constitution may imply an account of this form. Griffith wrote that, in the context of the United Kingdom constitution:

> ...the constitution is no more and no less than what happens. Everything that happens is constitutional. And if nothing happened that would be constitutional also.[18]

In a similar vein, others have treated rules as regularities of behaviour coupled with some observable negative consequence if the regularity is departed from.[19] These behaviouralist approaches to rules may be productive for some purposes and, in some contexts, may even be a sensible definition to adopt.[20] But for our purposes they are inadequate.[21] By ignoring the internal aspect of rules, these accounts obscure the important difference between two different meanings of 'rule'—that is, between a statement of repeated behaviour (as a 'rule' I walk my dog in the mornings) and a statement of rule-guided behaviour (I scoop up after my dog because there is—now—a social rule which requires this behaviour).[22] In the context of social groups, this distinction is especially significant. It is only by examining the motivation of actors that we can distinguish between mere sets of people and social groups. A set of people is connected by a common factor—for instance, the set of red-headed men, the set of people standing in Trafalgar Square. The boundaries of the set may even be reinforced through the threat of sanctions—perhaps, for example, the people standing in Trafalgar Square have been told to remain there by the police whilst some emergency is tackled. In contrast, a social group is bound together through shared obligations and entitlements.

Those who shy away from scrutiny of the mental states related to social rules do so for seductive reasons. As we have already seen, it will often be hard to determine whether a regularity of behaviour exists because of a social rule or for some other reason. Indeed, a regularity of behaviour may start as rule-governed but, over time, may lose its rule-governed quality.[23] Imagine a social rule emerging which requires

---

[18] J. Griffith, 'The Political Constitution' (1979) 42 MLR 1, 19. See also F. Ridley, 'There Is No British Constitution: A Dangerous Case of the Emperor's New Clothes' (1988) 41 Parliamentary Affairs 340.

[19] For example, E. Posner, *Law and Social Norms* (Cambridge Mass: Harvard University Press, 2000), 8, 34.

[20] See Posner's defence of his narrow definition of social rules: Posner, note 19 above, 46.

[21] Raz, note 2 above, 56–8. See also J. Jaconelli, 'The Nature of Constitutional Conventions' (1999) 19 Legal Studies 24, 31–2, discussing S. E. Finer, 'The Individual Responsibility of Ministers' (1956) 34 Public Administration 377.

[22] See further, J. Coleman, *The Practice of Principle* (Oxford: Oxford University Press, 2003), 80–1.

[23] See further, B. Tamanaha, *A General Jurisprudence of Law and Society* (Oxford: Oxford University Press, 2001), 162–6.

that people should walk on the left-hand side of the pavement. At the start, the practice is maintained by vigorous criticism of back-sliders who walk on the right. People within the community start to walk on the left because of the rule: either because they accept the rule as providing a justified standard for conduct, because they fear criticism if they breach the rule, or because they are just following the herd, copying the behaviour of those who comply with the rule. At some point many of the subjects of the rule might stop thinking of their conduct as rule-governed:[24] walking on the left is now just what people do. If interrogated on the subject they might recognize that there was a rule that was being followed, but it might require some reflection before they came to this realization. To draw a term from social psychology, the rule has been internalized.[25] Obedience to the rule no longer depends on the fear of punishment or censure by the group, but simply because the person thinks of the conduct as the correct thing to do in the situation. Here, the rule has become unconscious: it can be brought to mind, but most of the time it is forgotten, part of that mass of social rules which make social life possible but of which we are only dimly aware.[26] But in our example a further stage may be reached. If the rule is practically universally followed people might continue to walk on the left simply because this was a sensible thing to do, given the conduct of everyone else. Those who tried to walk on the right would get knocked into the road, or banged into buildings. At this point, people might walk on the left not because there existed a directive which constituted a reason to act in this fashion, but simply because there were good (non-rule related) reasons to behave in this way. People's disinclination to walk on the right would be like our disinclination to stick our hand in a fire. There is, ordinarily, no social rule against such foolishness; if a person does stick her hand in the fire she will be criticized, but not for breaking a rule. Walking on the right in this community may come to take a similar form: people are criticized for their foolishness in putting themselves and others at risk, not for breaching the dissipated social rule.

A second example of the dissipation of social rules can be given. Imagine a prejudiced society in which the elite came to repent their prejudices. A social rule could be encouraged to emerge to combat such attitudes. People could be enjoined not to discriminate, or be rude to, or tell jokes against, the minority group. The social rule might gradually become internalized. Once again, people might start to follow the rule not because of social pressure, but because they regarded the rule as determining the right thing to do. Here, the community would have shifted from being a prejudiced community to being a prejudiced community in which the manifestation of prejudice was constrained by a widely internalized social rule. But finally, the rule may lead people to change their attitudes towards the minority group; the prejudice may disappear as it ceases to be a feature of the community. Now the social rule may

---

[24] See generally, Searle, note 1 above, ch 6.

[25] E. Aronson, *The Social Animal* (10th edn, New York: Worth Publishers, 2007), 37–41; A. Etzioni, 'Social Norms: Internalization, Persuasion and History' (2000) 34 Law and Society Rev 157, 161–65. D. Forsyth, *Group Dynamics* (4th edn, Belmont: Thomson Publishing, 2006), 172–3.

[26] N. MacCormick, *Institutions of Law* (Oxford: Oxford University Press, 2007), 62–8.

start to dissipate: people are no longer following the rule by refraining from discrimination, they are just not prejudiced against the group, and so have no more inclination to act in a discriminatory fashion than they have to stick their hands in fire. A person who now discriminates against the minority group is criticized for doing a dumb or immoral thing, not for breaching the now dissipated social rule.

This process—the emergence, internalization, and gradual dissipation of social rules—might occur quite frequently without any alteration in the behaviour of the subjects of the social rule, or clear demarcation between the stages in the life of the rule. Not all types of rule, however, can dissipate. Rules can dissipate when they establish conduct which then, in itself, provides a reason for people to conform or when the rule succeeds in removing an impediment to sensible social behaviour. But rules cannot dissipate when they are constitutive of social institutions. The continued existence of the rule is predicated by the institution. John Searle provides an elegant account of the rules which constitute the social institution of money.[27] Few of us have thought of—few of us could reason out as Searle does—the mass of interlocking rules which create this institution. But, however deeply internalized, our understanding of money requires that we comprehend the rules; we might not be able to articulate them, but we abide by them all the same.

(iv) A note on rules and norms

Before turning to consider rules in the particular context of social groups it is necessary to address a distinction that has been assiduously dodged so far: the distinction between rules and norms. Many philosophers, including Joseph Raz[28] and Neil MacCormick,[29] distinguish between the two, and generally couch their accounts of law in terms of norms rather than—as is the case here—rules. It seems that some rules are not norms, and that some norms are not rules. Given that I am using 'rule' to encompass things that these authors would label only norms, it is really only the second of these categories we need be concerned with (that is, those norms which are not rules). For the sake of clarity, though, it is worth including a few words on the first category as well (that is, those rules which are not norms).

Rules that are not considered norms include those rules which relate to the interpretation and application of norms. According to Raz, such rules should not be considered norms as they lack direct normative force, though they have indirect normative force.[30] So, for example, in the context of chess Raz identifies the rules relating to the number of players, the essential properties of the chess board, and the number of pieces as rules which are not norms. In contrast, the rule governing castling is both a rule and a power-conferring norm. In the context of law, Tony Honoré, has argued that, amongst other examples, laws which govern the inferences drawn

---

[27]　Searle, note 1 above, 41–52.

[28]　Raz, note 2 above, 9.

[29]　MacCormick, note 26 above, 24–6.

[30]　Raz, note 2 above, 117.

from evidence, laws which create or destroy legal entities, and laws which determine the scope of other laws are examples of rules which are not norms.[31]

The second category—norms which are not rules—is of greater significance to
this chapter. The account of rules I have provided is broad enough to encompass all
norms. Against this, it is often argued that rules require a quality of generality that
norms need not possess.[32] Under this analysis, the prison sentence specified by a
judge, the orders issued by a police officer regulating a demonstration and an award
of damages by a court would amount to norms, but would not count as rules. In
some contexts this distinction may prove useful—and may, perhaps, be justified by
the meaning attributed to 'rule' in philosophy more generally—but for our purposes
it is an unhelpful complication. There are at least three complexities raised by the
distinction which a wider account of the nature of rules avoids. First, once we move
beyond very specific commands, generality seems to be a matter of degree, rather
than an absolute quality. The number of people governed by the statement and the
number of occasions on which the statement operates vary. A court order making a
group of a hundred people severally liable for a thousand pounds, paid at a hundred
pounds a month, could be regarded as having a significant degree of generality or a
significant quantity of specificity. Secondly, the extent to which the norm is expressed
in generalized language may be a matter of chance. A social club might include the
names of its officers and the address of its premises in its constitution, or it might
phrase the provisions in vaguer terms. Finally, there are some very specific laws
which many of us would normally regard as rules. There are statutes which dissolve
marriages, award pensions to individuals, determine ownership of particular tracts
of land, and so forth.

Neil MacCormick stipulates a slightly different distinction: rules are explicitly
articulated norms. That is, a norm is a rule when some element of authority is
attached to its articulation.[33] The issue MacCormick raises by this distinction is an
important one, and will be discussed later in the context of the formalization of
rules. Once more, the difference is one of degree, though, rather than a distinction
between two fundamentally different entities. The extent to which rules should be
considered to have been explicitly articulated by a person in authority will often be
unclear. Social rules can emerge in reaction to the statements or conduct of char-
ismatic figures. Legal rules, in contradistinction, sometimes emerge from a mass
of legal materials, without it being possible to ascribe authorship to a single
institution.

The distinctions drawn by Raz and MacCormick may prove helpful in some contexts, but for our purposes, that is, the purposes of those primarily interested in the
study of social and political life, they are not essential, and may risk causing confu-

---

[31] T. Honoré, 'Real Laws', in P. M. S. Hacker and J. Raz, *Law, Morality and Society* (Oxford:
Oxford University Press, 1977); J. Raz, *The Concept of a Legal System* (2nd edn, Oxford: Oxford
University Press, 1980), ch 7.

[32] Raz, note 2 above, 49–50; G. Christie, *Law, Norms and Authority* (London: Duckworth,
1982), 2–3; F. Schauer, note 4 above, ch 2.

[33] MacCormick, note 26 above, 24–26.

sion. Even those who advocate the distinction sometimes slip into presenting norms as rules.[34] The arguments that have been presented against the distinction between rules and norms are not conclusive. Those who wish to maintain one or other of the distinctions should feel free to modify the claims of this chapter if they wish. For them, the constitution will consist of rules and norms, though the difference between these elements is vague rather than sharp.

SOCIAL RULES AND SOCIAL GROUPS

All social groups are constituted by rules. Even the very simplest social group consists of a collection of people bound together by shared rules—though the rules may be so basic, so elemental, that members of the group may be unaware of them. At a minimum, there needs to be a shared rule setting the purpose of the group, that is, the objective the group is aiming to achieve, and a rule determining membership of the group. This may consist merely of a resolution to act together. Groups of friends often meet up with the intention of undertaking an activity together, without any clear idea of what that activity will consist. Members of the group break this rule, and incur criticism, when they undertake activities inconsistent with this purpose. Our simple social group also requires a further rule which determines who is bound by the rules of the group. Strangers walking past the group do not violate its rules by failing to participate in its activities. Finally, there must also be a rule which determines the manner in which the group makes decisions. In simple groups this rule is set at the 'default' position: unanimity. Because the group lacks a mechanism to accommodate disagreements, all of its members must agree to changes in the group's objectives or membership. In the event of the group needing to make a decision it may develop a new rule to resolve conflict or, as is commonly the case, it may get by through putting pressure on recalcitrant members. Their desire to remain part of the group will often be sufficient to pressure them towards agreement.

(i) A special type of constitutional rule?

Is there a special type, or a special set of types, of constitutional rule? John Searle draws a distinction between regulative and constitutive rules.[35] Constitutive rules take the following form:

'X counts as Y' or 'X counts as Y in context C.'[36]

Y is an institutional fact constituted by the rule; X, at its most basic, consists of a group of brute physical facts. So, a piece of paper covered in certain patterns of ink

---

[34] Raz, note 2 above, 9.

[35] Searle, note 1 above, 27–29, ch 2; J. Searle, *Speech Acts: An Essay in The Philosophy of Language* (Cambridge: Cambridge University Press, 1969), 33–42. See also J. Rawls, 'Two Concepts of Rules' (1955) 64 Philosophical Review 3.

[36] Searle, note 1 above, 28.

(X) counts as money (Y) in a certain territory (C). In a constitutive rule, Y assigns a new status to the facts set out in X. This new status generally changes the powers of some individuals, enabling or disabling, requiring or proscribing, action.[37] It is an important aspect of Searle's account that the X quality can, itself, be the product of a constitutive rule; constitutive rules can operate in layers. So, money (X) counts as a deposit (Y) when paid to a landlord (C). In this rule there are nested—at least—three lower constitutive rules determining 'money', 'paid', and 'landlord'.

Of the two formulations of constitutive rule which Searle gives, the former (X counts as Y) perhaps should be preferred to the latter (X counts as Y in context C). It is difficult to see how the rider 'in context C' adds to the rule. Whatever is placed in C could, equally well, be thought of as part of the group of elements contained in X. To return to the earlier example, it is difficult to see why it is less correct to treat the requirement of territory as part of X than include it as a separate feature C.

In Searle's account, all social institutions are constituted by constitutive rules. Social groups are a particular form of social institution. If Searle's distinction between constitutive and regulative rules holds, we might have a test through which the constitutive rules of a social group—and, eventually, the constitution of a state—could be distinguished from the other rules which affect group members. Unfortunately, Searle's distinction does not hold up to scrutiny. Searle provides us with two ways in which regulative rules differ from constitutive rules. First, he claims, the two rules differ in form. In contrast to constitutive rules, regulative rules take the form 'Do X', or, 'If Y do X'.[38] Secondly, regulative rules regulate antecedently existing activities, whereas constitutive rules create the very possibility of certain activities.[39] A rule demanding that houses not be sold on a Sunday, for example, regulates the existing practice of house-selling, whereas a rule specifying the conditions under which a house is sold creates this practice. As many have demonstrated, most rules, perhaps all rules, can be described in either regulative or constitutive terms.[40] The actions which must be undertaken to sell a house, for example, could either be seen as regulative (the contract of sale must be signed if the house is to be sold) or constitutive (a house is sold when a contract of sale has been signed). To put the point another way, we could either conceptualize the rules about house-selling as a set of conditions the would-be seller is obliged to satisfy, or as a set of conditions the satisfaction of which results in a sale. This ambiguity carries over to those rules which are constitutive of social groups. Is the rule which says a charity cannot be run for the sole purpose of

---

[37] Searle, note 1 above, 104–10.

[38] J. Searle, *Speech Acts: An Essay in The Philosophy of Language* (Cambridge: Cambridge University Press, 1969), 34.

[39] Ibid, 33.

[40] Raz, note 2 above, 108–10; N. MacCormick, 'Law as an Institutional Fact', in N. MacCormick and O. Weinberger, *An Institutional Theory of Law: New Approaches to Legal Positivism* (London: Kluwer Publishing, 1985), 23–4; E. Lagerspetz, *The Opposite Mirrors: A Conventionalist Theory of Institutions* (London: Kluwer Publishing, 1995), 17–19. Schauer, note 4 above, 6–7.

enriching its employees a constitutive rule—defining what a charity is—or a regulative rule—defining what a charity may do? The answer is, of course, that it is both.

Though Searle's distinction between regulative and constitutive rules fails, it would be a mistake to underestimate the importance of his work on the role rules play in constituting social institutions. First, Searle's account brings forward the complex relationship of social rules and social groups. As a social institution, such groups can only exist where they are constituted by social rules. But, conversely, social rules can only exist in the context of a social group. The operation of a social rule requires the existence of a group, a group defined by—at a minimum—their common acceptance of the rule, coupled with an awareness of their common acceptance. If no such group exists, the mooted rule is merely a potential social rule, or a collection of similar personal rules.

Second, Searle emphasizes the part that such rules play in constructing our world.[41] A significant part of our reality consists of institutional facts: social entities that exist because of our continued acceptance of constitutive rules. Brute facts, like trees and mountains, exist whatever we think of them. The words and categories we use to identify these brute facts are, of course, partly arbitrary, but the stuff the words refer to exists separate from us; everyone in the world could die tomorrow, but the mountains and trees would remain. In contrast, institutional facts only exist as a function of their constitutive rules. Like brute facts, our choice of words used to capture these institutional facts (money, *geld, argent*) is variable and partly a matter of chance. Like brute facts, an institutional fact could exist in a community which lacks the language to identify it. And like brute facts, a person might fail to correctly identify an incidence of an institutional fact—believing, for example, that a television personality is a qualified doctor, whereas she is, actually, not. But in contrast to brute facts, institutional facts exist because we—collectively—accept the rules that constitute them. If folk suddenly forgot the rules that constitute the institution of money, money would cease to exist.

Finally, Searle's formulation of constitutive rules illuminates the extent to which such rules can be non-optional. Raz, in the course of a telling critique of the distinction between regulative and constitutive rules, suggests that Searle's account of constitutive rules is best understood as an early conception of power-conferring rules.[42] This may be correct, but in shifting from Searle's constitutive rules to Raz's power-conferring rules, there is a risk that we may lose sight of the extent to which people's choices are curtailed by constitutive rules. A police officer making an arrest can *only* execute that arrest as a police officer. She cannot make a 'citizen's arrest' whilst in uniform. When the Prime Minister makes a public attack on the leader of a foreign country, he does so on behalf of the United Kingdom—whether or not he wishes to speak on behalf of the state. In each of these cases a constitutive rule simultaneously

[41] See especially, Searle, note 1 above, ch 5; see further, C. Taylor, 'Interpretation and the Sciences of Man', in C. Taylor, *Philosophy and the Human Sciences: Philosophical Papers Vol 2* (Cambridge: Cambridge University Press, 1985), 32–8; Galligan, note 2 above, 105–9.

[42] Raz, note 2 above, 111.

empowers and disempowers a person. She is given a power to act in one capacity, but is stripped of the power to act in another.

(ii) Internal and external rules

The rules that constitute social groups can be divided into two broad sets: those rules that are internal to the group and those that are external to the group. Internal rules are those which the members of the group have adopted in their capacity as group members. External rules are those rules which are set for the group by other social groups, in particular, and most importantly, the wider community of which the group is a part. So, for example, a charity will have a set of internal rules that define its objectives, the powers of its office-holders and so forth. These rules have been chosen by those founding and running the charity. The charity is also partly structured by a collection of external rules which provide a template for charitable groups: they may not pursue political objectives, for instance, and any profits they make must be put towards their charitable purposes, not divided up amongst the directors. These rules have not been chosen by members of the group, save that they have chosen to form a charity. Frequently, external rules are set by law, but there can also be non-legal social rules which constitute the group. These social rules can also form part of the template that people form groups within: the charity may be partly constituted through such social rules. The wider community may, for instance, require that the charity meets higher ethical standards in its treatment of employees than those demanded by the law. This may be one of the general rules that define what a charity is.

Social groups may also be shaped by rules which are not part of their constitution, but which constitute aspects of the broader environment within which they operate. There are numerous rules of this type. Linguistic rules, rules of social morality, and etiquette can all serve to constrain the ways in which people interact, and, consequently, the forms which social groups within that community take. These rules are not part of the group's constitution because they do not directly relate to the group. They are not external rules of the group because they are not part of the template set by the community for groups of that type. The boundary between those rules which directly relate to the group—and are therefore included within the group's constitution—and those rules which are not part of the group's constitution but still shape it by defining the environment within which the group operates, is a very fine one, and may be hard to detect in practice.

There is often no tension between the internal and external rules constituting the group, with the two collections of rules working happily together. Indeed, frequently a person will be a member both of the group which is subject to the rule and the wider group which has adopted the rule: a single person may experience the same rule both as an internal and as an external rule. So, English law has been determined—in a far from straight-forward fashion—by members of the community within which the law applies. This determines some of the rules which structure charities. A person may be both a member of the community which sets English law, from which perspective charity law is internal, and a member of a charity, from which perspective charity law is external.

On occasion, the external rules purporting to constitute the group will be in tension with the internal rules that the group has purported to adopt. For example, a company may be liable for corporate manslaughter even though it sought to create an internal structure which would isolate it from the negligent acts of its employees. The carelessness of the employee and the death thus caused are ascribed back to the company—irrespective of the company's own, more limited, rules. Sometimes a group's internal rule may be directly contradicted by an external rule. A policeman who refuses to leap into a river to save a drowning child might be correctly following the internal rules of the police service and, in that sense, be a successful member of the police force (which is, of course, a social group), but the social rules of the community which determine success in that office may take a different view.

Where there are conflicting rules constituting the group it might sensibly be asked which is the 'real' rule, which of the two rules actually does play a part in constituting the group. Sometimes it may be possible to answer this question. A charity might adopt a policy of spending money on political campaigning, only to discover this is not permitted by charity law. Several options are open to it. First, the charity could change its policy in light of the rule. It made a mistake, and now seeks to conform to the restriction. Secondly, the charity could become a lobby-group. Its members accept the construction of a charity contained in the law and decide to carry on the activity in a different guise. Thirdly, and most interestingly, the group could persist in its political campaigning but also continue to claim to be a charity. This rule-breaking might be done in a covert fashion or it might reflect a sincere disagreement about the rules which ought to constitute charities. Each of these possibilities will be considered in turn.

Sometimes the act of breaking a rule contains a tacit acceptance of the rule. If the charity decides to conceal its lobbying from its donors and the public, this may indicate that its members accept that the rule prohibiting such conduct applies to their institution, and defines what a charity is, but are trying to avoid the negative consequences of rule-breaking by deception. On many occasions, this will amount to simple dishonesty: one type of institution (a lobby group) is seeking to abuse the benefits accorded to another type of institution (a charity) by misrepresenting its true nature. But it is possible that there may be a virtuous motivation animating the deception: perhaps the limitations on the activities a charity can pursue are unjust, and surreptitious action by the group is the only way this injustice can be countered.

Things become more complicated when there is open disagreement about the rule. The charity which is engaged in political campaigning might disagree with the rule which prohibits such conduct. Its members might believe that charities ought to engage in such acts, that the external rule purporting to define charitable conduct is mistaken and inapplicable. In this situation the external rule is rejected: the members of the group regard themselves as a charity, whilst members of the wider group challenge this identity.

Frequently disagreement of this type occurs within a connected set of social groups. Members of the charity who wish to engage in lobbying are also members of the larger social group, the state, in our example, which has resolved that charities should not engage in this activity. Furthermore, the state claims that it is entitled to determine the rules which define a charity. Consequently, it is not simply the case that one group is asserting another group *ought* to adopt a constitutive rule, the state is, rather, asserting that it is entitled to set the rules which shape this institution. That particular charity, says the state, must accord with the template of a charity as determined by the state.

Principled disagreement of this type might be resolved by reference to an adjudicative body. The 'charity' might accept that a court is entitled to have the final say about the scope of charitable activities. But sometimes it may not be possible to resolve the dispute; there may not be an adjudicative body whose authority is accepted by both sides. On these occasions, it may not be possible to say definitively whether the rule is part of that constitution or not. Sometimes the best that can be said is that there are rival rules purporting to structure the group, and the content of the group's constitution depends on the perspective we adopt. One group seeks to impose a rule on another group that the other rejects. From the perspective of one group, the rule is not part of its constitution, but from the perspective of the other group it is.

It might be objected that a rule which is not acknowledged or followed by members of a group cannot form part of the constitution of that group. Such an objection underestimates the extent to which the group's actions and intentions, its purposes, successes and failures, are rule-defined and, consequently, relative to the set of rules that is referred to. An action may be that of the state under international law, but the act of private individuals under domestic law. There may be no 'correct' answer to what the state did, just different answers relative to different rules.

The position is different when there is a complete disjuncture between the group advocating the constitutive rule and the institution which is the subject of this advocacy. If, say, an anthropologist identified 'charitable' groups within a tribal community which did not fully accord with the rules of charities in her home society, she could either conclude that she had made a mistake in labelling these groups charities, or she might conclude that these groups were best understood as versions of charities—like her domestic charities in some respects, but different in others. It would be strange, and inappropriate, to conclude, though, that these groups were unknowingly breaking a constitutive rule.

(iii) The formalization of rules and creation of institutions within the group

Simple social groups can be constituted by rules which are largely unconscious: unspoken and deeply internalized. As the group becomes bigger these rules become less effective. At a certain point—the size has been estimated at between ten and fifteen members,[43] depending on the tasks of the group—the group can no longer function merely through consensus or the supervision of a strong leader. The group requires internal structures which delineate responsibilities and provide mecha-

[43] M. Argyle, *The Psychology of Interpersonal Behaviour* (5th edn, London: Penguin, 1994), 178–80.

nisms for making decisions and resolving disputes. The development of these structures requires the formalization of some of the rules that constitute the group. A rule becomes formalized when it is articulated in a definitive fashion. This is a matter of degree. At one end of the scale a social rule may start to become formalized when it is expressed by community leaders whose statements begin to clarify the rule. At the other end of the scale, law provides an example of an extremely formalized set of rules: it contains rules which are frequently written in canonical fashion, coupled with institutions empowered to resolve disputes that may arise over their interpretation.[44]

Complicated groups like states are constituted by a large number of rules, and, in contrast to simple groups, most of the rules that constitute them are not intuitive.[45] States require rules that define and empower office-holders, enable the group to make decisions, resolve disputes between members, and many other tasks besides. All of these rules can have different contents and take different forms. Consequently, for the state to exist, a more or less conscious choice must be made between various possible options. The selected rule must therefore be, to an extent, formal.

In tandem with the formalization of the rules comes the creation of institutions within the group: all social groups are institutions, but more complex groups contain multiple institutions within themselves. Once processes emerge through which new rules can be created, at least two categories of group-membership are formed: the category of group-members involved in the production of the rules, and the category of group-members who are subject to the rules once they are produced. The group now contains an institution which its members, or some of them, can occupy. Entering an institution alters the powers and duties of the individual in respect of the group. A group-member who enters the institution through which the group's rules can be created enjoys a different relationship with the group to the group-member who is merely expected to abide by those rules—though, of course, these two figures may be the same person acting in different capacities. It is a short step from this to the creation of many and various further institutions within the group, allowing for significant division of labour in pursuit of the group's objectives. The state has a vast array of such institutions. Some of these are concerned with the process of formalizing the rules of the constitution—most obviously, courts and legislatures—others are concerned with the execution of the state's projects—including, in most states, the army, police force, and, in many states, the provision of healthcare, schools, and universities. Within these institutions there are often further, yet smaller, institutions. The process reaches down to offices—a form of institution—that are occupied by a single person who enjoys particular powers to act for the group.

---

[44] Though, as Galligan notes, the creation of formal rules often indirectly leads to the creation of informal rules surrounding these rules: Galligan, note 2 above, 62–3.

[45] See generally, N. MacCormick, *Institutions of Law: An Essay in Legal Theory* (Oxford: Oxford University Press, 2007), 22–4.

CONCLUSION

This chapter has developed an account of rules, an account which has been directed towards illuminating the part that rules play in the existence and operation of social groups. It has brought forwards some of the ambiguities of rule-governed behaviour: in particular, the difficulties of distinguishing between action guided by rules and action undertaken for other reasons, and the possibility of quite fundamental disagreements within a social group over the existence and content of rules. The next chapter will continue to pursue these questions in the context of an extremely formalized social group: the state. It will be argued in that chapter that some of the uncertainties surrounding the nature of rules have led to uncertainties about the nature and content of state constitutions. The account of rules developed in this chapter will help us to resolve some of these uncertainties, allowing us to determine the boundaries of the state's constitution and giving some clarity to the rules which form part of that constitution. As well as resolving some longstanding questions about state constitutions, the work in this chapter will also be used to open up some new questions. The understanding of rules developed here provides the foundation for the discussion of legal and constitutional pluralism, found later in the book.

5

The State and its Constitution

The content of the constitutions of states is remarkably unclear. We should anticipate that particular constitutional rules will be disputed and debated—such rules are, after all, often vague or incomplete—but even the scope of the constitution appears ambiguous. It is far from obvious what rules should be counted as part of the state's constitution, and what rules, in contrast, act on the state indirectly, mediated through other institutions and groups. This chapter seeks to provide an outline of the types of rules which are found within state constitutions. It argues that state constitutions contain both legal and non-legal rules, and, further, that constitutions may include laws drawn from a number of different legal systems.

The chapter begins by reflecting on Hans Kelsen's account of the constitution and, by derivation, state. Kelsen's legalistic account of the constitution is introduced not only because of its inherent interest, but also because it has proved attractive to many British writers on the constitution. This attraction is curious, as it is in conflict with an established feature of British constitutional scholarship: the recognition of the plurality of sources of the constitution. This chapter will argue that an appreciation of the strengths of this approach requires the rejection of the Kelsenian model. Legalistic accounts of state constitutions provide a distorted picture of the state.

LEGALISTIC MODELS OF STATE AND CONSTITUTION

Hans Kelsen thought that the constitution only contained legal rules. Kelsen distinguished between the constitution in the formal sense and the constitution in a material sense.[1] Kelsen's constitution in the formal sense is what we might term a Constitution with a capital 'C'; a single document which purports to define the institutions of the state and delineates their relative powers and duties. Typically, such a document has special legal force, taking precedence over any conflicting law.[2] Not all states have a Constitution in this sense—the United Kingdom famously lacks such

---

[1] H. Kelsen, *General Theory of Law and State*, trans A. Wedberg (New York: Russell & Russell, 1961), 124–5. Compare T. Janoski, *Citizenship and Civil Society* (Cambridge: Cambridge University Press, 1998), 38–9.

[2] J. Raz, 'On the Authority and Interpretation of Constitutions: Some Preliminaries' in L. Alexander, *Constitutionalism: Philosophical Foundations* (Cambridge: Cambridge University Press, 1998), 152–4. K. Wheare, *Modern Constitutions* (2nd edn, Oxford: Opus, 1966), ch 1.

a canonical document. Kelsen's constitution in the material sense, in contrast, consists of those legal rules that regulate the production of other (general) legal rules; the constitution is the highest level of law within national law. Every state, according to Kelsen, had a material constitution.

Kelsen's legalistic account of the constitution complements his legalistic account of the state.[3] Once more, Kelsen distinguished between the formal and the material concepts of the state.[4] Kelsen equated the formal concept of the state with the totality of an effective national legal order. Kelsen's state is a legal order which manages, to some significant extent, to centralize and control the use of coercive power. In order to achieve this centralization the legal order requires a set of working institutions—courts, a legislature, and, presumably, an executive branch—that can make the legal system effective.[5] Kelsen argued that, as the state equates with a legal order, all of the classical features of a state should be understood as features of that order. Members of the state, the state's citizens, are invested with citizenship by the legal order.[6] The territory of the state is determined by the reach of the legal order;[7] going as far into the sky and as deep into the earth as its officials are able to police.[8] Finally, the actions of the state are undertaken through the legal order: the state can only act when the legal system attributes the conduct of individuals to it.[9]

This final point, the attribution of actions to the state, presented a difficulty for Kelsen. The state can not be invariably equated with the legal order as it can also act within that order on occasion. States employ people, buy property, and are liable for civil wrongs; indeed, it is common to talk of courts adjudicating between the state and its citizens, common to find references to the state in statutes and cases. Kelsen resolved this problem by introducing a second concept of the state: the material concept of the state. The material concept of the state is that understanding of the state found within the legal order. It is this 'state' which is to be found in statutes and law reports, able to sue and to be sued. The material concept of the state presupposes the formal concept of the state, but is not identical with the formal concept.

Kelsen was right to distinguish between the state and the conception of the state contained within a given legal system. Most, possibly all, legal systems contain concepts of the state. Domestic legal systems commonly determine which institutions are parts of the state and which fall outside of the state: a line is drawn between the public and the private. Frequently public bodies are burdened by special duties—the

---

[3] See the discussion in N. MacCormick, 'The State and the Law' in N. MacCormick, *Questioning Sovereignty* (Oxford: Oxford University Press, 1999), 21–2.

[4] Kelsen, note 1 above, 192–4.

[5] These criteria permitted Kelsen to distinguish primitive legal orders and international legal orders from states: Kelsen, note 1 above, 338–9.

[6] *Ibid.*, 233–42.

[7] *Ibid.*, 207–18.

[8] *Ibid.*, 217–18.

[9] *Ibid.*, 191–2.

rules of administrative law and some parts of human rights law—that private bodies ordinarily escape, and are accorded special legal powers which are denied to private bodies, the power to coerce and spend public funds, for example. The international legal order also contains an account of the state, setting the qualities an entity must possess before it is regarded as possessing statehood under international law.[10] However, it would be a mistake to think that these legal concepts of the state determine the nature or boundaries of the state outside of the confines of these legal orders. Legal concepts of the state are reflections—sometimes usefully distorted reflections—of the more basic account of the state provided in this book. Most obviously, the account of the state in international law varies significantly from this account. For example, under international law it is arguable that, in some circumstances, entities which have been created unlawfully or in violation of democratic principles will not be treated as states.[11] There are good political reasons for imposing such limitations if they deter unlawful aggression or promote democracy within fledgling states, and it would be a mistake to criticize their invocation solely because they are not 'really' essential to statehood. Consider Taiwan, for example. For policy reasons, Taiwan has not been recognized as a state by the international community.[12] But it clearly falls within the account of the state developed in previous chapters: China does not exercise control over Taiwan's territory, even if the precise relationship between China and Taiwan is left deliberately unclear on each side.[13] On the other hand, sometimes states are extinguished, yet remain in existence within the framework of international law. When Kuwait was occupied by Iraq in 1990 it continued to be regarded as a state by the international community, even though the government-in-exile lacked control of the territory.[14] Consequently, an entity can amount to a state and yet fail to have this quality recognized at an international level, or can fail to amount to a state but be characterized by international law as enjoying statehood.

Kelsen's legalistic understanding of the state echoed, or shaped, much of British constitutional scholarship.[15] So for example, in a short essay in the 1930s Sir Ivor Jennings presented the state as a collection of institutions that create and which are created by the law; an entity defined by the rules of a legal order.[16] When Geoffrey Marshall addressed the question he provided the reader with a thorough, and

---

[10] For a classic discussion of the state in international law, see J. Crawford, *The Creation of States in International Law* (2nd edn, Oxford: Oxford University Press, 2006) and I. Brownlie, *Principles of Public International Law* (7th edn, Oxford: Oxford University Press, 2008), ch 4.

[11] See Crawford, note 10 above, ch 3.

[12] Ibid., 198–219.

[13] A similar point could be made about Rhodesia: *Ibid.*, 128–31.

[14] *Ibid.*, 688–9.

[15] So far as it bothered with an account of the state: C. Harlow and R. Rawlings, *Law and Administration* (2nd edn, London: Butterworths, 1997), 4–7. See also J. Bryce, *The American Commonwealth* (Indiana: Liberty Press, 1995), vol 2, 1210.

[16] I. Jennings, 'The Institutional Theory' in I. Jennings (ed), *Modern Theories of Law* (Oxford: Oxford University Press, 1933), 80–1.

surprisingly amusing, survey of the uses of the term 'state' and related terms in statute and case law.[17] Legal positivists also found Kelsen's account of the state attractive: Neil MacCormick reported that Herbert Hart described it as 'a triumph'.[18] In
short, Kelsen's state is compatible with the positivistic, non-mystical style of British
scholarship. It provides a clear, straightforward picture of the state, one which fits
comfortably within the confines of legal theory: an understanding of law brings with
it an understanding of the state.

The temptation to endorse Kelsen's account of the state should be resisted.
Despite its superficial attractions for British constitutional scholars, Kelsen's model is
fundamentally incompatible with a central strength of their scholarship: the recognition of the plurality of sources of constitutions.

THE CONTENT OF CONSTITUTIONS

(i) Legal rules and state constitutions

In order for the state to maintain its essential connection with people within its territory, and in order for the institutions of the state to exist, the state must contain and
control at least one discrete legal order within its borders. A state stripped of a functioning legal order ceases to be a state. This might happen if the state is conquered
by another or collapses into anarchy. However, whilst there must be at least one
legal order in the state, it is quite possible for there to be more than one domestic
legal order within the state, these legal rules bound together, but left distinct by, a
collection of legal and non-legal constitutional rules. Furthermore, it is possible for
the state to be partly constituted by non-domestic legal orders: both by international
law and, less commonly, by the rules of foreign legal systems.

(a) A plurality of domestic legal orders
The United Kingdom is a perfect example of a state constituted by a variety of legal
orders. England and Wales, on the one hand, and Scotland, on the other, have distinct legal orders.[19] Though both of these territories accept the Westminster
Parliament as the highest legislative body, they do so by virtue of different rules. The
Scottish courts apply Westminster statutes because of an obligation imposed by
Scots law. English courts, in contrast, apply Westminster statutes because of a rule
of English law. It is arguable that the content as well as the source of these two rules
differs. In *MacCormick v Lord Advocate*[20] the Scottish Court of Session suggested that
Scots Law might not recognize Westminster statutes that were contrary to the
Treaty of Union, leading T. B. Smith to suggest that English law had inherited the

---

[17] G. Marshall, *Constitutional Theory* (Oxford: Oxford University Press, 1971), ch 2.

[18] MacCormick, note 3 above, 22 ftn15.

[19] The Isle of Man and the Channel Islands also have distinct legal orders. See generally,
P. Jackson and P. Leopold, *O. Hood Phillips and Jackson: Constitutional and Administrative Law*
(London: Sweet and Maxwell, 2001), 767–9.

[20] 1953 SC 396, 1953 SLT 255. See also *Gibson v Lord Advocate* 1975 SLT 134.

pre-1707 doctrine of sovereignty, whilst Scots law had inherited a more limited understanding of Parliament's powers.[21] This example demonstrates that the power of a single constitutional institution, the Westminster Parliament, may be differently defined by the rules of these multiple legal systems.

These considerations might have compelled Kelsen to conclude that England and Scotland are separate states, but practical British scholars have long recognized that the United Kingdom is a single state partly constituted by multiple legal systems. England and Scotland have different legal systems, but share a great many institutions. Parliament is the supreme law-maker in each territory; citizenship is common across the state. These institutions are constituted by a mix of English and Scots law, and a number of non-legal rules besides. Furthermore, there is a rich collection of such non-legal rules—of which the Sewel[22] convention is only the most obvious—that bind the people, officers and institutions of England and Scotland together in a common recognition of the statehood of the United Kingdom.

Not all of the rules of the domestic legal order of a state are part of the constitution of that state. Some of these rules only play an indirect role in constituting the state, or have no role at all in this process. Whilst the rules of private law may sometimes indirectly shape the state, they are not part of the constitution of the state, that is, part of the set of rules which directly relates to the formation and regulation of the institutions of the state. This can be quite a fine line to draw. When state institutions agree contracts that restrict their discretion, for instance, the rules of contract law are not part of the state's constitution, though the state interacts with these rules and is shaped by them. However, the rules contained within particular contracts (which directly relate to the state institution) are part of their constitution.

The laws of the domestic legal system are acts of the state, the products of pronouncements of its institutions—in particular, the legislative and judicial branches. The character of the state, an aspect of the state explored later in this book, is partly established by these laws. Whilst the private law of contract is not part of the state's constitution, it still creates and reveals the character of the state. A law which prohibits racial discrimination in employment, for example, may not be part of the state's constitution, but is still an articulation of the character of that state.

Though the bulk of private law rests clearly in the private realm, there are some areas of law which have both a public and a private character, where public and private law overlap. On occasion, public law alters the operation of private law when one of the parties is a state institution. Sometimes contracts will not be enforced

---

[21] T. B. Smith, 'The Union of 1707 as Fundamental Law' (1957) Public Law 99,
N. MacCormick, 'The United Kingdom: What State? What Constitution?'
in N. MacCormick, *Questioning Sovereignty* (Oxford: Oxford University Press, 1999)
and N. MacCormick, 'Is there a Constitutional Path to Scottish Independence?' (2000) 53
Parliamentary Affairs 721, 727. See also Lord MacDermott, 'The Decline of the Rule of Law'
(1972) 23 NILQ 474 for attempt to apply a similar argument to Northern Ireland.

[22] The Sewel convention places constitutional (but not legal) limits on the capacity of the
Westminster Parliament to legislate in areas devolved to the Scottish Parliament; see
Devolution Guidance Note 10.

against public bodies when this would fetter their capacity to advance the public interest. Sometimes tort claims against public bodies fail because courts wish to preserve public funds—or succeed because the law demands a higher standard of public bodies than it does of private individuals. These rules are part of public law and they do relate directly to, and partly constitute, state institutions. The tension which often arises in these situations is testament, perhaps, to the uncertain relationship between the objectives of public and private law.

(b) Non-domestic legal orders—international law

The legal rules of a state's constitution need not be exhausted by its domestic legal orders: non-domestic legal orders can also have a part to play in the constitution. The least controversial of these, perhaps, are rules of international law. The common response of those attracted to legalistic models of constitutions—such as that provided by Kelsen—to the inclusion of international law in the constitution is predictable. International law is only part of the constitution, they say, when it is incorporated within the legal order by a rule of domestic law and has, by incorporation, ceased to be part of international law. When it is not so incorporated, it cannot be considered to be part of the state's constitution. This is a mistake. Rules of international law that are not incorporated into domestic law may still be followed by state officers and institutions. This is an example of the role of external rules, discussed in the previous chapter, operating in the context of state constitutions. An unincorporated rule of international law may still form part of the constitution of a state if a significant portion of those within the state—crucially, those within state institutions—treat it as binding on them, and act accordingly. So, for example, the European Convention on Human Rights was ratified by the United Kingdom in 1951 but was not incorporated into domestic law until the Human Rights Act 1998 came into force. During this period the Convention had a significant impact on the United Kingdom's constitution. It was widely accepted that both the legislature and the executive were bound by its provisions: they ought to legislate and act within the confines set by the Convention. Furthermore, when the European Court of Human Rights ruled against the United Kingdom, there was a duty to change the law to bring it into line with the Convention. These duties were not—directly—part of domestic law,[23] but they still shaped how the United Kingdom acted and partly determined the relationship between the governing institutions of the state and its people. A complete account of the constitutional rules of the United Kingdom in this period would include an account of the Convention.

Even after incorporating a rule of international law it may still be the case that a difference exists between the incorporated rule and the international law rule. The incorporated rule is absorbed within, and becomes part of, the domestic legal order. The international law rule will enjoy a distinct life as part of the system of international law. Either of the two rules—the international rule or its domestic version—may change over time. If state officials continue to follow the international law rule, both the domestic and international versions of the rule will form (distinguishable) parts of the constitution.

---

[23] They did have some legal consequences: see M. Hunt, *Using Human Rights Law in English Courts* (Oxford: Hart Publishing, 1997).

(c) Non-domestic legal orders—foreign law

Perhaps more controversially, there is no reason why the rules of a foreign legal order could not form part of a state's constitution, in much the same manner as the rules of international law. It is hard to think of any clear example of this, but it could occur if officials in one state endorsed a portion of the rules of another state, adopting them as a guide to their conduct in certain areas. Imagine, for instance, a notoriously corrupt state whose rulers resolve to improve standards of governance. A neighbouring state is famous for its high standards of integrity in public life, and its strict legal rules governing—amongst other things—the giving of 'gifts' and campaign contributions to politicians. The rulers of the corrupt state decide to follow these rules. The easiest—and most obvious—way for them to do this would be to incorporate the rules of the neighbouring state into their own legal order. If they did so, these rules would change in character and become part of their domestic law. However, it is possible that the officials of the corrupt state might accept and follow the rules of the second state without transposing them into domestic law. They might even commit themselves to accept any changes to these rules made by the neighbouring state. The rules of the foreign state might then become part of the constitution of the corrupt state, without the corrupt state incorporating them into domestic law or placing itself under the legal order of the foreign state.

(ii) Non-legal rules and state constitutions

Perhaps the strongest reason British constitutional scholars could have for rejecting Kelsen's legalistic model of the constitution is that its adoption would produce a bizarre account of the United Kingdom's constitution, a constitution in which non-legal rules play a crucial role. Legalistic descriptions of the constitution, resembling those advocated by Kelsen, were popular during and prior to the eighteenth century, achieving their most developed form in Sir William Blackstone's *Commentaries*. Blackstone's account encompassed only the legal dimension of the constitution and excluded, or ignored, non-legal rules.[24] As early as 1832 the artificiality of Blackstone's account was subject to criticism: J. J. Park noted how far such legalistic accounts of the constitution diverged from reality.[25] One of the great advances of Victorian legal scholarship, championed by Albert Venn Dicey, was the recognition of the importance of non-legal constitutional rules.[26] Non-legal rules are an aspect of every functioning constitution, but in an unwritten, political, constitution like that of the United Kingdom, an understanding of these non-legal rules is essential to a plausible

[24] W. Blackstone, *Commentaries on the Laws of England* (1st edn, Oxford: Clarendon Press, 1765). See also: J. L. de Lolme, *The Constitution of England* (1st edn, London: T. Spilsbury, 1784).

[25] J. J. Park, *The Dogmas of the Constitution* (London: B. Fellows, 1832), 94.

[26] A. V. Dicey, *An Introduction to the Study of the Law of The Constitution* (10th edn, London: Macmillan, 1959). See further, O. Hood Phillips, 'Constitutional Conventions: Dicey's Predecessors' (1966) 29 MLR 137, and C. Munro, 'Dicey on Constitutional Conventions' (1985) Public Law 637.

account of the constitution. As Dicey commented, Blackstone's account had the effect of 'ascribing…to a modern monarch and constitutional King the whole, and perhaps more than the whole, of the powers actually possessed and exercised by William the Conqueror'.[27] It is non-legal rules that limit the power of the monarch, define the office of the Prime Minister, and, more recently, have shaped the relationships between Westminster and the devolved institutions.[28] Indeed, if we were to adopt Kelsen's model of the state, in which state offices are defined by law,[29] the office of the Prime Minister would barely scrape a mention.

The non-legal rules which structure the constitution have been accorded a variety of labels. They are the 'unwritten maxims' of 'constitutional morality',[30] forming the 'system of political morality' that underpins the constitutional order,[31] serving to shape constitutional institutions through the force of 'usage' and 'custom'.[32] Dicey wrote in sweeping terms of '…conventions, understandings, habits or practices…'[33] In recent years the phenomenon has been rediscovered in other jurisdictions. Keith Whittington writes of the construction of constitutional norms within the realm of American political practice, distinct from constitutional law, but intertwined with it.[34]

In constitutional scholarship non-legal rules are now commonly referred to as 'constitutional conventions'.[35] Much has been written on the nature of these rules.

---

[27] A. V. Dicey, *An Introduction to the Study of the Law of the Constitution* (10th edn, London: Macmillan, 1959), 7–8.

[28] R. Rawlings, 'Concordats of the Constitution' (2000) 116 LQR 257.

[29] Kelsen, note 1 above, 192–193.

[30] J. S. Mill, 'Considerations on Representative Government', in J. Mill, *On Liberty and Other Essays*, J. Gray (ed) (Oxford: Oxford University Press, 1991), 270.

[31] E. Freeman, *The Growth of the English Constitution* (3rd edn, London: Macmillan, 1876), 114–20. Hood Phillips, note 26 above, 144–145.

[32] A. Todd, *Parliamentary Government in England* (London: Longmans, 1889–90), vol 2, 141. Hood Phillips, note 26 above, 143.

[33] Dicey, note 27 above, 24.

[34] K. E. Whittington, *Constitutional Construction: Divided Powers and Constitutional Meaning* (Cambridge Mass.: Harvard University Press, 1999), esp ch 1.

[35] Philosophers also talk of conventions, but the meaning they give to 'conventions' sometimes differs from that ascribed by constitutional scholars. The leading philosophical work on the topic is by David Lewis (D. Lewis, *Convention* (Oxford: Blackwell, 2002)). The focus of Lewis' interest is a particular type of coordination problem: those in which there are two or more possible solutions, each of which is about as attractive at the other to all of the participants. A 'convention' then arises where a group of people pick one of these options. Constitutional conventions can take the form of a Lewisian convention, but they do not all fit Lewis' model. In some instances constitutional conventions help create an institution rather than solve a pre-existing coordination problem of Lewis' type, and, moreover, there are sometimes a variety of more or less attractive versions of the constitutional convention open to the participants, who may rightly disagree about which should be adopted. See further A. Marmor, 'On Convention' (1996) 107 Synthese 349, and J. Dickson, 'Is the Rule of Recognition Really a Convention?' (2007) 27 Oxford J Legal Studies 373.

Geoffrey Marshall distinguished two groups of understandings of conventions: the 'positive morality' and the 'critical morality' interpretations.[36] In the 'positive' camp he placed, amongst others, Sir Kenneth Wheare and O. Hood Phillips. These writers tried to provide a model of conventions that did not require the describer to adopt a position on their value or purpose. Wheare wrote, for instance, that a convention was '. . . a rule of behaviour accepted as obligatory by those concerned in the work- ing of the Constitution'.[37] Whilst O. Hood Phillips declared them to be '. . . rules of political practice which are regarded as binding by those to whom they concern'.[38] The 'critical' group was led by Sir Ivor Jennings, with his rather vague claim that, in addition to the features identified by Wheare and Phillips, there must be a 'reason for the rule'.[39] A far more satisfying version of the 'critical' definition was provided by Marshall himself: '. . . conventions are the rules that the political actors *ought* to feel obligated by, if they have considered the precedents and reasons correctly'.[40]

Wheare's and Phillips' definitions square with the account of social rules provided in the previous chapter. To flesh out their accounts, a convention operates when: (1) in general, people act in conformity to the rule; (2) when so acting, the rule forms part of the causal explanation of their conduct; (3) a portion, at least, of the political community accepts the rule as a valid standard for conduct. And, as Joseph Jaconelli reminds us, (4) a convention is a *constitutional* convention when it is constitutional in nature; not all social rules are constitutional conventions.[41]

What, then, are we to make of those advocating a 'critical morality' approach to conventions? Marshall regards it as a positive feature of his model that it allows 'critics and commentators to say that although a rule may appear to be widely or even universally accepted as a convention, the conclusions generally drawn from earlier precedents, or the reasons advanced in justification, are mistaken'.[42] This appears a hazardous benefit: if a rule is widely accepted and followed by political actors, it would be odd for a constitutional commentator, or even for one of those political actors, to deny that it was a convention. Conventions are rules and, like laws, they purport to provide reasons for action that pre-empt, to use Raz's term, consideration of the reasons on which they depend.[43] The convention should be the

---

[36] G. Marshall, *Constitutional Conventions* (Oxford: Oxford University Press, 1984), 10–12.

[37] K. Wheare, *Modern Constitutions* (2nd edn, Oxford: Oxford University Press, 1966), 122.

[38] P. Jackson and P. Leopold, *O. Hood Phillips and Jackson: Constitutional and Administrative Law* (8th edn, London: Sweet and Maxwell, 2001), 24.

[39] I. Jennings, *The Law and the Constitution* (5th edn, London: University of London Press, 1959), 136. A test adopted by the Canadian Supreme Court: *Re Amendment of the Constitution of Canada (Nos 1, 2 and 3)* (1982) 125 DLR (3d) 1; see also I. Harden, 'The Constitution and Its Discontents' (1991) 21 British J Political Science 489, 494–6.

[40] G. Marshall, *Constitutional Conventions* (Oxford: Oxford University Press, 1984), 12.

[41] J. Jaconelli, 'The Nature of Constitutional Conventions' (1999) 19 Legal Studies 24, 35–9.

[42] Marshall, note 40 above, 12.

[43] J. Raz, *The Morality of Freedom* (Oxford: Oxford University Press, 1986), 57–62. Jaconelli also notes this quality of conventions: see J. Jaconelli, note 41 above, 24, 28.

product of these reasons, but it also stands separate from them. If constitutional commentators began to refuse to acknowledge the rules that political actors treat as conventions simply because there were not, or were not perceived to be, adequate reasons to support them, we might again fall foul of Dicey's charge of artificiality in our interpretation of the constitution: there would be one set of rules governing the functioning of the constitution, and another set in the writings of constitutional scholars.

However, Marshall's and Jennings' accounts should not be dismissed out of hand. The demand that we consider the reason behind a constitutional convention is well-founded. But to understand what this demand entails we need to think a little further about what a 'reason' implies in this context, and the distinct questions which an account of a convention might be seeking to answer. First, a writer might attempt to provide an account of the emergence of a constitutional convention. In this context, the 'reason' for the convention is contained within the explanation of how it came to be as it is. So, for example, the (historical) reason why there is a convention that the British monarch sign bills placed before her by Parliament is, to simplify, that the Crown was defeated in its tussles with Parliament in the seventeenth and eighteenth centuries. Secondly, a writer might attempt to provide an account of the current operation of the convention. In this context, the (psychological) reason for the convention includes an explanation of why people adhere to the convention. To speculate, the reason the monarch adheres to the bill-signing convention is because she values tradition or, perhaps, because she wants to keep her job. Finally, a writer may try to explain why people should adhere to the convention. In this context, the (justificatory) reason for the convention is the benefit or value that following the rule obtains. So, the reason for the bill-signing convention may be that it facilitates democracy. Every operative constitutional convention possesses a 'reason' in senses one and two, but need not possess a 'reason' in sense three: some conventions may just be pointless, or wrong. Those subject to the convention must be aware, at some level, of the reason in sense two, but need not be aware of the reason in senses one and three.

A complete and satisfying account of a convention would include an exploration of all three senses of 'reason' set out above. Each of the three is important and interesting; which one has priority will depend on the type of account of the convention we are seeking to provide. The third sense, though, the normative account of the reason behind a convention, is of especial importance to scholars writing for the community in which the convention operates. This is because such an account may affect the content and development of the convention when read by those subject to the convention. In this context, the line between political actors and constitutional scholars becomes blurred: scholarly work shapes the content of the convention, providing a resource which can be consulted in times of difficulty[44] and, also, reinforces certain readings of a convention where there are a number of rival interpretations. Consequently, it is impossible for a scholar to merely describe a convention, as that

---

[44] See Lord Wilson, 'The Robustness of Conventions in a Time of Modernisation and Change' (2004) Public Law 407, 408.

description may change what it describes.[45] She is in the same position as an academic lawyer whose work is read by barristers and judges. Within the elastic confines of the interpretations of the convention provided by political actors and other writers, she must try to identify the (justificatory) reason for the convention, and then clarify the rule in the context of that reason. She has a responsibility to her community to seek to show the convention in its best light or—if this cannot be done—to advocate that it be discarded or changed.

(iii) The place of customs and principles within the constitution

From time to time it has been argued that, in addition to rules, constitutions include customs and principles. Each of these will be considered in turn.

Most states contain customs, or practices, that have arisen within their institutions.[46] It is necessary to distinguish between pure customs and customs that have ossified into rules. A pure custom exists where people tend to behave in a certain fashion, and behave in this way because others in the past have acted in a similar manner, but there is no normative underpinning to their conduct. For example, it is customary to serve soup first at a dinner party, but whilst a host who decided to serve it as a second course might have broken with custom, she would not have broken a social rule.[47] A person considering breaching a pure custom will not be subject to social criticism when she departs from this practice.[48] Pure customs are not part of the constitution. They may influence conduct, but they do not guide it. Customs that have ossified into rules, in contrast, are included within the constitution. These customs have gained normative force and trigger social disapproval when breached. Not only do we expect people to behave in this way, we believe that we are entitled to expect people to behave in this way. Even apparently pointless practices can turn into social rules over time. Often this is because the rules serve a symbolic function, signalling that the rule-follower is part of a particular social group. The social rules which determine fashion in clothes are sometimes of this type. A man who turns up at a formal dinner without a tie might be understood by stuffier diners to have breached a rule defining the dining community. He has indicated that he is not part of their group and is not willing to accept their rules. Customary rules

[45] See generally, C. Taylor, 'Social Theory as Practice' in C. Taylor, *Philosophy and the Human Sciences: Philosophical Papers*: Vol 2 (Cambridge: Cambridge University Press, 1985).

[46] Sometimes also described as practices or usages of the constitution. See R. Brazier, 'The Non-Legal Constitution: Thoughts on Convention, Practice and Principle' (1992) 43 *NILQ* 262, 270–2; G. Marshall and G. Moodie, *Some Problems of the Constitution* (5th edn, London: Hutchinson, 1971), 26–8.

[47] Marmor suggests that there is a convention that folk in our community eat using their fork with the left hand. I suspect this is a pure custom, rather than a convention, as it lacks normative force. Marmor, note 35 above, 364.

[48] Jaconelli, note 41 above, 30–1; K. Wheare, *The Statute of Westminster and Dominion Status* (5th edn, Oxford: Oxford University Press, 1953), 10.

of this type are common in state constitutions, with all manner of rules governing modes of address, social precedence, uniforms and so on. Sometimes these serve to create a sense of solidity and community within the institution, and may be of greater importance than they seem at first sight.

A further set of features which have sometimes been included within the constitution are principles.[49] The inclusion of principles within the constitution recalls Ronald Dworkin's classic attack on Hart's rule-based account of law.[50] Hart, Dworkin claimed, could not accommodate legal principles within his understanding of law. Dworkin drew a contrast between principles and rules. Principles, according to Dworkin, have a dimension of weight that rules lack. Whereas rules function in a binary fashion, either requiring a result in a given instance or not, principles provide an impulse towards a result, but may need to be balanced against other, competing, principles. Constitutional documents often do contain some very broadly worded clauses. Some of these do resemble the type of principles to which Dworkin was referring. The German constitution, for example, requires the state to respect human dignity[51] and ensure equality before the law.[52] Some make even more ambitious connections: the preamble to the Irish constitution acknowledges the state's obligation to Christ, and enjoins observance of prudence, justice, and charity.[53] The Egyptian constitution calls for movement towards Arab unity,[54] whilst the basic law of Israel calls for the state to respect both Jewish and democratic values.[55]

Sometimes declarations of this type are just meaningless waffle, with little or no significance for the state. Sometimes, though, they do make a difference. The right to dignity and equality in the German constitution, for instance, has significant legal consequences. Even when the clause appears to have no legal effect it could still be understood as a directive constitutional principle: requiring the legislature and executive to follow certain policies or principles even if these are not legally enforceable.[56]

Given that constitutions do contain broad principles of this type, is it necessary to amend our model of the constitution to include constitutional principles alongside constitutional rules? Hart's reply to Dworkin answers this question. Hart rejected

---

[49] I. Harden, 'The Constitution and its Discontents' (1991) 21 British J Political Science 489, 504–5; T. R. S. Allan, Law, *Liberty and Justice* (Oxford: Oxford University Press, 1993), 92–8; Brazier, note 46 above, 272–5; F. Snyder, 'The Unfinished Constitution of the European Union' in J. H. H. Weiler and M. Wind (eds), *European Constitutionalism Beyond the State* (Cambridge: Cambridge University Press, 2003), 60–2.

[50] R. Dworkin, *Taking Rights Seriously* (London: Duckworth, 1977), 24–7.

[51] Art 1.

[52] Art 2.

[53] Preamble to the Constitution of Ireland.

[54] Preamble to the Constitution of Egypt.

[55] See, for instance, Basic Law: Human Dignity and Liberty (1992).

[56] See generally, J. Usman, 'Non-Justiciable Directive Principles: A Constitutional Design Defect' (2007) 15 Michigan State J Int L 643.

Dworkin's dichotomy.[57] There was no sharp divide between rules and principles. At one end of the spectrum there are rules that are very precise and narrowly drafted. At the other end there are rules which are framed in very general terms. These generalized rules can be called principles, but the difference between these principles and the narrower rules is one of degree, with no sharp boundary between the two. Very general expressions about the nature of the state in constitutional preambles should sometimes be understood as very general rules, which are, sometimes, not legally enforceable.

THE AMBIGUITIES OF STATE CONSTITUTIONS

Though this chapter has clarified some aspects of the constitution, it has also, in some respects, sought to make the content of constitutions a little less clear. Not only is the interpretation of constitutions beset by ambiguity, it can also—sometimes—be unclear whether a given rule is part of a constitution. A particularly troublesome task lies in distinguishing actions of states that are ascribed by, or are the product of, external constitutional rules, and actions of states that are merely reactions to external pressures. Like practically all other social groups, the state is shaped by its interaction with outside groups. Sometimes this is simply a response to the actions of those groups. A bomb attack on a capital city, for example, may cause a state to introduce new criminal legislation and create a new counter-terrorism unit in the police force. The terrorist group's actions have had constitutional implications, but no one would argue that the rules of the terrorist group are part of the state's constitution; their impact takes the same form as a flood or hurricane: an exertion of force to which the state responds. On the other hand, perhaps the rules adopted by the governing political party to choose its leader should be considered part of the state's constitution. Some of the significant actors in the state accept these rules as binding upon them, and the rule affects the running of the executive branch. These are external rules imposed on the state by the political party, just as the laws regulating political parties are external rules imposed on parties by the state.

A further complexity arises when an outside group purports to impose a rule on the state that many within the state reject. For instance, the international community might insist that when soldiers commit a war crime they do so on behalf of the state, irrespective of the state's internal rules. This situation is considered further in later chapters. In this case, it seems that there are two rival sets of rules constructing the state. It may not be possible, or helpful, to say which of these is the 'true' constitution. There is the international law construction of the state, which empowers the soldiers to act on the state's behalf, and the domestic construction of the state, which does not empower the soldiers. The plausibility of the rival constructions of the state in this context will depend on the plausibility of the claim of the outside group to be entitled to set rules for the state. The example given is attractive because

---

[57] H. L. A. Hart, *The Concept of Law* (2nd edn, Oxford: Clarendon Press, 1994), 259–63; J. Raz, 'Legal Principles and the Limits of the Law' (1972) 81 Yale LJ 823.

the international community can make a plausible claim to be a wider social group which encompasses states and state members within its reach. If the rival construction of the constitution was advanced by a group unconnected with the state, it would look much less persuasive: such an account would more closely resemble an argument for constitutional reform than an attempt to set out the rules of an existing constitution.

CONCLUSION

This chapter has attempted to clarify the boundaries and content of state constitutions. It has rejected claims that the constitution can be reduced to a unified, ordered, set of legal rules. In place of this Kelsenian model it has argued that a plurality of rules make up the constitution. This plurality has two dimensions. First, there may be a plurality of different, distinct, legal orders which contribute rules to a single constitution. Second, state constitutions practically invariably also include non-legal rules, constitutional conventions. The ground work undertaken in the previous chapter was utilized to draw this map of state constitutions, and to give some clarity to the nature of constitutional conventions. The recognition of the plurality of constitutional sources raises questions about how these sources interrelate, and about the implications of this plurality for the state's capacity to act. These questions dominate the latter half of this book. The next chapter considers the relationship between laws and constitutional conventions in more detail, arguing that the distinction between the two is a matter of degree, and that the boundary between the two is a soft one. The book then turns to consider the state's ability to form intentions and undertake actions, making use of the plurality of sources of the constitution to cast light on the state's capacity to act beyond, and potentially in defiance of, its domestic legal order.

6

Laws and Conventions

The previous chapter introduced the idea of constitutional conventions, discussing their nature and place within the constitution. It left at least one important feature of conventions unexplored: their relationship with law. The task of identifying the differences between laws and constitutional conventions has caused British constitutional theorists a great deal of trouble. It would have caused non-British constitutional theorists trouble too, had they reflected on the issue, but the unusual significance and quantity of conventions in the United Kingdom's constitution has rendered the question of especial interest within that territory. Two possible distinctions are frequently canvassed. First, that laws are enforced by courts, with legal sanctions following their breach, whilst conventions are enforced only by political pressure. Second, that laws are systematic, a set of rules bound together by other rules, whereas each constitutional convention stands alone. A sophistication of this second distinction focuses on the special claims that law makes. Even if conventions can, sometimes, form systems, this system does not make the claims which are characteristic of legal systems. This chapter will argue that neither distinction can be sustained. The difference between law and convention is one of degree: laws and conventions can be placed upon a spectrum of types of social rules, a spectrum gradated in terms of the formalization of rules. Laws lie at the most formalized end of this spectrum, but there is no single, definable, point at which rules shift from being conventions into being laws. Alongside this argument, it will be contended that conventions can become laws through judicial intervention, and that conventions can 'crystallize' into laws over time by becoming increasingly formalized.

COURTS AND THE ENFORCEMENT OF CONVENTIONS

In contrast to laws, contended Albert Venn Dicey, constitutional conventions are neither 'enforced or recognised by courts'.[1] Implicit in Dicey's account is a division between laws on the one hand—that are recognized and enforced by courts—and conventions on the other—that are neither recognized nor enforced by the courts. A number of challenges can be advanced against this clear division. First, the sharp division will fail if it is conceivable that there are some conventions which are

---

[1] A. V. Dicey, *Introduction to the Study of the Law of the Constitution* (10th edn, London: Macmillan, 1962), 417.

enforced by the courts, or which are recognized but not enforced by the courts. Secondly, the sharp division would also fail if it were conceivable there are some laws which are not recognized by courts, or which are recognized but not enforced by the courts. If any of these challenges succeeds, Dicey's division will have been shown to be inadequate. It may still be the case, however, that Dicey has identified an important characteristic of laws and constitutional conventions. It may be an important characteristic of laws that they are (normally) enforced by courts and an important characteristic of constitutional conventions that they are (normally) not, even if some unusual instances can be shown where these features are absent.

(i) The recognition and enforcement of constitutional conventions by courts

The first element of Dicey's claim, that courts will not, or cannot, recognize conventions, is plainly too broad.[2] Courts can recognize anything they wish to recognize. Judges frequently make reference to dictionaries, encyclopaedias, and a host of other things. It would be surprising if they never recognized constitutional conventions. The interest in Dicey's claim lies in the difficult divide between recognition and enforcement—the extent to which recognition can be equated with enforcement. Judicial enforcement of convention can be divided into two groups. First, there are those occasions when the convention is indirectly enforced because of its connection with a distinct legal right. Secondly, and more controversially, there may be occasions when conventions are directly enforced by courts without the support of a pre-existing legal right.

Courts indirectly enforce many things. A court faced with a tricky word in a statute might turn to a dictionary for clarification. In a sense, perhaps, the court then 'enforces' this definition. Similarly, a court adjudicating on the reasonable use of a hedge-trimmer in an action for negligence might look at the guidance for safe use contained in the instruction manual. If the judge concludes that a user who ignores these rules has contributed to her own accident, the judge might be said to have 'enforced' the guidance. Constitutional conventions can have a similar role in the court. Judges can use conventions as an interpretative aid to clarify the meaning of statutes.[3] Sometimes statutes make reference to conventions, and interpretation of the statute requires an interpretation of the convention. Sometimes statutes are passed in the context of conventions; the structure of the statute presupposes the parallel operation of these rules. A court which ignored conventions in this context would risk producing an impractical interpretation of the statute. Conventions can also form part of the background set of facts which are relied upon to make out a legal right. Like the safety warnings in the instruction manual, the judge may turn to

---

[2] G. Marshall, *Constitutional Conventions: The Rules and Forms of Political Accountability* (rev. edn., Oxford: Clarendon Press, 1986), 12–17; P. Jackson and P. Leopold, *O. Hood Phillips and Jackson: Constitutional and Administrative Law* (London: Sweet and Maxwell, 2001), 138–41; C. Munro, 'Laws and Conventions Distinguished' (1975) 91 LQR 218, 229–31.

[3] For instance, *British Coal Corporation v The King* [1935] AC 500; *Copyright Owners Reproduction Society Ltd. v EMI (Australia) Limited* (1958) 100 CLR 597; Marshall, note 2 above, 12–17.

convention to establish whether conduct is reasonable, or whether someone's legally enforceable expectations have been frustrated.

T. R. S. Allan argues that the recognition of a convention by a court implies approval of it,[4] and amounts to an acknowledgment that the convention is the manifestation of a constitutional principle which ought to be ascribed 'the dignity of law'.[5] For Allan, conventions express 'conclusions of political principle, and so cannot, in the last analysis, be distinguished from the law'.[6] In the following sentence, Allan writes that: 'In matters of constitutional significance, legal doctrine and political principle are inevitably interdependent and intertwined.' This latter statement is certainly correct, but is Allan right to go further than this, and insist on the equation of conventions with legal principles?

Recognition of a convention by a court will often imply the court's approval of the convention. Sometimes the expression of approval will be implicit within the test adopted for the recognition of the convention. Sir Ivor Jennings' test, it will be recalled, included a requirement that there be a reason for the convention,[7] whilst Geoffrey Marshall wrote that conventions were those rules which political actors ought to feel bound by, if they had construed the precedents correctly.[8] If either of these tests was adopted, the court's identification of a convention would require it to have identified a (justificatory) reason for the convention, that is, a reason why the political actors ought to have considered themselves bound by the rule. Furthermore, the legal context within which the convention is invoked may also require that judges express approval of the convention. If a judge concludes that it was irrational for a minister to depart from a convention the judge must, at a minimum, hold that the convention was of sufficient worth to warrant consideration by the minister in the course of making a decision. Similarly, if the court finds that a minister has frustrated a person's legitimate expectation that a convention be honoured by departing from it, the convention must be at least attractive enough to entitle people to think that it will be followed.

Despite the attractions of Allen's argument, there are a number of difficulties with the conclusion that the identification of a convention invariably implies approval. The previous chapter discussed the part that the (justificatory) reason for a convention should play in its identification and interpretation. Whilst a person describing a convention should attempt to identify the (justificatory) reason for a convention, and interpret it in light of this reason, such a reason may not exist for every convention. Some conventions may just be mistakes; rules that are followed, but which would be better ignored. There may be pragmatic arguments for a court to adopt Jennings' or Marshall's tests where mere recognition of a convention is likely to

---

[4] T. R. S. Allan, *Law, Liberty and Justice* (Oxford: Clarendon Press, 1993), 244.

[5] *Ibid*, 240.

[6] *Ibid*, 253.

[7] I. Jennings, *The Law and the Constitution* (5th edn, London: University of London Press, 1959), 136.

[8] Marshall, note 2 above, 12.

encourage observance of it. When the Canadian Supreme Court, for instance, was asked to decide whether it was a convention of the Canadian constitution that the federal government should obtain the consent of the provinces before requesting the Westminster Parliament to change legislation relating to the powers of those provinces,[9] the adoption of Jennings' test made some sense.[10] Knowing that a declaration of the existence of the convention made it more likely that the federal government would adhere to it, the court wished to be sure that there was value to the convention. However, on other occasions judicial reliance on Jennings' test might be a mistake. Bad conventions, conventions which are not backed by justificatory reasons, might also require judicial recognition in certain situations. Statutes might be enacted in the context of bad conventions, and require an appreciation of those conventions when being interpreted. Bad conventions might also ground legitimate expectations: whilst no one could have a legitimate expectation that a truly evil convention would be adhered to, a convention that was merely silly, or had only a moderately negative effect, might ground a legitimate expectation. In short, in some situations judges could and should recognize conventions without approving of them.

Even if it were conceded that recognition of a convention does equate to approval of it, Allan would still not have shown that recognized conventions amount to legal principles. A further step is needed: Allan would need to demonstrate that all rules which judges recognize and approve of should be considered laws. This is an ambitious claim. Judges recognize and indicate approval of lots of rules which are not, ordinarily, considered laws. A paragraph of hand-written rules taped to a municipal lawn-mower, a list of instructions on the back of a packet of soup, guidance on the correct way to tie up a parcel, all of these might be recognized and approved of by a court. None of these would normally be thought of as laws.

A distinction needs to be drawn between those occasions where conventions are indirectly judicially enforced and those in which conventions are directly judicially enforced. A convention is indirectly judicially enforced where the court, having successfully identified a convention, interprets or applies a pre-existing legal rule in such a way that the obligation of the convention is rendered, in that instance, legally obligatory. So, for example, a Minister who wanted to publish cabinet discussions the day after a cabinet meeting might find that the Common Law doctrine of confidentiality prevented the publication.[11] The convention of collective responsibility would form part of the background from which the legal duty of confidentiality is derived. The court would have indirectly enforced the convention against the Minister, but only because of the operation of a separate and established rule of law. In contrast, a court directly enforces a convention when it relies on the convention

---

[9] *Re Amendment of the Constitution of Canada (Nos 1, 2 and 3)* (1982) 1 SCR 753.

[10] A. Heard, *Canadian Constitutional Conventions: The Marriage of Law and Politics* (Oxford: Oxford University Press, 1991), ch 5; R. Brazier and St. J. Robilliard, 'Constitutional Conventions: The Canadian Supreme Court's Views Reviewed' (1982) Public Law 28.

[11] The example is a modification of *Attorney-General v Jonathan Cape* [1975] QB 752.

as generating a legal obligation without the presence of a separate legal rule which is being interpreted or applied.

In a recent article, Mark Elliott argues that judges should directly enforce conventions when shaping and developing constitutional law.[12] Part of Elliott's argument is relatively conservative—that those parts of constitutional law which are built upon constitutional conventions ought to be interpreted in light of these rules—but Elliott also argues for a further, stronger, role for conventions.[13] Developing Allan's argument, Elliott contends that conventions reflect, or are generated by, underlying constitutional values. Elliott argues that judges could properly transform at least some of these conventions into legal limitations on Parliament.[14] Whereas Allan contends that these constitutional values, and the conventions they produce, are already law, Elliott advances the jurisprudentially more cautious claim that it would be good if judges turned them into laws. According to Elliott, the limitations on Westminster's power to legislate over matters handed to the devolved assemblies and, perhaps, the obligations which surround the Human Rights Act 1998 might prove suitable candidates for juridification.

One way of interpreting Elliott's argument is as a call to the courts to render some conventions legally binding even though there is no legal rule entitling them to make this change: it is a call for juridification through bare-faced judicial *fiat*. Such a development is perfectly possible. Judges often have more power to change the law than the legal system accords them. Constitutional institutions, including the courts, are empowered by both legal and non-legal rules. Sometimes the law does not accord a constitutional actor a power, or perhaps even prohibits its exercise, but the non-legal rules of the constitution do grant the power. So, for example, the Prime Minister has the power to declare war, even though, legally, this power is held by the Monarch. Judges can also possess a constitutional power to change the law which is not conferred by the law. This is most commonly seen in times of crisis. Courts frequently adjudicate on the 'legality' of revolutions, even where the legal rules empowering the court forbid such adjudication.[15] Courts have also departed from the law when adherence to it would produce disastrous results. In *Re Manitoba Language Rights*[16] the Supreme Court of Canada considered the constitutionality of the laws of

---

[12] M. Elliott, 'Parliamentary Sovereignty and the New Constitutional Order' (2002) 22 Legal Studies 340; see also T. R.S. Allan, 'Law, Conventions, Prerogative: Reflections Prompted by the Canadian Constitutional Case' (1986) 46 Cambridge LJ 305; see the discussion in J. Jaconelli, 'Do Constitutional Conventions Bind?' (2005) 64 Cambridge LJ 149, 162–3.

[13] See also I. Harden, 'Review Article: The Constitution and Its Discontents' (1991) 21 British J Political Science 489, 504 and Allan, note 4 above, 240.

[14] Elliott, note 12 above, 375–6.

[15] See generally, T. Mahmud, 'Jurisprudence of Successful Treason' (1994) 27 Cornell Int LJ 49; F. M. Brookfield, *Waitangi and Indigenous Rights* (Auckland: Auckland University Press, 1999), ch 1; N. W. Barber, 'The Doctrine of State Necessity in Pakistan' (2000) 116 LQR 569; N. W. Barber, 'The Doctrine of State Necessity and Revolutionary Legality in Fiji' (2001) 117 LQR 370.

[16] [1985] 1 SCR 721; see the discussion in P. W. Hogg, 'Necessity in a Constitutional Crisis' (1989) 15 Monash University L Rev 253.

Manitoba that had been passed since 1890. Manitoba's constitution (The Manitoba Act 1870) required that all laws should be enacted in English and French, but a statute—The Official Language Act 1890—provided that laws only needed to be passed in English. It had already been determined that the 1890 Act was unconstitutional,[17] and the *Language Rights Case* considered the constitutionality of the monoglot laws passed after 1890. The Supreme Court held that the laws were invalid, but had temporary validity whilst they were translated and re-enacted. The decision appeared to run contrary to an express requirement of the constitution,[18] but its obvious good sense muted criticism.

One possible analysis of cases such as these is that the court makes a legal 'mistake', and the rules governing judicial error render it binding. In many situations an *ultra vires* ruling by a judge is binding until it is set aside. The same could, it might be argued, be true of supreme courts when they act contrary to the law: their decisions are permanently effective, but only because there is no higher court to correct the error. However, supreme courts can correct their own errors in subsequent cases.[19] If we really believe that these decisions were mistakes, these are mistakes which can be set right. We could declare that the *Language Rights Case* was such a mistake, and attempt to unpick its consequences. That we do not, and the generally positive reception the case was given, suggests that even if the case lacks a legal basis, the judges are still generally regarded as having acted constitutionally.

A court may, then, enforce a convention even where there is not a pre-existing legal rule which the convention helps interpret, or which renders the convention of legal significance. In some situations it may even be constitutionally legitimate for the court to innovate in this way. Elliott's wider claims about the enforcement of conventions surrounding the devolution settlement and the Human Rights Act are questionable—Parliament chose not to make these rules legally enforceable for a number of reasons—but his broader point is correct. Indeed, as Elliott notes, the *Factortame* litigation[20] could be interpreted as an instance of the courts giving legal force to a convention that governed the relationship between English and European Law.[21] At the time of the *Factortame* decision there was no legal precedent for the suspension of an Act of Parliament. Sir William Wade described the decision as 'revolutionary';[22] it was a radical change to the legal system effected by an institution

[17] *A-G Man v Forest* [1979] 2 SCR 1032.

[18] Hogg, note 16 above, 257–9.

[19] See, for instance, *R v Shivpuri* [1987] AC 1.

[20] *R v. Secretary of State for Transport exp Factortame (No 2)* [1991] 1 AC 603; Elliott, note 12 above, 371.

[21] A. Martin, 'The Accession of the United Kingdom to the European Communities: Jurisdictional Problems' (1968–1969) 6 Common Market L Rev 7. See also F. A. Trindade, 'Parliamentary Sovereignty and the Primacy of European Community Law' (1972) 35 MLR 375, 385–6. Compare Munro's account of the relationship prior to *Factortame*: C. R. Munro, *Studies in Constitutional Law* (London: Butterworths, 1987), 132.

[22] W. Wade, 'Sovereignty—Revolution or Evolution?' (1996) 112 LQR 568.

which did not possess legal authority to make that change. In his response to Wade, Allan posed a dilemma: either the judges in *Factortame* acted contrary to law, and their decision should be condemned as illegitimate, or they acted in conformity to law, and Wade's allegedly positivistic understanding of the nature of law was shown to be too narrow.[23] However, *Factortame* can be analysed in a similar fashion to the *Language Rights Case*. Once again, the court acted outside of its legal powers, but, again, remained within its constitutional powers in limiting Parliament's law-making capacity.[24]

(ii) The recognition and enforcement of law by the courts

So far it has been argued that, contrary to Dicey, courts can and do recognize and enforce conventions. It has even been suggested that, on rare occasions, the direct enforcement of conventions by courts is both desirable and constitutional. The second side of Dicey's equation asserted that laws are invariably recognized and enforced by the courts. This claim also requires qualification.

Whilst it is hard—though not, perhaps, completely impossible—to imagine a court refusing to recognize a law of the legal order of which the court is a part, there are occasionally laws of that order which the court cannot enforce. Not all laws are enforceable by courts. First, there are those laws which are enforceable only by institutions that are not courts. The clearest example is found in that set of rules which regulates the conduct of representatives in legislatures. Frequently, interpretation and application of these rules is reserved to the legislature in order to insulate the legislature from the courts. The courts may recognize, for certain purposes, these laws, but they are forbidden from enforcing them.[25] Colin Munro, defending Dicey, contends that such laws are court-enforced because Parliament is a court, the highest court in the land.[26] This seems a little artificial. Parliament may, for historical reasons, retain the title of a court, but it has long since lost the functions of a court and it lacks the structural characteristics of a court. Furthermore, many other states accord similar powers to their legislatures without according them the title of 'court'. Secondly, some constitutions contain directive principles within the constitution. These principles are legally binding on the state, but are not enforced by the court. Examples of such directive principles can be found in both the Irish and Indian

---

[23] T. R. S. Allan, 'Parliamentary Sovereignty: Law, Politics and Revolution' (1997) 113 *LQR* 443, 445.

[24] On the reception of the decision, see D. Nicol, EC Membership and the Judicialization of British Politics (Oxford: Oxford University Press, 2001), ch 7. A second, less clear, instance of a convention becoming a law through judicial activism might be found in the exclusion of lay peers from the Judicial Committee of the House of Lords. See R. E. Megarry, 'Lay Peers in Appeals to the House of Lords' (1949) 65 *LQR* 22; R. Stevens, 'The Final Appeal: Reform of the House of Lords and Privy Council 1867–1876' (1964) 80 *LQR* 354.

[25] See generally, J. Chafetz, *Democracy's Privileged Few* (New Haven: Yale University Press, 2007).

[26] C. Munro, 'Laws and Conventions Distinguished' (1975) 91 *LQR* 218, 255–6.

Constitutions.[27] The prerogative duty to protect citizens in English Law is also a principle of this type.[28] These non-enforceable legal principles are frequently created where the authors of a constitution wish to set social goals for the state which will require positive action. Given that the ability of the state to pursue these goals will depend on complex and changing economic and political factors, it is sometimes thought inappropriate that courts should regulate action in these areas.[29]

Courts may also fail to recognize or enforce the rules of legal orders of which they are not part. English courts may not recognize the rules of a foreign legal system and, even if these rules are recognized, may decline to enforce them. Albert Venn Dicey, the author of a classic book on conflicts of law, would, of course, have been well aware of this rather obvious point. The distinction he drew between laws and conventions related to the domestic courts of the legal systems of the United Kingdom and the national constitution. Nevertheless, just because the courts of standard national legal orders fail to enforce constitutional conventions, it need not follow that conventions are not court-enforced. There may be courts, or court-like bodies, which exist as part of the state's constitution, but which are not part of the standard national legal order. This question will be returned to later in the chapter.

FORMALIZED CONSTITUTIONAL CONVENTIONS

Colin Munro asserts that one crucial difference between a rule of law and a convention is that a rule of law is contained within a system, whereas conventions have no system.[30] Munro's account of law, building on that of Hart's, is unobjectionable.[31] Munro draws attention to interaction of primary and secondary rules in a legal system. In a legal system there are rules which identify the content of that system, determining whether a particular rule is part of the system or not. Allied to this, there are rules which govern legal change and adjudication. In a functioning legal system these rules also have an institutional dimension: legal orders require the existence of law-making and law-applying bodies such as legislatures and courts. In short, law is a heavily formalized form of rule governing. Conventions, according to Munro, lack these features. They form a 'discrete unconnected set'.[32] There is no authoritative mark of their existence, no rules which determine whether or not political actors ought to regard them as binding. There are no rules which regulate their production, no institutions to adjudicate upon their breach. It would obviously be going too far to

---

[27] See generally, J. Usman, 'Non-Justiciable Directive Principles: A Constitutional Design Defect' (2007) 15 Michigan State J Int L 643.

[28] *China Navigation Company v Attorney-General* [1932] 2 KB 197.

[29] See generally, J. A. King, 'Institutional Approaches to Judicial Restraint' (2008) 28 Oxford J Legal Studies 409.

[30] Munro, note 26 above, 231–4.

[31] H. L. A. Hart, *The Concept of Law* (2nd edn, Oxford: Oxford University Press, 1997), especially chs 5 and 6.

[32] Munro, note 26 above, 233. Quotation marks in original.

claim that conventions are completely non-systematic: it is actually quite hard to conceive of a social rule which does not, in some way, rely on or interact with other rules. But Munro's claim is plausible: perhaps the lack of those formalizing features of law provides a sharp line between constitutional conventions and laws?

In the previous chapter it was contended that the formalization of social rules is a matter of degree. At one extreme, there are unspoken, deeply internalized, rules which function at an unconscious level. At the other extreme there are those rules contained in statutes: these rules have been given an authoritative formulation and are interpreted by institutions which prize clarity and certainty. This is a spectrum: law is at one end, but even legal systems are susceptible to a greater or lesser degree of formalization. In principle, at least, a particular rule could progress along this scale, becoming more formalized over time. If it could be shown that some constitutional conventions have progressed up this scale, the softness of the divide would have been demonstrated, and some doubt—at least—would have been cast on the sharp divide drawn by Munro between laws and conventions. Furthermore, if successful, we might be able to unearth one of the holy grails of Commonwealth constitutional scholarship: a constitutional convention which has 'crystallized' into a law.

Whilst a few constitutional lawyers have speculated that conventions might 'crystallize' into laws,[33] none have satisfactorily explained what the metaphor signifies.[34] It suggests that, over time, conventions can change in nature, becoming increasingly law-like until, one day, they mature into legal rules. This process, if it occurs, is distinguishable from the transformation of conventions into laws by the intervention of the court, discussed in the previous section. In those instances the convention was instantly transformed into a law by virtue of the court's law-making capacity. When a convention 'crystallizes' into a law, in contrast, the process is a gradual one, without a defining intervention by a law-making body. The rule becomes increasingly formalized over time until it starts to resemble the most formalized type of rule—a law. A clear, if hypothetical, description of this process can be found in an unlikely source: H. L. A. Hart's masterpiece, *The Concept of Law*.

In *The Concept of Law* Hart provided us with an account of one of the ways in which a legal system might come into existence.[35] Hart imagined a primitive community which is governed by a collection of unrelated rules that have developed over time. These rules provide standards which members of the group expect each other to adhere to, and which will lead to criticism when violated. Over time, the group begins to recognize three deficiencies in this mechanism of governance. First, there is no provision by which ambiguities in these rules can be clarified, no body that can authoritatively determine the meaning of the rules in the event of a dispute. Secondly, the rules are static; without a process whereby they can be formally

---

[33] See, for instance, R. Brazier and St. J. Robilliard, 'Constitutional Conventions: The Canadian Supreme Court's Views Reviewed' (1982) Public Law 28, 32–33. Allan, note 4 above, 314.

[34] J. Jaconelli, 'Do Constitutional Conventions Bind?' (2005) 64 Cambridge LJ 149, 154 n 16.

[35] Hart, note 31 above, 91–95.

changed, they will be slow to adapt to new situations. Finally, there is no mechanism by which breach of the rules can be authoritatively ruled upon, no agency which can determine a violation and channel social pressure against offenders. For these three ills, Hart prescribed three groups of secondary rules: rules of recognition, change, and adjudication. The rules of recognition identify rules as part of the system, setting criteria for inclusion within the set. Rules of change empower bodies to alter these rules, responding to varying circumstances. And, finally, rules of adjudication empower bodies to adjudicate on breaches of the rules.

Hart's account of the emergence of a legal system is unsatisfying in two, connected, respects. First, and least importantly, his historical tale is probably the wrong way around, at least in most cases. Often, the seeds of a legal system lie in the emergence of social institutions which are generally accepted by people as possessing the authority to resolve disputes within the community. The 'primary' rules which Hart speaks of, those rules which tell individuals what they should or should not do, often come later, as the institutions develop rules to guide their discretion.[36] Secondly, Hart underestimates the importance of institutions within his account of law. Whilst he presents the union of primary and secondary rules as the key to jurisprudence, the existence of law-making and law-applying institutions is a necessary corollary of secondary rules. As many have noted, law possesses an institutional dimension, it cannot be fully understood just as an intermeshing of rules.[37]

Nevertheless, Hart's account of the emergence of a legal system is plausible: it is conceivable that a legal system might come about in the manner he describes. There might be a group which regulated itself through a collection of distinct rules, and which, over time, embarked on a slow process of formalization; developing mechanisms to interpret and shape the obligations that they imposed. As Hart recognized, there may not be a single moment when it becomes correct to say that the group possesses 'law': there are a series of stages in which the governing mechanism increasingly resembles law, until it reaches a point at which the community possesses an unequivocal instance of a legal system.[38]

In principle, at least, the formalizing process identified by Hart could occur to constitutional conventions. They could also become more formalized, being gathered together into a set, with rules emerging to govern membership of the set, determining the manner of their change and providing mechanisms to resolve disputes about their meaning. These disparate rules could, gradually, crystallize into law, becoming more and more law-like over time as they accreted a clearer and fuller legal character. Given that, as Hart has shown, this is possible, can it be seen to have occurred in the context of constitutional conventions? There are several groups of constitutional conventions which have developed law-like qualities. The strongest example is provided by the growing formalization of the conventions of ministerial responsibility in the United Kingdom constitution.

---

[36] D. Galligan, *Law in Modern Society* (Oxford: Oxford University Press, 2007), ch 4.

[37] J. Raz, 'The Institutional Nature of Law' in J. Raz, *The Authority of Law* (Oxford: Clarendon Press, 1979).

[38] Hart, note 31 above, 94.

Ministers are responsible to Parliament for the running of their department and for their conduct in public life.[39] Before 1945, these conventions were unwritten and uncodified. The test for ministerial propriety depended on the expectations of the political community around Westminster. In 1945 Clement Attlee produced a document entitled 'Questions of Procedure for Ministers' designed to give new Labour Cabinet Ministers information about their role. An enlarged version of this document was published in 1992, and gained its present name—the Ministerial Code—in 1997. The most recent version of the Code was published in 2010 and runs to 25 pages. It does not cover every aspect of ministerial responsibility, but it does codify and formalize many of the key parts of the doctrine. Amongst other issues, the Code outlines Ministers' duties towards Parliament,[40] the extent to which they can receive gifts and payment from private bodies,[41] and their relationship with the Civil Service.[42] The Ministerial Code also makes reference to, and reminds Ministers of their duty to abide by, domestic and international law,[43] the Civil Service Code,[44] the *Guidance on Government Communications*,[45] and the rules governing the registration of Members' or Peers' interests.[46]

Since its publication in 1992, the Code has grown in political strength. In recent years those alleging ministerial misconduct have frequently argued that the Code has been violated. When, for instance, it was discovered that Tessa Jowell's husband had received a substantial sum from Silvio Berlusconi, the challenge to her integrity was framed within the Code. Her critics argued that this was a gift, and should, under the Code, have been reported to her Permanent Secretary. The Prime Minister concluded, after an investigation by the Cabinet Secretary, that by the time Jowell knew of the money the Inland Revenue had classed it as earnings, and it consequently did not need to be declared under the Code.[47] On both sides of the controversy the Code was accepted as the source of the relevant constitutional obligation. The Code has been invoked in a similar fashion in other recent political battles. Controversies surrounding Lord Sainsbury's loans to the Labour Party,[48] David Blunkett's intervention in an application for a visa,[49] and John Prescott's stay at a

---

[39] On the Ministerial Code, see P. Leopold, 'Standards of Conduct in Public Life' in J. Jowell and D. Oliver (eds), *The Changing Constitution* (6th edn, Oxford: Oxford University Press, 2007), 419–20.

[40] *Ministerial Code* (London: Cabinet Office, 2010), para 1.2(b)–(e); section 9.

[41] *Ibid.*, section 7.

[42] *Ibid.*, section 5.

[43] *Ibid.*, para 1.2.

[44] *Ibid.*, para 1.2(j); para 5.1.

[45] *Ibid.*, para 6.3.

[46] *Ibid.*, 7.24.

[47] See Statement of Tony Blair on the conduct of Tessa Jowell MP, BBC Website, 2 March 2006.

[48] *Financial Times* report, 3 April 2006.

[49] A. Budd, *An Inquiry Into An Application for Indefinite Leave to Remain*, HC 175, December 2005.

ranch and receipt of a 'cowboy outfit',[50] have all been fought out within the context of the Code.

The focus of political attention on the Code suggests the emergence of a new convention: one of the rules of ministerial responsibility now places a duty on Ministers to follow the rules set out in the Code. Failure to do so will lead to political censure and may end with the Minister leaving office. This new convention does not fit into our traditional model of constitutional conventions. It is a rule which identifies a formalized set of rules, and which, by recognizing them, renders them constitutionally obligatory. The convention tells Ministers—and those who wish to criticize them for falling short of their duties—that they should look to the Code for an authoritative statement of at least part of ministerial responsibility. To return to Hart's tale of a primitive legal order, discussed earlier, the uncertainties and ambiguities surrounding the plethora of conventions of ministerial responsibility have led to the adoption of a unified set of rules, identified by a 'secondary' rule that strongly resembles Hart's rule of recognition. What of Hart's other secondary rules, those rules of change and adjudication, which he also identified as aspects of his account of law? The rules of change are clear: the Prime Minister is the author of the Code, and is entitled to alter it whenever he sees fit. One of David Cameron's first acts as Prime Minister was to publish a revised version. The rules of adjudication are a little more tricky. At present, the Prime Minister is the ultimate enforcer and arbiter of the Code, but the investigative mechanism for assessing Ministers' conduct has become steadily more formalized. On a number of occasions senior civil servants have been asked to ascertain the facts relating to allegations of ministerial misconduct.[51] In 2006 Sir John Bourn, the Comptroller and Auditor General, was appointed as an independent advisor on ministerial interests, a role which empowers him to investigate allegations of breaches of parts of the Code on invitation of the Prime Minister.[52] Since 2008 this post has been held by Sir Philip Mawer. Recently, the House of Commons Public Administration Select Committee recommended that an independent investigative capacity be expanded to cover the whole Code, though the ultimate decision about whether the Code was violated should continue to rest with the Prime Minister.[53] The recommended expansion of the Independent Advisor's role has now been accepted by the Government.[54] It is easy to imagine a

---

[50] 'Prescott Escapes Sanctions over Ranch Visit', *The Guardian website*, 21 July 2006.

[51] See Sir Alan Budd, *An Inquiry Into An Application for Indefinite Leave to Remain*, HC 175, December 2005; Statement of Tony Blair on the conduct of Tessa Jowell MP, BBC Website, 2 March 2006.

[52] HC Deb, 23 March 2006, col 33WS.

[53] Public Administration Select Committee, Seventh Report of Session 2005–06, *The Ministerial Code: the Case for Independent Investigation*, HC 1457.

[54] Public Administration Select Committee, Seventh Report of Session 2007–08, *Investigating the Conduct of Ministers*, HC 381, para 13; Public Administration Select Committee, Ninth Special Report of Session 2007–08, *Investigating the Conduct of Ministers: Government Response to the Committee's Seventh Report of Session 2007–08*, HC 1056, para 4.

future in which an independent investigator could develop into an independent adjudicator of the Code.

If Hart's account of a legal system were contrasted with the Ministerial Code, it would appear that the Code has slipped, over time, from a collection of conventions into a set of laws. The Code possesses the union of primary and secondary rules that Hart commended as the core of a legal system.[55] Hart's internal attitude also is present:[56] the Code is regarded by members of the political community as setting standards for ministerial behaviour, and deviation from it will provoke criticism and censure. After Hart, others pointed to additional features that are thought to characterize a legal system. Legal systems contain law-making and law-applying institutions,[57] and have a coercive dimension, backsliders may be punished.[58] Both of these aspects are also present in the context of the Ministerial Code. It possesses an institutional quality: the office of the Prime Minister is a constitutional institution, constructed largely by convention. It also possesses a coercive quality: Ministers who transgress its demands suffer harm to their reputations and may, ultimately, lose their jobs.

In at least one important respect, though, the Ministerial Code differs from the typical case of a legal system. Legal systems normally claim to provide a comprehensive set of their subjects' legal obligations. People are only required to act as the system demands, any further duties they accept are voluntary, a matter of personal choice. Joseph Raz relies on this common quality of legal systems to distinguish between legal systems and other formalized systems of rules within a community. Raz stipulates that law is the most important formalized system found within that community.[59] His observation plays out in three characteristic features of a legal system. First, that legal systems are comprehensive, in that they claim authority to regulate any area of activity.[60] Secondly, that legal systems claim to be supreme, in that they claim to be superior to other normative orders.[61] Finally, legal systems are open systems, in that they incorporate the rules of other systems and, in doing so, render those rules binding within the legal system.[62] In specifying these features, Raz hopes to be able to distinguish law from other systems of rules—such as the rules which regulate certain sports and some religious codes. The requirement would certainly exclude the Ministerial Code from

[55] Hart, note 31 above, 99.

[56] *Ibid*, 88–91.

[57] J. Raz, *The Concept of a Legal System* (2nd edn, Oxford: Oxford University Press, 1980), ch 8.

[58] H. Kelsen, *General Theory of Law and State*, trans A. Wedberg, (New York: Russell and Russell, 1945), 18–20. The issue is discussed more broadly in G. Lamond, 'Coercion and the Nature of Law' (2001) 7 Legal Theory 35.

[59] J. Raz, 'The Institutional Nature of Law' in J. Raz, The Authority of Law: Essays on Law and Morality (Oxford: Clarendon Press, 1979), 116.

[60] *Ibid.*, 116–18.

[61] *Ibid.*, 118–19.

[62] *Ibid.*, 119–20.

the category of formalized systems that can be given the title of law. The Code acknowledges the superior and prior force of domestic law.[63]

Raz recognizes that the test is not a sharp one, that whether a system counts as 'law' or not will be a matter of degree,[64] but even this concession may not be sufficient. The softness of the line between informal social rules and a legal system has long been recognized by legal academics with a sociological turn of mind.[65] Legal pluralists have made much of the ways in which other formalized normative systems resemble law as classically described and can interact with the legal systems of the state. Their claim is that some of the systems that writers like Raz would exclude from the legal world are better thought of as variations on the forms law takes.[66] On their more liberal reading, many formalized, institutionalized, systems of rules would count as law. The most radical legal pluralists claim that practically all social rules are 'law' in a sense, providing the concept with a terrifyingly wide reach.[67]

Deciding between narrower and broader understandings of law is a difficult business, but in recent years consensus has, perhaps, shifted towards a broader definition. Raz's account would exclude many systems we commonly think of as law. As Brian Tamanaha points out, if Raz's requirements were accepted, most 'law' of the medieval period would have to be re-titled.[68] Perhaps even more worryingly, Raz's account would exclude European Law: whilst European Law claims supremacy over national law, it does not claim authority to regulate all areas of domestic life, nor does it claim that national law is incorporated within European Law.[69] Indeed, the extent to which a system of rules meets Raz's account may be a matter of chance. A system of religious law, for instance, might include a rule stating that it is subservient to national law, or it might include a rule purporting to incorporate and validate national law. It might explicitly confine itself to devotional issues and deny that it has authority outside these areas, or it might claim to be entitled, in principle, to regulate all areas of life—but still confine itself to matters of religious ceremony and organization. A given system of religious law might have included all of these rules at some point in its existence, and it might be unclear which rule is presently part of the system. Raz's account excludes from 'law' some phenomena commonly thought of as law, and turns on marginal factors that most would not think of sufficient importance to determine the boundaries of law.

---

[63] *Ministerial Code*, para 1.2.

[64] Raz, note 59 above, 116.

[65] See the discussion in Galligan, note 36 above, chs 9 and 10 and B. Tamanaha, *A General Jurisprudence of Law and Society* (Oxford: Oxford University Press, 2001), esp ch 6.

[66] See generally, J. Griffiths, 'What is Legal Pluralism?' (1986) 24 J Legal Pluralism 1.

[67] B. de Sousa Santos, *Towards a New Common Sense: Law, Science and Politics in Paradigmatic Transition* (London: Routledge, 1995), 428–36; Tamanaha, note 65 above, 181–6.

[68] Tamanaha, note 65 above, 139–40.

[69] See generally, K. Alter, *Establishing the Supremacy of European Law* (Oxford: Oxford University Press, 2001), ch 1; J. Weiler, 'The Autonomy of the Community Legal Order' in J. Weiler, *The Constitution of Europe* (Cambridge: Cambridge University Press, 1999).

Recent writers coming from the same tradition as Raz have been willing to expand the range of systems that can claim the label of 'law'. Neil MacCormick, for example, cites the law of the state as just one form of law amongst many others: international law, the law of the European Union, canon law, shari'a law, and the laws of sporting organizations are listed by him as examples of legal systems which exist separate from the state.[70] The answer to the conundrum addressed by Raz is that law lies at the formalized, institutionalized, end of a spectrum of systematic social rules, with no sharp divide existing between it and other, similar, systems of rules. The features identified by Raz are commonly found in legal orders, but are not invariable features of such orders.

Even if constitutional scholars baulk at the claim that the Ministerial Code is a legal system, the Code has become steadily more law-like over recent years. It is not a clear, or central, instance of a legal system, but it now possesses many of the characteristic features of a legal system. There may come a point, indeed, we may even have reached this point, when the Code joins the pack of normative systems that roam in the penumbra of law. Along with religious law, international law, *lex mercatoria* and other such entities, the Code provides an example of the softness of the line between law and other formalized normative systems.

CONCLUSION

The objective of this chapter has not been to argue that laws and constitutional conventions are identical, but rather to argue that the differences between them are a matter of degree. Constitutional conventions and laws are two brands of social rule which differ in the extent of their formalization. Laws and constitutional conventions behave in similar ways and share many common qualities. This makes it possible for courts, as well as legislatures, to transform conventions into laws on occasion. Furthermore, because the difference between conventions and laws is a soft one, it can sometimes be hard, perhaps even impossible, to decisively state whether a rule should be thought of as a constitutional convention or a law. Conventions can become more formalized over time as political actors create authoritative statements of their content and mechanisms which can create, modify, and adjudicate upon, these rules. This chapter has further argued that this process of formalization is not just an abstract possibility, it can also be detected within the British constitution: the Ministerial Code is an instance of a set of conventions which are in the process of crystallization.

[70] N. MacCormick, *Institutions of Law* (Oxford: Oxford University Press, 2007), 11.

∽ 7 ∽

The Mentality of the State

We routinely talk about, and think of, social groups as creatures possessing intentions and undertaking actions. So natural and convenient is this attribution that it is easy to overlook just how very strange it is. When a natural person forms an intention or undertakes an action at least part of the explanation is biological: chemicals mix, brain-cells fire and electrical impulses shoot around the body. A social group, of course, lacks a brain. It acts in the physical world through the bodies of its members: it can only act and intend through their actions and intentions. But are the actions and intentions of a social group identical to the actions and intentions of its members? It seems unlikely. To say a group has acted in a certain way cannot necessarily be equated with the statement that every member of that group has acted in that same way: when an army invades a country not every soldier need play a part in the invasion.[1] Similarly, to say that a group possesses an intention cannot be equated with the statement that every member of that group shares that intention: a trade union may enter negotiations with an employer intending to secure the best possible deal for its members—but some of those members may not even be aware the negotiation is taking place. When considering the acts and intentions of social groups we need to explain in what sense groups can be attributed such qualities, and, further, the complicated relationship between the intentions and actions of the group and the intentions and actions of the group's members.

These questions are of particular importance to those interested in the state. We need to understand how and in what sense the state can possess intentions and undertake actions if we are to understand what the state has done, what it is responsible for, and what character it possesses. These questions are inherently interesting, but they are also important because they have implications for citizenship. It is a bad thing to be a citizen of a state which has done bad things, or of a state which possesses unpleasant characteristics. The life of a citizen of a bellicose or a racist state is made, all else being equal, less successful than it would otherwise have been by reason of her membership of this failing group.

It will be contended in this chapter that when we talk of states possessing intentions and acting we use these terms in an analogous sense to their primary use in the context of individuals. To talk of a state intending a thing amounts to a claim that it

---

[1] See generally, J. Finnis, 'Persons and Their Associations' (1989) 63 Aristotelian Society Supp Vol 267, 271–3.

shares sufficient features in common with a person intending a thing to make the statement sensible; it does not amount to a claim that the state intends things in the same sense as a person intends things. This chapter will begin by considering two collections of rival approaches to this issue: individualism and holism. Individualists contend that it is inappropriate to attribute mental states to groups: it confuses rather than assists our understanding of the world. Holists, in sharp contrast, contend that groups can possess some mental states in the same sense as individuals. It will be argued that there is something to be learned from each of these traditions. An account of the intentions and actions of social groups based on the rules which constitute those groups will be advanced; it will be contended that it is plausible to talk of groups acting and intending, even if they do not exhibit these features in precisely the same sense as individuals. The chapter will conclude by exploring the limits to which the attribution of mental qualities to social groups in general and states in particular can usefully be pushed. Do states have an unconscious? Can they become emotional? Can they even, perhaps, experience neurosis?

INDIVIDUALIST AND HOLIST ACCOUNTS OF SOCIAL GROUPS

Towards the end of the nineteenth century a number of sociologists who studied social groups made some quite radical, and quite surprising, claims about their nature. Within some social groups, it was argued, the personality of group members is entirely subsumed and a wholly new identity emerges at the level of the group. The group can come to possess an independent mind and enjoy a capacity to act and form intentions which is distinct from that of its members. This extreme version of holism can be found in the work of two of the leading sociologists of the period: Gustav Le Bon and Émile Durkheim. Le Bon contended that people in crowds lose their individuality and regress to a more primitive mode of behaviour,[2] labelling this process the 'law of mental unity of crowds'.[3] In crowds a collective mind emerges which dominates the minds of individuals. Le Bon contended that, in consequence, there is no point studying the individual within the crowd: her individuality is completely displaced by the mob.[4] Durkheim, in his classic work on suicide, similarly asserted that when people come together in association their consciousnesses combine, forming 'a psychical existence of a new species, which consequently has its own manner of thinking and feeling.'[5] This entity is external to the individual, interacting with her and shaping her expectations, values and self-understanding.

---

[2] G. Le Bon, *The Crowd* (New Jersey: Transaction Publishers, 1995), ch 1. For a contemporary assessment of Le Bon, see S. Reicher, 'The Psychology of Crowd Dynamics' in M. Hogg and S. Tindale, *Blackwell Handbook of Social Psychology: Group Processes* (Oxford: Blackwell, 2001).

[3] Le Bon, note 2 above, 44.

[4] *Ibid.*, 62.

[5] E. Durkheim, *Suicide*, trans J. A. Spaudling and G. Simpson (Abingdon: Routledge, 2002), 275; P. A. French, *Collective and Corporate Responsibility* (Columbia: Columbia University Press, 1984), 98–102.

Perhaps predictably, this approach to sociology was quickly countered with a robustly individualistic alternative, an approach to social groups which entirely rejected the holism of Le Bon and Durkheim, and challenged the analytical utility of studying social groups as such.[6] Talk of social groups is, it claimed, a form of intellectual sloth; an unwillingness to engage with the complexities of the interlocking behaviour of individuals. In the 1920s the social psychologist Floyd Allport vigorously asserted that group activity is nothing more than the sum of a collection of individual activities, and it is these individuals, not the group, that should be the focus of study.[7] Max Weber advanced a similar claim in his writings on society.[8] The individualist approach to social groups was bolstered, perhaps, by a fear that regarding groups as possessing an identity distinct from their members immunized members of the group from responsibility for actions of the group.[9] Shortly before Le Bon wrote his work on crowds, Scipio Sighele, an Italian socialist, had advanced an account of the group mind which purported to provide individuals with a defence against criminal responsibility for acts of the group of which they were a member.[10] It was the crowd, not the individual, who had acted, and it was the crowd, not the individual, who was responsible for these actions.

In light of this type of reasoning, it is hardly surprising that Allport and Weber, amongst others, insisted on a redirection of attention back towards the individual. Of the two writers, Allport was the most extreme, arguing that groups should not be studied by psychologists: the actions of groups are nothing more than the sum of individual actions, which can—and should—be considered separately.[11] As Weber realized, though, it is impossible to entirely eradicate social groups from our understanding of society. Even if we accept that the actions of social groups depend upon the actions of individuals, the social group as a whole still interacts with the individual who is a member of that group.[12] The member has an understanding of the group which affects her behaviour. The social group is not, therefore, simply the

---

[6] For discussion, see R. Brown, *Group Processes* (2nd edn, Oxford: Blackwell, 2000), 4–5; D. Forsyth, *Group Dynamics* (4th edn, Belmont: Thomson, 2006), 19–20.

[7] F. H. Allport, *Social Psychology* (New York: Houghton Mifflin, 1924), 5–8.

[8] M. Weber, *Economy and Society*, G. Roth and C. Wittich (eds) (California: California University Press, 1978), 13.

[9] A. Quinton, 'Social Objects' (1975) 75 Proceedings of the Aristotelian Society 67; French, note 5 above, viii–ix. See also R. Ekins, *The Nature of Legislative Intent*, D.Phil submitted to Oxford University, 2009, chapter 3.

[10] S. Sighele, *La Folle Delinquente* (1891) cited in R. A. Nye, Introduction to Le Bon, note 2 above; see also J. van Ginneken, *Crowds, Psychology and Politics, 1871–1899* (Cambridge: Cambridge University Press, 1992), 33–44. For a recent, and much more cautious, version of this argument, see P. Pettit, 'Responsibility Incorporated' (2007) 117 Ethics 171, 196. For criticism see S. Veitch, *Law and Irresponsibility* (London: Routledge-Cavendish, 2007), especially ch. 2.

[11] Allport, note 7 above, 5. Allport later backed away from this extreme position: Forsyth, note 6 above, 24–5.

[12] Weber, note 8 above, 14.

sum of the distinct actions and beliefs of its members: the existence of the group alters these actions and beliefs. This interaction has a number of significant consequences. Social psychologists have demonstrated, for instance, that group cohesion cannot be equated with the attraction that members of that group feel for each other.[13] Social groups can remain cohesive even when their members dislike each other and would, but for the group, have no wish to interact. Furthermore, the corporate opinion of a social group on an issue often differs from the average opinion of its members on the same issue. Group members tend to shift their opinion in response to the views of others in the group[14] in an apparent desire to reach consensus, and can settle on a different option to that which would have won a vote conducted prior to group discussion.[15]

Once it is conceded that the group can affect the individual, as well as the individual having the capacity to affect the group, the individualist approach to groups appears the more attractive. The discussion by Le Bon and Durkheim of group mentality and collective imagination begins to look worryingly mysterious, possessing a disturbing whiff of the magical. People may behave differently in a crowd, but they are still people and they are still the ones doing the behaving. Before setting aside the holist tradition, though, it is worth considering whether there is anything to be learned from a more cautious form of holism, one which is compatible with the recognition that groups are collections of people and are dependent for their existence and functioning on their members. If we assume that holists are not arguing for the emergence of a group mind through some form of telepathy, at least two plausible re-interpretations of their claims are open to us. First, some of the descriptive terms we apply to individuals may also be applicable to social groups. These words describe observable behaviour, and a group may exhibit such behaviour in precisely the same fashion as a person. Second, holists may have used terms which are normally considered to possess a physiological aspect in a metaphorical or analogous sense. These terms have different, but closely related, meanings when applied to social groups and to individuals. Each of these possibilities merits further discussion.

There are some descriptions of behaviour which can be attributed to both people and groups without requiring any artificiality or distortion of their meaning. Both people and social groups can vote, sell property and adopt positions on contentious political issues, for instance. When a person votes, she chooses from a number of options and registers her preference for one of those options over another, alongside others who are engaged in the same undertaking. When a group votes—a trade union, say, voting for the leadership of the Trade Union Congress—it does precisely the same thing. Of course, the manner in which the vote is produced and decided upon is different in these two situations, but in each case the act of voting has occurred.

---

[13] Forsyth, note 6 above, ch 5; Brown, note 6 above, 44–6.

[14] Forsyth, note 6 above, ch 7, 348–52.

[15] See also J. Surowiecki, *The Wisdom of Crowds* (London: Abacus, 2004), ch 1.

Behaviouralists argue that scientific study should adopt descriptions of behaviour that exclude analysis of interior biological processes and, perhaps, we could regard Le Bon and Durkheim as forerunners of this school of psychology.[16] The central claim behind behaviouralism is that we should study the things people do, rather than the psychological states which lie behind these activities: feelings and motives are too difficult to scientifically measure and cannot be objectively assessed.[17] Consequently, we should confine our attention to the actions of individuals and seek to correlate these actions with the observable stimuli that led to them. Some ostensibly physiological attributes should therefore be redefined so that they take the same form as these action-descriptions. Alan Turing, for example, famously claimed that a machine could be said to 'think' when a person communicating with the machine was unable to determine if she was communicating with a machine or a person. If it behaves as if it were thinking, it is thinking. Applying this to social groups, we could argue that a group has a mind when it behaves as if it had a mind. Philip Pettit, who is certainly not a behaviouralist, provides an account of group rationality that fits comfortably with this approach. Pettit argues that we should regard collectivities as intentional subjects, and ascribe beliefs and desires to such social groups, if the collectivity exhibits 'rational unity'.[18] If its actions appear rational, if the group appears to have consistent objectives over time and appears to act on those objectives, we should regard the group as an intentional subject.[19]

The trouble with behavioural accounts of psychological states is that whilst they may provide a useful set of descriptors for groups, they risk impoverishing our understanding of individual psychology. In the hundred years following Le Bon and Durkheim's work the methods available to us for assessing people's drives and motivations have become increasingly sophisticated. It is now possible to study the biological processes of the brain/mind in far greater detail and with far greater accuracy. The divide between those who study the physical processes of the brain and those who study the psychological processes of the mind has come to look ever more artificial. Whilst we cannot reduce mental states to biological recipes, it seems likely that they will turn out to possess a physiological aspect. To strip concepts like mind, intention, and emotion of their physicality risks inhibiting our understanding of the individual, even if it may have once assisted our understanding of social groups.

The second interpretation treats the holists as applying mental attributes in a metaphorical sense. Social groups may not hold intentions or experience emotions in precisely the same sense as individuals do, but there may be sufficient points of similarity to warrant the application of the same term in each context. A social group

---

[16] B. F. Skinner, 'The Operational Analysis of Psychological Terms' (1945) 52 *Psychology Rev* 270 cited and discussed in R. Harré and P. F. Secord, *The Explanation of Social Behaviour* (Oxford: Blackwell, 1972), ch 6; see also the discussion in J. Searle, *Mind: A Brief Introduction* (Oxford: Oxford University Press, 2004), 35–9.

[17] See Eric Posner for a behaviouralist account of social norms: E. Posner, *Law and Social Norms* (Cambridge Mass: Harvard University Press, 2000).

[18] P. Pettit, 'Collective Persons and Powers' (2002) 8 Legal Theory 443, 457–60.

[19] *Ibid.*, 460–3.

experiences anxiety about its identity, for example, when the group fails to adequately specify the goals it seeks to achieve, and this failure causes the group to function ineffectively. A person experiencing anxiety about her identity will suffer a similarly disabling lack of clarity about her life, but this will be accompanied by biological changes, the physiological aspects of stress.

These two interpretations may be complementary. Sometimes it will not matter whether the term being applied to the group is one which is best understood in purely behavioural terms or whether it is being used metaphorically. If our focus of interest lies in social groups, we do not need to resolve the question of whether the term has a biological dimension. For example, philosophers who study intention in the context of individuals can profitably debate whether the concept of intention should include, or at least allow for, a biological element. Those who study social groups, in contrast, need not have this debate. To talk of a group intending a thing is either to invoke (individual) intention directly, if it is taken as a purely behavioural description, or to invoke (individual) intention metaphorically, if it is taken as including a biological element.[20] In either event, the application of the term to the group possesses the same meaning. Such philosophical modesty is especially useful when it is far from clear which descriptors should be given a biological aspect: the issue can be left to one side for debate on another day.

THE INTENTIONS AND ACTIONS OF THE STATE

Our discussion of individualist and holist understandings of groups began by presenting them as two polar extremes, but as the more implausible forms of each school were discounted, a middle ground emerged. The claim that groups have minds and possess mental states in the same sense as individuals is implausible. But the claim that we can replace the study of groups with the study of discrete individuals is equally unattractive. Social groups have an existence which is dependent upon, but distinguishable from, their members. Social groups interact with their members and with non-members. These groups behave in ways that resemble persons: they appear to hold intentions, have attitudes towards people and things, and act. And we tend to think of social groups in this fashion; we conceptualize the group, and not simply the people who comprise the group, as possessing these features.

(i) The intentions of states and other social groups

Social groups possess intentions when the rules which constitute the group determine objectives and processes which the group ought to pursue or follow. The intentions of the group consist of these identified objectives and processes. In very simple situations the group's intentions may simply consist of an intention to retain group unity and to act together. Lacking these minimal intentions, the social group

[20] For a similar argument in a different context, see C. Boudreau, M. D. McCubbins and D. Rodiguez, 'Statutory Interpretation and the Intentional(ist) Stance' (2004–2005) 38 Loyola of Los Angeles L Rev 2131.

ceases to be a group and becomes a set of individuals. Consequently, every social group must possess some intentions. As the rules that constitute the group become more complex, the intentions of the group may also become more complicated. The group can intend to achieve a diverse collection of things through a diverse collection of mechanisms and processes.

The easiest group intentions to identify are those which are expressed in formalized constitutional rules and acted upon by the group. Looking at the United Kingdom, for example, we can say that the state intends to be run (more or less) democratically, that it intends to provide healthcare for, and education to, its members. These are all intentions which are embodied in explicit, formalized, rules, rules which are (again, more or less) put into practice by officers and institutions of the state. This simple picture of group intention becomes cloudier in two instances: first, where the explicit rules of the group are not carried out, and, secondly, when the rules are deeply internalized.

Sometimes social groups adopt rules which they do not follow. There may be an innocent explanation for this. A group may identify an objective it plans to work towards at some stage, but at present it lacks the time or resources to pursue this goal. A charity might, for example, set out to tackle poverty in Rwanda and Sudan, but only undertake activities in Rwanda for the time being. In this situation the charity intends to work in both countries, but has yet to act on this intention in the second. On other occasions, the failure to act on a rule may look a bit more sinister. Some states include lofty celebrations of democracy in their constitutions which appear to have no practical effect on the way their governments function. The North Korean Constitution boldly asserts that the state will guarantee the democratic rights and liberties of its citizens,[21] and will uphold freedom of speech, assembly, and the operation of political parties.[22] Constitutional rules of this type are window-dressing, included in order to fool the unwary observer and hoodwink the more gullible members of the state. In situations like these the ineffective rule is part of the constitution—because it is part of that formalized section of rules which do not need to be effective to be constitutional—but the intentions of the state cannot be deduced from the rule. The state no more intends to be a democracy than the conman intends to safeguard the money his mark hands him for safekeeping. The purported declaration of the state's intention is a lie. In such a situation the ostensible rule of the constitution is negated by a concealed constitutional rule: the officers of the state are obligated to act to prevent democracy being established, and are required to ignore the overt rule.

The position will not always be as clear-cut as this. The formal rule contained in the constitution may not be directly countermanded by a concealed constitutional rule, but may be qualified and limited in its application by other rules. In these situations the intentions of the group should be deduced from the totality of the rules within its constitution. The United States Constitution requires a strict separation of

---

[21] Constitution of North Korea, Article 63.

[22] Constitution of North Korea, Article 67.

the church and the state. Religion, asserts the Constitution, ought to be kept within the private sphere.[23] Yet religious symbolism and rhetoric can be found throughout the institutions of state. To an outsider, the character of the American state appears dominated by, and imbued with, religion to a far greater extent than many countries—such as the United Kingdom—which have a formal connection with a faith. Alongside the constitutional exclusion of religion are found a host of other rules which admit religion back in to public life. This does not mean that the Constitution is ineffective, merely that its effectiveness is qualified. Consequently, whilst it may be correct to say America intends to operate a system of government which is not dominated by a religious group, it is not correct to claim that America intends to maintain a secular collection of state institutions.

These thoughts draw us into a further area of ambiguity: where the rules of the group are so deeply internalized that members of the group may not immediately be aware of them, or, at least, may not understand them as rules.[24] Imagine a golf club which consists entirely of men. It might be that this situation exists by chance: that only men have applied for membership. It might be that this situation has been brought about by the conscious, even if concealed, adoption of sexist rules of admission. But it could be that the club is partly defined by a deeply internalized rule which the men share, but of which they are not aware. When women come up for admission to the club the committee agrees that each candidate does not quite fit in, that they are not the right type of person for the club. An individual member of the committee who disagreed would face criticism, and doubts would be expressed about his judgment. He has violated an unspoken rule of the club. If challenged, the committee could provide plausible explanations for rejecting each candidate, and might even believe those explanations. Over time, though, this unconscious sexism will be revealed through a pattern of admissions decisions. The internalized rule which limits admission to the club forms part of the intention of the social group; the club intends to maintain a men-only association.

When pressured to confess that this rule guides their decision-making, members may disclaim its operation—sometimes using quite indignant language. To confess that the rule exists would be to confess that a group of which they are a member is not as successful as they believe it to be. And, given the success of his life is partly determined by the success of this group, an admission of the failures of the group by a member is, more or less directly, an admission of his own failings. There is a pressure, perhaps also a temptation, to avoid facing up to the sexist rule. Psychologists would have little trouble identifying this attitude as one of denial, a psychological defence mechanism which involves the disavowal of aspects of reality which it would be painful to acknowledge. Denial may operate at the level of the group as well as at the level of particular members when the attempt to bring the rule to the consciousness of the group is subject to collective censure: the group denial is instantiated in a rule which seeks to prohibit recognition of the sexist rules of admission.

---

[23] First Amendment to the Constitution of the United States.

[24] See further, I. J. Janis, *Groupthink* (2nd edn, Boston: Houghton Mifflin, 1982).

On a more cheerful note, it is in the nature of an internalized rule that it has the potential to be rendered explicit, that it can be brought to the consciousness of those whom it regulates. As any therapist will tell you, whilst denial is a powerful psychological mechanism, it can be overcome. The golf club is capable of acknowledging reality, facing up to the internalized admission rule and making changes. It could be that once this is done, the golf club will rapidly reform. It may be that its members—at a conscious level, at least—would not wish to be part of a sexist organization, and will quickly reject the rule once they reflect critically upon it.

The presence of deeply internalized rules in the constitution of a group provides a sense in which we can talk of the group as possessing an unconscious; a set of rules which operates within the group without the conscious awareness of group members. These rules can specify objectives of which the group is unaware, yet which still shape the actions and character of the group. As with an individual's unconscious intentions, the unconscious intentions of the group may conflict with its conscious intentions. The group may be animated by intentions it would repudiate if it came to be aware of them. And, in a further point of comparison with the individual, the group's effectiveness will be inhibited by this unresolved and unacknowledged conflict.

(ii) The actions of states and other social groups

A social group acts through the actions of people where those persons are empowered to act on behalf of the group by a rule constituting that group. Group action may be deliberate or accidental. Deliberate actions are those which are undertaken by people within the scope of an empowering rule in accordance with the intentions of the group. Accidental actions may be further subdivided between those which are voluntary and those which are involuntary. Voluntary accidental actions are those which are undertaken by people within the scope of an empowering rule, but contrary to the intentions of the group. Involuntary accidental actions are actions which are a consequence of actions undertaken within the scope of empowering rules, but which are not themselves mandated by a rule constituting the group.

A group undertakes a deliberate action where a person empowered by a rule of the group acts in conformity with the intentions of the group. The rule which empowers this action may be legal or non-legal. In the context of the state, Kelsen recognized the importance of rules in connecting the actions of people to the actions of the state, but he confined this process to the operation of law.[25] Once it is recognized that the constitution includes non-legal as well as legal rules, an additional layer of complexity is added to the attribution of actions to the state. Even if the law does not accord a person the power to act on behalf of the state, a non-legal rule may do so. The unformalized nature of non-legal rules can make the attribution of actions to states contentious—though attribution through law can also be subject to debate—but this process is a common feature of our constitutional life. When, for

---

[25] H. Kelsen, *General Theory of Law and State*, trans A. Wedberg (New York, Russell & Russell, 1961), 192–3.

example, the Australian Prime Minister apologized for his country's treatment of aborigines it was recognized that this was an apology by the state, and not just a personal statement. There was no legal rule which empowered this action, just a widespread social recognition of the Prime Minister's constitutional capacity to make such statements.[26] Such non-legal rules can be quite nuanced: different state officials can have the capacity to speak for the state on different issues. This capacity is lost if their comments stray outside their remit.

Sometimes the social rules which empower officers to act on behalf of the state will be broad enough to include exercises of power which the legal rules of the constitution seek to exclude. This dual empowerment of officials and institutions can have desirable and undesirable consequences.[27] First, it can enable officials and institutions to side-step legal limitations on their power. Courts and legislatures may be able to issue laws and rulings which, as a matter of law, they are not empowered to produce. Whilst this presents the risk of an abuse of power, it also enables constitutional bodies to escape legal constraints which have become inappropriate. Constitutional bodies ought not to adhere to the demands of the legal part of the constitution if doing so would precipitate disaster,[28] or would frustrate the achievement of a new constitutional consensus.[29] Second, this dualism may prevent institutions escaping the actions of their officers. The legal rules which regulate the police force might hold that an officer who harasses innocent folk steps outside of the area of her office and acts as a private citizen. The community in which the police officer works, in contrast, may regard the harassment as an act of the police: it is the police as an institution who have undertaken this action, through the medium of that particular officer.

Just because an action is voluntary, it need not follow that it was undertaken pursuant to an intention of the group. A tax officer is empowered to issue demands for tax. These demands amount to an act of the state, executed by the officer. She is obliged to issue demands for the correct amount. The state intends that people be asked to pay the correct amount of tax. When she sends out correct tax demands, the state acts deliberately and in conformity with its intention. Whilst the tax officer is required to send out bills for the correct amount, erroneous bills still count as tax demands and must be either paid by their recipients or challenged through a formal process. So, in this system, the tax officer is obliged to issue correct tax demands, but is empowered to issue incorrect tax demands. When she issues incorrect demands the state has acted voluntarily, a person empowered to act has acted on behalf of the state, but it has not acted in conformity with its intention. The state has acted, but it has made a mistake.

---

[26] See generally, E. Gibney and E. Roxstrom, 'The Status of State Apologies' (2001) 23 HRQ 119.

[27] For a critical view of dualism, see D. Dyzenhaus, *The Constitution of Law: Legality in a Time of Emergency* (Cambridge: Cambridge University Press, 2006), 185–90.

[28] See, for instance, *Re Manitoba Language Rights* [1985] 1 SCR 721.

[29] See, for instance, *R v Secretary of State for Transport ex p Factortame (No 2)* [1991] 1 AC 603.

A further sense in which a group can be said to have acted accidentally is when the act is the product of the rules of the group, but is not mandated, or even permitted, by any rule of the group. A dress code, for example, can have the effect of excluding certain religious groups from playing a part in an institution. Such exclusion could be against both the intention of the group and the intentions of the members of the group: they might have no wish to discriminate and be unaware of the consequences of the rules they have adopted.

These two forms of accidental group action may shed some light on one of the most controversial pieces of institutional labelling made in recent years: the claim that some groups manifest 'institutional racism'.[30] It is sometimes unclear what this allegation entails, but it probably invokes some combination of the two forms of accidental group action. When people claim to have identified institutional racism they are not ordinarily alleging that the institution includes a rule which mandates racist behaviour, even in a deeply internalized sense. Rather, the claim is that the institution is behaving in a racist fashion without possessing racist intent. It is a claim that either some of the officers of the institution are exercising their powers in a racist fashion, or that some combination of the rules of the institution produces racist effects.

Our discussion of the accidental actions of groups is related to a topic which will be explored in the next chapter: the responsibility of social groups. A group is certainly responsible for its intentions and its actions, including its accidental actions, but it can also be held responsible for the actions of others. The law may require the group to compensate for the actions of its officers even if they have stepped outside their scope of authority. This may be because the group has failed to properly supervise them in some way—the group is held to have acted negligently in failing to stop the conduct—or because the law demands that the group compensate for the action, irrespective of any wrong-doing by the group. The attribution of actions to groups then shades into the attribution of responsibility for those actions. It may sometimes be unclear whether an officer of the group has acted for the group, thus incurring group responsibility for the action, or whether the officer has stepped outside her area of authority, but responsibility for the action is attributed back to the group nonetheless. The position may be especially unclear when the group has attempted to block the attribution of action by creating internal rules which purport to limit the authority of its officers. The internal rules of a company might, for instance, forbid the management from forming anti-competitive agreements with its business rivals. If the senior management, ignoring these rules, reached such a deal, it may be unclear if they were acting as individuals or as officers of the group. When the competition authorities fine the company they may not need to specify whether the company is being fined for reaching the agreement—irrespective of the sham internal rule—or if the company is being held vicariously liable for the unauthorized acts of company officers.

---

[30] See the discussion in C. McCrudden, 'Institutional Discrimination' (1982) 2 Oxford J Legal Studies 303, and *The Stephen Lawrence Inquiry: Report of An Inquiry by Sir William MacPherson of Cluny* (London: HMSO, 1999) para 6.34.

(iii) A note on the claims of the state

In earlier chapters much was said about the authority 'claims' of the state. Whilst some space was devoted to considering what this claim entailed, little consideration was given to how the claim could be made. It might be contended that talk of the state making claims is an unhelpful personification of the state, an unnecessary fiction.[31] It seems unlikely that the state makes claims in precisely the same way that people make claims. The state lacks vocal cords, for a start. But we can ascribe claims to the state in the same way that we ascribe actions and intentions to it. The claims of the state can be deduced from the content and implications of the rules which constitute the state and, connectedly, from the pronouncements of those empowered to speak on behalf of the state.[32]

For our purposes, a person can be understood as making a claim when she makes a statement which attributes a fact to a thing. So, the statements that London is the capital of the United Kingdom and that Hitler was a bad person, connect facts (status as a capital city and badness) to things (London and Hitler). These statements are claims: they assert a connection and are correct if this statement is true, and untrue if the statement is false. States often make claims. The North Korean constitution claims that Kim Il Sung was a great human being.[33] This claim is true if he was a 'great human being' and untrue if the statement is false. Sometimes these claims are part of a rule. A constitutional rule which asserts that a person is a tyrant and is not permitted to enter the territory of the state contains both a claim (the person is a tyrant) and a prohibition (who may not enter the territory). Some claims made by the state conceal rules. A claim in the constitution that the leader is an especially virtuous person might conceal an obligation on the people of the state to publicly acknowledge this supposed fact. It may be worth noting that in these instances the truth or falsity of the claim (that a person is a tyrant or the leader is especially virtuous) need not affect the existence or operation of the rule. People may still be required to accept that the leader is a great person, even if it is plain that he is a fool. Finally, some claims made by the state are neither part of particular rules nor conceal rules. These claims are, however, identified as claims of the state by rules which empower the institution to make such claims, and which require people to acknowledge that these claims have been made on behalf of the state—though there may not be a duty to accept the claims as correct. So, for example, a Minister for Culture may be empowered to declare that an artist's work has shown that artist to possess especial talent. Others may not be required to agree with this claim, but they are required to accept that it was made by the Minister within the powers accorded to her by the constitution, and was made on behalf of the state.

[31] As Dworkin contends in the context of the discussion of the claims of law: R. Dworkin, 'Thirty Years On' (2002) 115 Harvard L Rev 1655, 1666–1667. See the discussion of Dworkin's position in J. Gardner, 'Law's Aims in *Law's Empire*' in S. Hershovitz ed, *Exploring Law's Empire: The Jurisprudence of Ronald Dworkin* (Oxford: Oxford University Press, 2006).

[32] See the discussion in P. Soper, 'Law's Normative Claims' in R. P. George, *The Autonomy of Law* (Oxford: Oxford University Press, 1996).

[33] Preamble to the North Korean Constitution.

When people discuss the claims of the state—and its close neighbour, the claims of law—they are not normally interested in the variety of claims that *could* be made, but rather the claims that *must* be made, the necessary claims of this institution. In a recent paper on the claims of law, John Gardner makes much of the language and assertions of legal officials in manifesting law's claims.[34] Defending Joseph Raz's assertion that law claims moral authority, Gardner points to the pronouncements of legal officials. These people only speak on behalf of law when they speak in language which claims moral authority for law: this is implicit within the legal discourse of rights, duties, powers and immunities. A legal official who sought to speak outside of this discourse would cease to speak as an official. It is, Gardner claims, therefore a necessary feature of law that it claims moral authority, and this claim is to be found in the claims of its law-applying officials.

The nature and manner of claims made by the state cannot be directly equated with those of the law. As has been argued, it is a mistake to interpret the claims of law as necessarily including a claim to comprehensiveness or supremacy—though many legal systems do make these claims—whilst states do, necessarily, assert that they make the ultimate determination of the rights and duties of the citizen. Furthermore, even if we accept that Gardner is correct in tying the claims of law to the claims of law-applying officials, it is far from clear a similar restriction should be placed on the state. The state advances its claims through law-applying officials, but it also makes claims through other mechanisms. The state can additionally make claims through legislation produced by its law-making bodies, and through its Constitution, however that document was created and enacted. The state can also make claims through its executive officers acting in their official capacity. The Prime Minister can apologize—admit culpability—on behalf of the state. The sources of the claims of the state may consequently be wider than the sources of the claims of law.

(iv) The character of states and other social groups

The attribution of intentions, actions, and claims to social groups allows us to ascribe character to those groups. When people talk of aggressive groups or charitable groups, they mean that the group holds aggressive or charitable intentions and acts in aggressive or charitable ways. States can also exhibit character in this fashion. A secretive state is one which routinely conceals information about its activities. A bellicose state is one which demands that its members respond quickly to perceived slights, and takes violent action against those with whom it disagrees. Furthermore, states can also suffer from the problems that afflict agents capable of intention and action. The state may be indecisive, it may be unable to form clear intentions or it may hold conflicting intentions which prevent it from acting. The state may make mistakes: the intentions it adopts may be foolish, or the actions it

[34] J. Gardner, 'How Law Claims, What Law Claims' (2008) Oxford Legal Studies Research Paper No 44/2008 and M. Köpcke Tinturé, *Some Main Questions Concerning Legal Validity*, D.Phil submitted to Oxford University (2009), ch 6.

undertakes in pursuit of those intentions may be misdirected or counterproductive. The accusation that a state has dithered or blundered is relatively common; organizations are often accused of failures of this kind. It might be possible, though, to push forward the range of mental failings that can be attributed to the state. If we accept the ascription of intentions and actions to the state, might it also be acceptable to ascribe to the state some of the sicknesses of mind that are sometimes suffered by individuals? In short, can the state ever suffer neuroses?

THE NEUROSES OF THE STATE

W. R. Bion, working within the psychoanalytical tradition, sought to identify the irrational features of group activity which interfered with groups achieving the goals they existed to pursue.[35] Though he applied the tools and concepts of psychoanalysis to groups, and wrote of the group possessing a mind, Bion made it clear that the behaviour of the group rested on the interaction of the group's members. The dysfunctions of some groups could, Bion claimed, be traced back to dysfunctional patterns of behaviour brought to the group by its members. Bion described these patterns as 'basic assumptions', and used them to produce three models of dysfunctional groups.[36] These models were not tightly differentiated: a particular group could slip between the models and show elements of each from time to time.

First, Bion identified *basic assumption dependency*. This arises when the group behaves as if its primary task is to provide for the needs of those within the group, and furthermore assumes that the leader is uniquely able to provide for these needs.[37] In Bion's analysis, the group is echoing the behaviour of a child, placing total reliance on, and trust in, its parent. Whilst this type of relationship may be healthy for a child, in an adult it amounts to a crippling lack of maturity; a pathological inability to take control and accept personal responsibility. A group entering this position acts like an immature adult. It avoids engaging with the problems that face it by placing blind trust in the leader, shunning difficult decisions and internal debate. Members of the group cease to function collectively and attempt to form direct personal relations with the leader.[38] They are united by a common allegiance, rather than by a shared commitment to work together as a team.

Second, Bion identified *basic assumption fight-flight*.[39] Here, the group becomes preoccupied with a perceived external threat to the group. The group maintains its

---

[35] W. R. Bion, *Experiences in Groups* (London: Routledge, 1989); J. Stokes, 'The Unconscious at Work in Groups and Teams: Contributions From the Work of Wilfred Bion', in A. Obholzer and V. Z. Roberts (eds), *The Unconscious At Work* (London: Routledge, 1994); R. de Board, *The Psychoanalysis of Organisations* (London: Routledge, 1990), ch 5.

[36] From a very different tradition, but making similar observations of dysfunctional groups, compare Pratkanis and Aronson on cults: A. Pratkanis and E. Aronson, *Age of Propaganda: The Everyday Use and Abuse of Persuasion* (rev ed, New York: Holt, 2001), 302–17.

[37] Bion, note 35 above, 78–86.

[38] *Ibid.*, 119.

[39] *Ibid.*, 63–5. See also Forsyth, note 6 above, ch 13.

unity by identifying an outside body opposed to the group, and then reacts to this threat through fear or aggression, ready to flee or attack.[40] In Bion's analysis, the group behaves like an individual who transfers feelings about an authority figure from her youth to others she meets in adult life. The aggression and fear experienced towards this person may be inappropriate; a set of behaviours formed in connection to a different person. A related interpretation of this situation presents the group entering a paranoid-schizoid state.[41] The group splits off part of its identity (the previous relationship with an authority figure) and projects it onto another—the schizoid element of the diagnosis. The group then adopts an attitude towards that other of inappropriate fear and hostility—the paranoid element of the diagnosis.

Finally, Bion identified *basic assumption pairing*. In this situation the group invests its hopes for the future in the pairing of its leader with another person.[42] The product of this pairing will be the group's salvation. If the attitude of the group in the first model could be described as one of inappropriate trust, and in the second as inappropriate fear, in this third situation the group is inappropriately hopeful.

These three models are reinforced and maintained by a sort of collective denial.[43] Anyone within the group who challenges the assumptions of the group, who attempts to get the group to face reality and move out of its pathological condition, is subject to criticism and hostility. A rule has developed in the group, probably a deeply internalized rule, that certain statements, certain observations, are no longer permitted. To point out that the group is relying on an incorrect factual basis violates this rule.[44] There is pressure within the group for its members to agree to the collective untruth; moving away from this position appears to threaten the identity and security of the group.

We have strayed a long way from constitutional theory. Though Bion's work is engaging and provocative, it is clearly subject to powerful criticisms which cannot be assessed here. Freud's work on the supposed Oedipus complex[45] coupled with the belief that people tend to relive relationships from their childhood in inappropriate forms in adulthood, pervade Bion's work on groups. The underpinnings of these ideas are deeply controversial and cannot be adequately defended or challenged here. However, what might be less controversial is the claim that Bion has succeeded in identifying a number of types of dysfunctional group which at a minimum echo the dysfunctions experienced by individuals. At least the first two types of basic

---

[40] Bion, note 35 above, 152.

[41] W. Halton, 'Some Unconscious Aspects of Organizational Life: Contributions From Psychoanalysis' in A. Obholzer and J. Stokes (eds), *The Unconscious At Work* (London: Routledge, 1994), 14–15.

[42] Bion, note 35 above, 150–3.

[43] Halton, note 41 above, 12–13. For a similar observation from a different tradition, see Forsyth, note 6 above, 355–7.

[44] See Le Bon, note 2 above, 132.

[45] Or, more precisely, Melanie Klein's development of it: see de Board, note 35 above, chs 4 and 5.

assumption can also be seen to operate at the state level: states can experience inappropriate dependency and can enter the paranoid-schizoid position.

States exist for the benefit of their members. This contrasts with some other social groups which meet together for a particular task—to help the sick or to build a road, for instance. If a charity spent all of its time caring for the needs of its staff, it would have failed in its primary task. A state which spends its time caring for the needs of its members is, in contrast, a success. The first element of dysfunction in Bion's basic assumption dependency model, that the group is preoccupied working for the benefit of its members, cannot, therefore, be directly applied to the state. The second aspect of Bion's model, that group members are inappropriately dependent on the group leaders, can, in contrast, be seen in some dysfunctional states. Where the people of the state come to place complete trust in one person, or one sub-group, for the satisfaction of its needs, they are invariably disappointed. As Aristotle wrote, kingship would be a desirable method of government if we could identify those with the capacity to govern as well as the gods, but in reality it is impossible to find such people, even if they exist.[46] The history of states which have adopted this dependent structure is, in general, a history of failure.[47] Perhaps the paradigmatic example of this type of state is the totalitarian state, a form of polity often characterized by a personality cult. Members of the state are enjoined to put absolute trust in the leader. The will of the leader is claimed to embody a wisdom that transcends the understanding of ordinary folk; their very ordinariness causes them to miss his sagacity. The institutions of the state spend their time trying to guess what the leader would decide on an issue, were she to address her mind to it. Hannah Arendt tells us that Hitler's Governor General of Poland, Hans Frank, expounded a perversion of Kant's categorical imperative. 'Act in such a way', wrote Frank, 'that the Führer, if he knew your action, would approve of it.'[48] As in Bion's model of basic assumption dependency, the leader of the state is regarded as a magical, otherworldly, messianic figure.[49]

Totalitarian states exhibit pathological dependency in its most acute form, but healthier states also suffer from this malady to a degree. In democracies competing political parties stir up unrealistic expectations of the institutions of the state, expectations which will be realized only if they are elected to power. People are encouraged to believe that state institutions can accomplish the impossible. Through the provision of healthcare, sickness will be banished and death indefinitely postponed.

[46] Aristotle, *The Politics and Constitution of Athens*, ed S. Everson (Cambridge: Cambridge University Press, 1996), VII.14, 1332b16–23.

[47] Though a non-democratic government may be preferable to anarchy or an evil democratic regime.

[48] H. Arendt, *Eichmann in Jerusalem: A Report on the Banality of Evil* (London: Penguin, 2006), 136.

[49] Bion, note 35 above, 84. See also R. Baron, K. Crawley and D. Paulina, 'Aberrations of Power: Leadership in Totalist Groups' in M. Hogg and D. van Knippenberg (eds), *Leadership and Power* (London: Sage, 2003), 170–3 and S. Reichter and N. Hopkins, 'On the Science of the Art of Leadership' in the same volume at 206–8.

Through education, everyone will develop outstanding intelligence and get a good job. Through the police force, complete peace and security will be established within the country. When institutions fall short of these impossible goals they are subjected to fierce criticism. What the work of Bion, and many others, shows is that people tend to believe these things because, at least in part, they want to believe these things. By parcelling off worries about mortality, children's development and our security to state institutions, we are absolved from worrying about them ourselves. Hence our sometimes disproportionate surprise and disappointment when we discover that these institutions are imperfect. Not only are they failing, but, in a sense, we are failing, too, by investing excessive faith in them.

Bion's second model of a dysfunctional group, a group dominated by the basic assumption of fight-flight, can also be seen in some states. This model had two elements: the inappropriate identification of another as a threat, coupled with an inappropriately aggressive or defensive reaction against that other. Sometimes, of course, states will face threats from outsiders and, sometimes, a violent reaction is the best way to respond to this threat. The situation becomes pathological when the state perceives outsiders as threats when they are not threats, over-estimates the extent of the threat, or reacts inappropriately to the threat. To be pathological, this attitude must be maintained over time. A healthy state can make an error and take action on the basis of that error. Its action would have been appropriate if the assumption it acted upon was correct, but is rendered inappropriate because of the mistake. The state in this context is like a person who misunderstands the comments of another and responds in a way she would not have responded if she had correctly understood the comment. A neurotic state, in contrast, makes persistent errors and makes no effort to correct those errors. Furthermore, the state comes to identify itself through this opposition: it is the enemy that defines the state. Nazi Germany provides an extreme example of a neurotic state characterized by the paranoid-schizoid model. The state spent much of its time identifying imaginary foes—Jews and Romany, amongst others—blaming them for the problems of the state and reacting aggressively towards them.

The temptation to allow or encourage the state to give way to this type of pathology is enormous. It provides a quick and easy project for the group to pursue, one which is simple to understand and which can appear, at least, to be of extreme importance: if the state does not defend itself, its members risk harm or death. Furthermore, as Bion argued, it panders to people's preconceived notions about how groups should behave. Consequently, the paranoid-schizoid model of the state will be popular to leaders: it provides an easy way to reinforce the unity of the state and to maintain the power of state institutions. It is hardly surprising that leaders throughout history have sought to bolster state power by picking fights with other countries and vilifying minority groups within their territory.

Whilst obviously unhealthy states embody the paranoid-schizoid character in its fullest form, more moderate expressions of it can be seen in comparatively healthy polities. States often wish, for good reason, to create a sense of national identity, invoking a set of factors that its members share and which bind them together. It is hard to do this without identifying, explicitly or implicitly, groups against which the state is contrasted. If the state invokes racial, ethnic or religious qualities as facets of its identity it will struggle to prevent its people drawing negative contrasts with other groups who lack these qualities. After all, it is possession of these features that supposedly makes the state special. An influx of people who lack these features, or political activity within the state by minority groups which lack these features, will threaten the state. The attempt to invoke some form of a national identity for the European Union has encountered problems of this type.[50]

Many constitutional lawyers reading the previous paragraphs will have been struck by a startling similarity between our discussion of pathological groups and the writings of one influential constitutional theorist: Carl Schmitt. Schmitt's account of the state has the unhappy distinction of combining features of Bion's dependency and paranoid-schizoid models of dysfunctional groups.[51]

Schmitt's account of the state centred upon the moment of state emergency,[52] a moment at which the legal order drops away and politics emerges in its rawest form.[53] This realm of the political is—according to Schmitt—a distinct and discrete normative arena. Just as the aesthetic arena is defined by a divide between the beautiful and the ugly and the moral arena is defined by a divide between good and evil, the political arena is defined by a divide between the friend and the enemy.[54] In the moment of emergency the sovereign steps forward to make the decisions which define the enemy, decisions which are a quintessential exercise of political power.[55] The state's nature and operation in normal times is to be understood by reference to its nature and operation in these exceptional times: there must exist a sovereign with the potential to make radical decisions in times of emergency, and this potential must be sufficient to permit the identification of a group of people who can be classed as the enemy, even in times of peace.[56] The existence of the enemy is of vital importance to Schmitt's state. It is the enemy which creates the possibility of a public sphere: the identification of the enemy by the sovereign allows the people of the state to form a viable political unity. Within the state, between those identified as friends, there can be disagreements and even hatred, but towards the enemy there is the continuing possibility of combat, violence, killing.[57] According to Schmitt,

---

[50] See the discussion in N. W. Barber, 'Citizenship, Nationalism and the European Union' (2002) 27 European L Rev 241.

[51] For a good introduction to Schmitt's work see E. Böckenförde, 'The Concept of the Political: A Key to Understanding Carl Schmitt's Constitutional Theory' in D. Dyzenhaus (ed), *Law As Politics: Carl Schmitt's Critique of Liberalism* (Durham: Duke University Press, 1998).

[52] Often translated as the 'state of exception': C. Schmitt, *Political Theology: Four Chapters on the Concept of Sovereignty*, trans G. Schwab (Chicago: University of Chicago Press, 2006), 5.

[53] Schmitt, note 52 above, 15.

[54] C. Schmitt, *The Concept of the Political*, trans G. Schwab, (Chicago: University of Chicago Press, 1996), 26.

[55] Schmitt, note 54 above, 49; Schmitt, note 52 above, 12–13.

[56] Schmitt, note 54 above, 28, 39.

[57] *Ibid.*, 32.

warfare is not the aim of politics, but it is necessary as an ever-present possibility if political behaviour is to occur.[58] Only once the enemy has been identified can friends engage in political debate safe in the knowledge that the debate does not pose a threat to the existence of the state.

One of the reasons that Schmitt's work is important is because it provides a useful counter-balance to Kelsen's legalistic model of the state. Whereas Kelsen presented the state as a creature of law, shutting out social and political aspects of its construction, Schmitt presented law as a creature of the state. Law, for Schmitt, was conditional on the sovereign's political act of defining friend and enemy; this was the miracle[59] that made the state and the practice of law possible. This characteristically political act occupied the same conceptual space as Kelsen's *Grundnorm*.

Schmitt's model of the state is remarkably similar to the pathological models of the state set out above. First, Schmitt's state appears to have fallen prey to the paranoid-schizoid group malaise diagnosed by Bion. Schmitt's state does not merely identify others as enemies when and if it is threatened, its identity requires that it manufacture an enemy—whether or not this other group actually poses a threat. Without an enemy Schmitt's state ceases to exist. Perhaps bizarrely, the vitality of Schmitt's state depends on the maintenance of the enemy grouping: if this grouping were destroyed, if the enemy were completely overcome, the state would loose its identity and integrity.

Secondly, Schmitt's state is characterized by inappropriate dependency. His analysis centres on the sovereign, but the precise nature of the sovereign is ambiguous. In particular, it is unclear the extent to which Schmitt's sovereign can be an institution rather than a person. In Schmitt's earlier work the sovereign was presented as a person, but in his later writings it appears that institutions could occupy this role as well.[60] The apparent logic of the moment of the exception—that someone must be able to step forward to take a decision in a time of crisis—would seem to push towards the reductive conclusion that the sovereign must be a person. Just as one institution could emerge in a crisis as the most powerful in the constitution, if the crisis percolated into that institution a sub-group of that institution might emerge as a sovereign, and if the crisis percolated into that sub-group then one person might emerge. If we assume, and it is a big assumption, that the body able to command loyalty in a time of crisis is already inherent in the state, and is not identified by the particular nature of the crisis, it is hard to resist the conclusion that Schmitt's sovereign must be a person. This individual is able to command the complete obedience of the people of the state. She is able to make decisions about life and death: who is included within the state and who is excluded from it. The sovereign is set apart from other members of the state in that she is not constrained by the rules of the state. Schmitt claimed that all modern concepts of the state are secularized theologi-

---

[58] *Ibid.*, 34.

[59] Schmitt, note 52 above, 36.

[60] R. Cristi, 'Carl Schmitt on Sovereignty and Constituent Power' in D. Dyzenhaus, *Law as Politics: Carl Schmitt's Critique of Liberalism* (Durham: Duke University Press, 1998).

cal concepts. The sovereign, it seems, should be understood as the constitutional parallel of God: an all powerful entity, the source of the miracle that allows the state to come into existence.[61] Schmitt's sovereign plays a role in the state which is practically identical to that of the leader in Bion's model of a group characterized by inappropriate dependency.[62] In each case, the individual is invested with almost divine capacities, in each case the members of the group are defined by their almost complete willingness to place their confidence in a single person. In a further parallel between Schmitt's state and Bion's dysfunctional group, the members of the group cease to have relationships with the group as a whole and instead form relations with the leader directly. Members of Schmitt's state will share some common identifying feature, often a common ethnicity, but their most important shared feature is a common loyalty to the sovereign. Interaction between citizens in Schmitt's state is not essential and, at least in the political realm, appears to be something which is permitted rather than encouraged.[63]

Of course, none of this means that Schmitt is wrong. Social groups are the products of humans, and they will reflect—in a more or less distorted form—the imperfections and malaise of their creators. It could be that Schmitt is right and that states are, by their very nature, destined to fall into dysfunctional forms of behaviour. Inappropriate dependency on leaders and excessive hostility towards outsiders could be inescapable aspects of human psychology that, sooner or later, will inevitably be manifested at the level of the state. Let us hope that this is not the case. Let us hope that, like the neurosis of individuals, the neurosis of the state can be mitigated or even cured.

CONCLUSION

This chapter has discussed the senses in which states, and other social groups, can form intentions and undertake actions. It has connected this capacity back to the rules which constitute the state, discussed in the previous chapters. The plurality of constitutional rules enables the state to act and intend beyond the capacities conferred on its officials by the domestic legal order. Furthermore, the possibility of the state acting and intending allows us to talk of the state possessing a character; a nature shaped and defined by the exercise of these capacities. This character may be praiseworthy or regrettable. Our discussion of these features of the state leads, unavoidably, to the further question of their significance for the members of the state. This is the subject of the next chapter, which considers the implications of the exercise of these capacities and formation of character for the state as a whole, and, more importantly, for members and officials of the state.

[61] Schmitt, note 52 above, 36.

[62] Bion, note 35 above, 84.

[63] A comparison could also be drawn with cult leaders, who also often make a point of flouting the rules they impose on their members: Baron, Crawley and Paulina, note 49 above, 182; Pratkanis and Aronson, note 36 above, 306.

⚮ 8 ⚮

The Responsibility of the State

States form intentions and undertake actions. They have successes and failures, embarking on commendable projects and vicious schemes. There are states which we should be grateful to belong to and states in which citizenship is a burden and a cause for regret. Generally states are, of course, a mixture of the good and the bad. Like most people, the life-story of most states is a combination of the vicious and the virtuous, with parts of their history of which their members should be proud, and parts of which they should be ashamed.

This chapter reflects on the scope and the continuity of the responsibility of the state. It considers the ways in which states are connected to situations in the world and the significance these connections have for their members. The chapter considers the ways in which this responsibility can continue, in some form, despite radical changes or breaks in the identity of the state. In undertaking this enquiry some light will be shed on one of the hardest questions of constitutional theory, a question even Aristotle dodged: the determination of the point at which one state ends and a new state begins.

RESPONSIBILITY

Responsibility is a tricky word. It is tricky because it is a word with a number of different meanings. Some of these meanings are closely related whilst others are only loosely linked. It is very easy to slip unknowingly between different senses of responsibility in the course of a discussion. This can cause confusion, and a small portion, at least, of the anger generated by discussion of the responsibility of states is caused by a lack of conceptual clarity. This is not the place for an extended or intricate discussion of responsibility—such an account could easily fill a book—but it is necessary to map the broad contours of responsibility in order to clarify discussion of it in the context of the state.

The various concepts of responsibility can usefully be divided into three broad groups: outcome responsibility, capacity responsibility and explanatory responsibility. These groups are not hermetically sealed: they could easily be broken down into further subsets and important connections can be demonstrated between the different collections.

(i) Forms of outcome responsibility

Outcome responsibility turns on the connection between the conduct of an agent and events in the world.[1] At least five different forms of outcome responsibility can be identified.

The weakest form of outcome responsibility is *causal responsibility*.[2] Causal responsibility points to a causal connection between an agent and a set of outcomes, whilst additionally implying that this connection is of some special interest to us. Even inanimate objects can be causally responsible in this sense. We might say, for example, that a meteorite is responsible for the damage done to the property it hit, or that an earthquake is responsible for the collapse of a house. In these cases the meteorite and the earthquake were causes of the damage, and, moreover, are causes we might be interested knowing about.

When it is a person who is linked to an outcome, we normally expect to be entitled to infer rather more from the story. The connection also purports to tell us something about that person's character; it advances a connection of *moral responsibility*. To say that Alf was responsible for damaging property implies more than an interesting causal link between Alf and the damage: it further implies that we can make a moral connection between the damage and Alf. If Alf was thrown out of a hot air balloon and damaged a house on his landing, we would not—ordinarily—say that Alf was responsible for the harm done, even though the causal connection mirrors that of the meteorite in our earlier example. When it is asserted that a person is morally responsible for an outcome, the connection drawn purports to tell us something of interest about that person's character; that the outcome was a manifestation of Alf's carelessness or malice, for example.[3]

A single state of affairs may be linked back to many people in a variety of different ways. A soldier who has carelessly shot a civilian is certainly (morally) responsible for the killing, but others may also bear forms of responsibility for the action. The commander may have acted in a way which contributed to the event, perhaps by giving careless orders or by failing to train the soldier properly. Similarly, the soldier's comrades may have encouraged the shooting or failed to take the opportunity to prevent the act.

Legal responsibility is similar to moral responsibility.[4] As a claim of moral responsibility asserts a morally significant connection between an agent and an event, a finding of legal responsibility asserts an analogous legal connection. As with moral

---

[1] T. Honoré, 'Introduction' in T. Honoré, *Responsibility and Fault* (Oxford: Hart Publishing, 1999), 9; T. Honoré, 'Responsibility and Luck' in T. Honoré, *Responsibility and Fault* (Oxford: Hart Publishing, 1999), 14–15. See also D. Miller, *National Responsibility and Global Justice* (Oxford: Oxford University Press, 2007), ch 4.

[2] The label is Hart's: H. L. A. Hart, 'Postscript: Responsibility and Retribution' in H. L. A. Hart, *Punishment and Responsibility* (2nd edn, Oxford: Oxford University Press, 2008), 214–15.

[3] Which Honoré labels the 'basic form of responsibility'. T. Honoré, 'Introduction' in T. Honoré, *Responsibility and Fault* (Oxford: Hart Publishing, 1999), 9.

[4] Hart, note 2 above, 215–22.

responsibility, agents may have an interest in denying or asserting responsibility. A person may strongly deny her legal responsibility for an accident, hoping to avoid being compelled to pay compensation, but, on another occasion, may loudly assert her responsibility for the composition of a tune, hoping to secure a share of the royalties. Moral responsibility and legal responsibility are intertwined. Our moral responsibilities are partly determined by the rules of the community in which we live, and a portion of these rules is found in the law.[5]

This discussion leads us to the fourth form of outcome responsibility: *role responsibility*.[6] Role responsibility is a subcategory of moral and legal responsibility. Communities create various roles which people can enter into, offices which bring with them special rights and special duties. These offices are fashioned by legal and social rules and, perhaps, in some instances, directly by unsocially mediated moral reasons. A person who enters into such a role may become responsible for certain events as a consequence of her occupancy of that role. To take an example given by Hart, a person who becomes a sea-captain acquires a set of new responsibilities. She is now responsible for the safety of her ship, the welfare of her passengers and for getting the vessel to its destination. Some of the rules which govern the responsibilities conferred by this role are legal. The law may, for example, determine what standard of sea-worthiness the ship must meet before making sail and require the captain to ensure this standard is met. Or these rules may be social: there may be no legal requirement to check the seaworthiness of the boat merely because this is thought to be so plainly the duty of a captain that it has never needed to be legislated. A captain who sails an unseaworthy ship breaks a rule which defines success in her office—and is (morally and, perhaps, legally) responsible for this breach.

Peter Cane usefully distinguishes between historic and prospective responsibility.[7] Our historic responsibilities connect us to events that occurred in the past, whereas our prospective responsibilities connect us to events which will occur in the future. Role responsibility can operate in each of these dimensions. If a member of a platoon has carelessly shot a civilian, the commander of that platoon is responsible for the civilian's death because of her role as a commander. Even if the orders she issued and the training she provided were faultless, the death of the civilian is still connected back to her in a morally significant way. She has not been as successful in this role as, save for the death, she would otherwise have been. Role responsibility can also connect a person to events which have yet to occur, outcomes which have yet to play out. Returning to the sea-captain, it is already determined that her success in this role will depend on the success of the voyage—but these events lie in the future.

A further form of prospective responsibility is *remedial responsibility*.[8] Remedial responsibility is a subcategory of moral and legal responsibility and exists where an

---

[5] P. Cane, *Responsibility in Law and Morality* (Oxford: Hart Publishing, 2002), 53–6.

[6] The term is Hart's: Hart, note 2 above, 212–14.

[7] Cane, note 5 above, 30–32.

[8] D. Miller, *National Responsibility and Global Justice* (Oxford: Oxford University Press, 2007), 83–5, 97–100.

agent is under a duty to put right a problem. There is a mess, and it is this person's duty to clear it up. Once again, the agent is responsible for future events: the success or failure of the remedial task. Frequently, remedial responsibility will be a consequence of a finding of moral responsibility. A person who is morally responsible for harming another today is normally responsible for remedying that harm tomorrow. But the two forms of responsibility can come apart: an arsonist is responsible for setting fire to a building; the fire-brigade is responsible for putting the blaze out. The distinction between direct moral and remedial responsibility is of particular importance in the context of states. Where there is a break in constitutional continuity between an old and a new state the new state will not inherit the moral responsibilities of the old. The new state may, though, bear remedial responsibility for the mess made by the old. Modern South Africa, for example, may not be (directly) morally responsible for the products of its apartheid predecessor, but it is remedially responsible for putting right the injustices of that period.

Discussion of responsibility often rapidly shades into discussion of how we should react to a finding of responsibility; when blame or punishment is an appropriate reaction to a person's conduct.[9] Sometimes when we talk of people being held responsible, or escaping responsibility, we do equate 'responsibility' with punishment. Inquiries into the nature of responsibility can morph into inquiries into the necessary prerequisites of punishment, raising questions about the significance of intentions, motives and so forth. It is unsurprising that we are quickly drawn from the question of what a person is morally responsible for, to the further question of how we and others should react to this responsibility. It is often the latter question which animates our interest in the former: we care about what people have done because we want to know how we ought to treat them.

David Miller uses the term 'moral responsibility' in a slightly different sense to that given above, a sense which connects the finding of outcome responsibility with the further question of the proper reaction to that finding. A person is morally responsible where, according to Miller, they should be praised or blamed for a state of affairs for which they are outcome responsible.[10] So, he argues, a naturally talented athlete is responsible for the outcome of winning a race, but is not morally responsible for the victory because it depends too much on natural talent and too little on intention to attract moral assessment. Setting aside the interesting questions raised by Miller's example—why do we praise a person's hard work and drive, but not their innate physical ability, when both may be equally determined by genetics and chance?—his definition of moral responsibility must be distinguished from that used in this chapter. When it is claimed here that a person is morally responsible for an event it does not follow that the person should be praised or blamed for it.[11] Later

[9] See, perhaps, Hart, note 2 above, 222–7.

[10] Miller, note 8 above, 89–90.

[11] See further, T. Honoré, 'Responsibility and Luck' in T. Honoré, *Responsibility and Fault* (Oxford: Hart Publishing, 1999).

in the chapter it is suggested that a contemporary citizen of Britain is morally responsible for the crimes of imperialism. If Miller were to make such a claim he would imply that the citizen should be blamed for this policy, that, in some sense, the modern citizen is implicated in a collective guilt for these past actions.[12] This may be correct, perhaps modern Britons still enjoy the wrongfully acquired benefits of empire, but when 'moral responsibility' is used here it signifies a more modest connection. To assert that a citizen of Britain is morally responsible for imperialism is to assert that imperialism constitutes a state of affairs which connects back to British citizenship, partly defining the character of that institution. It follows from this that a person who enters this institution must engage with imperialism—and may incur remedial duties as a result of actions undertaken during this period of history—but they need not be blamed for imperialist policies of the past. The account of moral responsibility in this chapter draws a line between the attribution of events to persons and the further consequences of this attribution. Beyond a few cautionary remarks at the end of the chapter, little will be said about the circumstances in which compensation should be paid or apologies should be issued by states. These are hard questions which would require a detailed account of justice and rights before they could be satisfactorily answered.

(ii) Capacity responsibility

We sometimes enquire whether a person is responsible for their actions, meaning to ask whether they have sufficient mental or physical capacity to permit a connection to be drawn between their action or inaction and a resulting state of affairs.[13] A person whose self-control is significantly impaired may cease to be a responsible agent: she is suffering from a limitation which means that stuff which she would ordinarily be held to be (morally) responsible for cannot be attributed to her.

The effect of a limitation of capacity on (moral) responsibility can be quite a complicated question. A person who is involuntarily drugged and who then causes harm as she collapses into unconsciousness would not normally be held responsible for this harm. She has ceased to be a responsible agent, and cannot therefore be held (morally) responsible for the damage: the fact of the harm does not connect back to her character. A person who has chosen to ingest the drugs may, in contrast, be held responsible. As our hypothetical examples multiply, the issue rapidly becomes nuanced. What if the drug merely reduced, rather than obliterated, her self-control? What if the recipient of the drug was reasonably or unreasonably confused about its effects? These dilemmas suggest that factors which go to capacity may sometimes qualify, or shape, moral responsibility rather than obliterating it. A drugged person may, sometimes, still be (morally) responsible for her actions, but the implications of that connection will depend on a variety of factors relating to her reduced capacity. Capacity and moral responsibility are inextricably intertwined.

[12] See especially, Miller, note 8 above, ch 6.

[13] Hart, note 2 above, 227–30.

(iii) The quality of responsibility

John Gardner asserts that what he terms responsibility 'in the basic sense' has a dia-chronic aspect, that is, it straddles two points in time: the moment of the act under consideration and the moment at which the actor must account for what she has done.[14] Basic responsibility is important, argues Gardner, because it embodies the activity of giving an account of oneself as a rational being,[15] a person whose life has been shaped and guided by rationality. Gardner draws attention to the presence of this sense of responsibility within the legal system. One of the most important functions of a courtroom trial is to give the defendant a public opportunity to show that her actions had a rational explanation: they were justified or, if not justified, then excusable.

Gardner's account of basic responsibility is a combination of various forms of moral and capacity responsibility described in the previous two sections. First, the capacity of the agent and the significance of her connection to states of affairs at the moment of the original event must be considered (was Bella intoxicated, did she kill Clive, did her intoxication negate or shape her responsibility for the killing). Second, the capacity and on-going ability of the agent to give an account for her actions is also relevant (does Bella presently have sufficient command of herself to be held answerable for her actions at the earlier point in time). As Gardner notes, both of these two temporal points germane to responsibility are recognized by the criminal law: a lawyer might argue that her client was insane at the time of the act or might argue that her client is presently unfit to plead.[16] Both, on Gardner's account, go to the legal standard of basic responsibility.

Gardner's paper brings forward a number of important elements relating to responsibility and demonstrates their connectedness. There is, indeed, a sense in which being a responsible person consists of being committed to provide rational explanations for our past actions in the present moment and, if no good explanation can be found, feeling regret or trying to make amends. A responsible agent is responsible for her own character—an attribute which is both a benefit and a burden.[17]

But we might question whether this should be understood as the 'basic' sense of responsibility. It is, as we have seen, built up of elements of different temporal moments of moral responsibility and capacity responsibility. In some situations it will not be helpful, or necessary, to insist that these be combined. A person may no longer be able to be responsible, in Gardner's basic sense, yet we might still care deeply about their responsibilities, in the moral sense. Ascertaining the moral responsibility of a person for an action may be important for those affected by that action—the victims or beneficiaries—and for those who have relationships with

---

[14] J. Gardner, 'The Mark of Responsibility' in J. Gardner, *Offences and Defences* (Oxford: Oxford University Press, 2007), 182–5.

[15] Gardner, note 14 above, 188.

[16] Ibid., 183.

[17] T. Honoré, 'Being Responsible and Being a Victim of Circumstance' in T. Honoré, *Responsibility and Fault* (Oxford: Hart Publishing, 1999).

that person—her family and friends. To take an extreme example, the dead are never responsible in Gardner's basic sense—they can no longer give an account of their actions—but the question of which outcomes they should be held morally responsible for, in the sense outlined above, is frequently a contested and important issue. Indeed, it is not uncommon for legal systems to contain mechanisms within which the responsibilities of absent or even deceased individuals can be debated and ascertained.

RESPONSIBILITY AND THE STATE

Do states have the capacity to be held morally responsible for the outcome of their actions? Are they a type of agent which enjoys the quality of responsibility? The previous chapter argued that social groups, including the state, bore a sufficient resemblance to persons to make talk of their forming intentions and undertaking actions plausible. We now need to consider whether it is similarly useful to talk of states as agents who, like persons, can be said to be responsible for the outcome of their actions and decisions.

(i) The capacity of the state to be held responsible

Philip Pettit argues that it is only when a group demonstrates rational unity in its intentions and actions that it should be considered a person, and it is only once it is fit to be considered a person that it has the capacity to be held responsible for its actions.[18] A group possesses rational unity when it forms and preserves intentions over time, and acts upon these intentions.[19] Whether a state can exhibit 'rational unity' and therefore, on Pettit's account, be properly held responsible for its actions, will depend on how exacting Pettit's test proves to be. For a state to exist it must be a *de facto* authority, at least to some degree.[20] This requirement was discussed in chapter 2, but one prerequisite of being a *de facto* authority is that people who are the addressees of the state's commands must, to some minimal extent, be able to rely upon them. A law-maker which continually changes its mind in the period between the making and promulgation of laws could not amount to a *de facto* authority—nobody could know the present content of the law, however eager they were to obey it. A functioning state must exhibit some level of rational unity to avoid collapsing into anarchy. Pettit's discussion of voting processes and his attack on simple majoritarian systems for their failure to create rational unity in groups suggests that he would not accept that this minimal level of consistency is enough to allow us to treat all states as persons. Perhaps on Pettit's analysis some states would count as persons, and have the capacity to be held

[18] P. Pettit, *A Theory of Freedom: From the Psychology to the Politics of Agency* (Cambridge, 2001), 67; see also P. Pettit, 'Responsibility Incorporated' (2007) 117 Ethics 171 and P. Pettit, 'Rationality, Reasoning and Group Agency' (2007) 61 Dialectica 495.

[19] P. Pettit, 'Collective Persons and Powers' (2002) 8 Legal Theory 443, 456–7.

[20] L. Green, *The Authority of the State* (Oxford: Oxford University Press, 1990), 25–8, 65–6.

responsible, and some states would not. Alternatively, perhaps, Pettit might argue that all states should be treated as if they are responsible agents because those states which lack rational unity can develop it, and we will encourage such development by holding them responsible.[21]

As Peter Cane points out, most of the examples that Pettit gives of collectives which exhibit rational unity are small groups making discrete decisions. It is not clear, argues Cane, that larger more complicated groups—and the state must be one of the largest and most complicated—could ever satisfy Pettit's strictures.[22] It might be questioned whether Pettit is correct to raise his demand for rational unity beyond the minimal level necessary in order for the group to act and form intentions. The basis for the inclusion of a more exacting standard is unclear. Why should we demand that collectives demonstrate a high degree of rational unity before we regard them as persons, when we do not make the same demand of humans? Humans often fail to demonstrate rational unity in their decisions and conduct. Most of us are vacillating or inconsistent some of the time—indeed, a few people seem proud of their unpredictability and irrationality. Yet none of this imperils our identity as persons. Provided people enjoy sufficient constancy to function, they count as persons who are morally responsible for their conduct. The same is true of social groups. A fickle social group, like a fickle person, can still act and can still be held responsible for the consequences of its actions.

In our discussion of capacity responsibility in the earlier part of this chapter it was suggested that factors which go to a person's capacity frequently should be considered to shape that person's moral responsibility for outcomes. This is also true of social groups. Instead of seeing the impairment of rational unity as obliterating responsibility, we should sometimes understand it as one of the factors which conditions that responsibility. A group that regularly makes inconsistent decisions can be held responsible for this inconsistency, as manifested in the products of its actions and intentions. Often this inconsistency will be undesirable—we normally value consistency in both people and groups—but sometimes inconsistency may be preferable to consistency. Firstly, because inconsistency, impulsiveness, and other flaws in rational unity can cut both ways in respect of the assessment of the character of both persons and groups. It is better to have done a bad action in a moment of impaired rationality than to have undertaken the same action in a moment of cool deliberation, whilst appreciating the moral content of the action and foreseeing its consequences. A state which enters into an unjust war in a climate of moral panic is, all other things being equal, less reprehensible than a state which enters into that same war whilst fully aware of its injustice. Secondly, it is better to be inconsistently good than consistently bad. A state could decide on a clear and coherent set of objectives to pursue, adopt effective measures for their achievement and show steadfastness in their pursuit. But if these objectives are immoral, this consistency appears a vice rather than a virtue; a commitment to doing wrong rather than a slip in a struggle to act morally.

---

[21] P. Pettit, 'Responsibility Incorporated' (2007) 117 Ethics 171, 200.

[22] Cane, note 5 above, 166–8.

A radical challenge to the capacity of the state to be held responsible is advanced by Scott Veitch. Veitch argues that the state facilitates what he describes as the 'dispersal' of responsibility, diluting and obscuring the responsibility of people for their actions.[23] Veitch illustrates the ways in which structures of rules such as those which constitute the state can appear to immunize individuals from responsibility for the state's actions.[24] When a state invades another, for instance, no single member of that state undertakes this action. Whilst the invasion is funded by tax revenue, ordinarily no designated element of any individual's tax goes to that action. The taxes are fed into a central pool, and monies from this pool fund the health service, education and other virtuous activities, alongside the vicious. Consequently, taxes are put through a process of ethical laundering: no defined portion of an individual's contribution pays for the war. Similarly, the decision-making and executive structures of the state fragment and dissipate responsibility. Politicians' conduct is mediated through a complex web of hierarchical committees. Even the most powerful person in the system must persuade others to support her policies: save in the most autocratic of states, the decision to go to war will require discussion and agreement. And once the decision is made, the politicians are then distanced from its execution. They ordered the invasion, but did not specify how it was to be carried out. Finally, the diffusion of responsibility continues within the army that carries out the politicians' orders. The soldiers work on the assumption the political direction given by the politicians is morally correct—it is not their job to question the propriety of the decision to invade—and within the army the conduct of the war is further subdivided within, again, a complex hierarchical command system. Set against the enormity of the war, the part played by an individual citizen, politician, or soldier is of vanishingly small significance.

Veitch's sorry tale certainly captures a common feature of our experience of states: a distance between the individual and the state which can be both disempowering but also, sometimes, comforting. However, whilst people may be tempted to take solace from this divide, they are mistaken if they believe it cuts them off from responsibility for the state's acts. Returning to our earlier discussion of the different ways in which a particular state of affairs can be connected back to multiple individuals, the answer to Veitch's challenge turns on the precise descriptions of the responsibilities of the various agents in their differing capacities. It is true that no individual is, as an individual, responsible for the invasion, but all of the members of the state are, individually, responsible for the actions of that state. They are members of the

---

[23] S. Veitch, *Law and Irresponsibility: On The Legitimation of Human Suffering* (London: Routledge-Cavendish, 2008), ch 2. For psychological study of such diffusion, see J. Cooper, K. Kelly and K. Weaver, 'Attitudes, Norms and Social Groups' in M. Hogg and S. Tindale (eds), *Blackwell Handbook of Social Psychology: Group Processes* (Oxford: Blackwell, 2003), 271.

[24] Peter French makes a somewhat similar argument from a radically different perspective, contending that a group can sometimes be blameworthy even though no member of the group merits blame: P. A. French, *Collective and Corporate Responsibility* (Columbia: Columbia University Press, 1984), 13–16.

state and the significance and worth of that role is partly constituted by what the state does.

(ii) The moral responsibility of state members for actions of the state

Veitch's concerns about the dissipation of responsibility through the state reminds us that when we discuss the responsibility of states our ultimate interest is—almost invariably—in what this has to tell us about the responsibility of people. The history of a group is, in itself, boring and unimportant, but the topic becomes both interesting and important when it is connected back to the members of that group. It is this connection that makes debates about the actions and responsibilities of groups like the state so controversial. People care about what states have done, what states are responsible for, because of the consequences these questions have for members of the state.

Group members can be morally responsible for the outcomes wrought by groups in at least two ways. First, members of the state bear responsibility for the state's actions by virtue of their membership. This is a form of role responsibility. A person's life-story is, in part, constructed through the groups to which she belongs. Belonging to a successful group means that, all else being equal, your life is more of a success than it otherwise would have been. Belonging to a failing group, in contrast, has negative implications. All state members are, in a sense, responsible for the outcomes for which the state is responsible. They may not have undertaken—they may not even have supported or known of—the relevant action of the state. But it is still an action of a group of which they are members, and its actions, and the products of these actions, are connected back to their lives in a morally significant way. Indeed, rather than insulating individuals from responsibility—as Veitch suggests—membership of groups such as the state dramatically broadens people's responsibility.

The significance of responsibility flowing from bare membership of the state may be quite restricted. States can bear responsibility for the outcomes of actions undertaken many generations ago, before any of the current state members were born. These acts and their products may still shape the character of the state, and members may still, therefore, be said to bear responsibility for them. But as time elapses, this connection may become of less significance. Members of the British state are responsible for the war on Iraq, colonialism, the support of the United Kingdom for the slave trade, and much else, but as these events recede into history their implications for the current character of the state reduces. There may come a point at which it is implausible to claim that a modern state remains responsible for the actions of its ancient ancestors.

Secondly, members of the state are responsible for actions of the state which they are, in some way, personally implicated in. Office holders are directly and personally responsible for the actions they undertake on behalf of the state, or for their participation in processes which lead to state action. For example, the president who orders an invasion is responsible for the outcomes of issuing that order. Her responsibility is different from that of the soldier who goes into battle or the generals who plan the war, though it will be partly conditioned by their conduct. Policemen, judges, legislators, and diplomats, amongst many others, have the capacity to act in ways which are then attributed to the state. That the state is responsible for their actions does not absolve them of personal responsibility for what they have done.

This type of direct personal responsibility for the actions of the state is one of the characteristic features of citizenship. Citizens of the state enjoy a special type of relationship with the state. As we saw in chapter 3, a share in the control of the state is at the core of the institution of citizenship. Citizens consequently have a direct personal responsibility for the current actions and outcomes of these actions, a responsibility which is distinct from that conferred by mere state membership. Unlike a subject—whose opinions, in her capacity as a subject, have no influence on the state—the citizen possesses a capacity to participate in, and consequently to influence, the decisions of the state. As well as bearing responsibility for the state's actions as a member of the state, the citizen is also personally responsible for the part she has played in these actions. Citizens are most obviously responsible for those actions they support, but they are also responsible for actions they oppose or are neutral towards. Of course, the significance of this responsibility for the individual is defined by the attitude of the citizen towards the policy. A citizen who opposes a policy is responsible for the outcome of this opposition: for succeeding in stopping the measure or for failing to convince her fellow citizens she is right. It is better to have been a citizen who opposed a bad policy, and failed, than to have been a citizen who defended this measure—but it is far better still to have succeeded in stopping your state embarking on a misguided action.

The responsibility which state members bear for the activities of the state might appear unduly onerous. After all, sometimes state members are the victims of wrongs done by the state. To say that members of a persecuted group are responsible, in any sense, for their own persecution might appear both wrong and offensive. But the offence would rest on a misunderstanding of the implications of responsibility for those individuals. In this case, membership of the oppressive state would be a form of tragedy: not only are they persecuted, they are persecuted by a group of which they are members. That they are members of the state and, in this capacity, partly responsible for its actions, makes their plight worse, if anything. At some point, though, persecution by the state reaches a level at which it amounts to the exclusion of the persecuted group. When the institutions of the state make it plain that members of the persecuted group are not people whose well-being the state seeks to advance, the status of such people as state members is called into doubt.

When a person believes that their state is about to embark on a radically misguided course of action, she may wish to resign her membership; to cease to be part of the state, and to cease to bear responsibility for the state's actions. Escaping from the state can be surprisingly difficult. In simple social groups, merely deciding to abandon group membership is sufficient to exit the group. In complicated groups, like the state, the mechanisms of entry and exit are more formalized and, frequently, more difficult. States sometimes create mechanisms through which citizenship can be renounced, but normally a person can only abandon one state after she has secured membership of another. It is possible to be stuck with state membership: to be unable to escape the pull of the state.

(iii) A note on responsibility and non-state social groups

The state is not the only social group which can incur responsibilities in the sense discussed above. All social groups are capable of action, and all social groups can be responsible for events which occur in the world. Even very simple social groups can act, and can be properly considered responsible for the products of that action. A riotous mob is a simple social group. In some situations it may be useful to treat this group as a responsible agent, and then to regard the individual rioters as bearing responsibility for the actions of the group through their roles as group members. The question of the responsibility of social groups is ordinarily of more significance, however, when we consider social groups which are complex and long lasting. Churches, universities, trade unions, amongst many other types of group, are capable of acting and existing over time, in just the same fashion as the state. Sometimes these other social groups interact with the state. The state can become dominated by another group which forms an elite, controlling the mechanisms of government. In this situation the dominating group will continue to bear responsibility for its actions even once it has lost control of the state.

One type of group which often has a special connection with the state is the national group. David Miller identifies a number of features which characterize national groups.[25] Nations, on Miller's account, are a particular type of social group. Like other social groups, they consist of people who are bound together by a set of obligations and entitlements which are generated by their membership of the group. Like other social groups, the nation has a purpose—and, like the state, the nation is partly characterized by its embrace of a distinctive purpose. Nations, contends Miller, aspire towards some form of political self-government. This need not amount to a demand for autonomous statehood; nations can achieve self-government within a federated or devolved constitutional structure.[26] A social group which did not endorse this aspiration would not be, on Miller's account, a nation. Three further factors distinguish nations from other social groups. First, national groups have a special connection to a territory, a homeland which they aspire to control. Secondly, national groups enjoy historical continuity.[27] The nation stretches back into the past and possesses a history which includes heroes and villains, triumphs and defeats, but also projects forwards: the nation is expected to exist long after its current members have died. Nations have an inter-generational quality, connecting members in the past, the present and the future. Finally, the nation has a public culture, a shared set of understandings and social norms which are manifested in common values, religious convictions, art,

[25] See D. Miller, *On Nationality* (Oxford: Oxford University Press, 1995), ch 2; Miller, note 8 above, 124–8. See also N. MacCormick, 'A Kind of Nationalism' in N. MacCormick, *Questioning Sovereignty* (Oxford: Oxford University Press, 1999), 169–74 and M. Canovan, *Nationhood and Political Theory* (Cheltenham: Edward Elgar Publishing, 1996), ch 6.

[26] D. Miller, *On Nationality* (Oxford: Oxford University Press, 1995), 114–18.

[27] Though national histories often need to be taken with a pinch of salt: E. Hobsbawm, *Nations and Nationalism Since 1780* (Cambridge: Cambridge University Press, 1990), 12.

language, and, perhaps, ethnicity.[28] A nation need not be distinctive in all of these ways, nor need each member of the nation be characterized by each facet of the national character. What is required is that members share sufficient in common to be thought of as belonging to the national group: individuals can connect with the nation in a wide range of different ways.

Whereas the state requires a collection of institutions and a, more or less, formalized set of constitutional rules, the nation need not possess either of these things. A nation can exist without institutions and without a clear set of constituent rules. This can make it difficult for the nation to undertake actions. It will often be unclear whether it is the national group which has acted or whether the action was undertaken by members of that group in a personal capacity. The push of nations towards statehood may, in part, be explained by a desire to develop institutions which permit and facilitate more complicated actions by the group.

Miller identifies two models of collective responsibility which may, on occasion, render members of national groups responsible for its actions. First, there is the like-minded group model of collective responsibility.[29] In this model, members of the group who are not directly involved in wrongful actions may still be held responsible where they show solidarity with the actors, or help sustain a climate of opinion in which the conduct occurs. It is the existence of the group, the community, which creates the cultural atmosphere in which the acts can take place, and those who contribute to that culture are collectively responsible for the resulting actions. The second model advanced by Miller is the cooperative practice model of collective responsibility.[30] Under this model members of a group are collectively responsible for actions of the group where they receive a fair share of the benefits of group activity and have a fair chance to influence the group's activities.

Each of these two models can lead to a member being responsible for the acts of her national group. First, national groups are—by definition—groups within which members have special obligations towards each other and share a common culture. When individuals act on behalf of the nation, when their actions are manifestations of the values or culture of that group, all of the nation is implicated in their acts.[31] Secondly, national groups provide benefits to their members, benefits which include, but are not confined to, the provision of a culture which is regarded by members as being of value to them.[32] Where nationals receive a fair share of this benefit and have a fair chance to influence the actions of the group, they may rightly be held to be

---

[28] See further, C. Geertz, 'The Integrative Revolution: Primordial Sentiments and Civil Politics in the New States' in C. Geertz (ed), *Old Societies and New States* (London: Free Press of Glencoe, 1963) and S. Tierney, *Constitutional Law and National Pluralism* (Oxford: Oxford University Press, 2004), 34–40.

[29] Miller, note 8 above, 118. See also L. May, *Sharing Responsibility* (Chicago: Chicago University Press, 1992), ch 2.

[30] Miller, note 8 above, 119.

[31] *Ibid*, 127.

[32] *Ibid*, 131.

collectively responsible for its actions, under the cooperative practice model. Each of these explanations of collective responsibility could operate in a non-democratic national group, but, as Miller notes, the presence of democratic structures makes it more likely that the conditions of each model will be satisfied in a particular case.[33] Where democratic structures exist it will be easier to demonstrate that, under the like-minded group model, an action is genuinely a manifestation of the nation's culture. And, under the cooperative group model, it will be easier to demonstrate that, in a democracy, nationals had a fair chance to influence the decision to undertake the action.

The first thing to note about Miller's account of national responsibility is that these are models within which individuals may be rightly criticized for acts of the group, they deserve censure. In the like-minded group model, they have helped create a culture in which the acts have occurred. In the cooperative group model, the control over the group which they enjoy, coupled with a share of the benefits generated by that group, requires that they also shoulder a share of the burdens, the wrongful acts of the group. It is hard, though, to maintain the view that an individual is blameworthy when her national group undertakes actions which she strongly and publicly opposes. To say, for instance, that a white South African who spent her life fighting apartheid should be *blamed* for apartheid seems wrong, even if she is a member of the culture which produced this regime, or she has had a fair chance (alongside other members of her racially defined national group) to influence apartheid policies. Miller qualifies his account of collective responsibility by asserting that a person can escape blame where she has taken 'all reasonable steps to prevent the outcome occurring'.[34] But where such a person does not or cannot leave the group she may still, on Miller's account, be outcome responsible without being to blame for the acts. This means that, amongst other things, she may incur a liability to pay compensation later on. Nestling within Miller's discussion of collective responsibility is, then, a weaker account of group member responsibility which is similar to the discussion of the moral responsibility of group members, discussed earlier in this chapter.

Much of Miller's account of national responsibility is concerned with the troublesome question of when a national group can be said to have acted. When the national group controls a state, or possesses state-like institutions, this task is relatively easy: the group can act in the ways discussed in the previous chapter. When a national group does not possess these mechanisms this attribution will be far harder to prove. It is this, in part, perhaps, that leads Miller to present an account of group responsibility which turns on the blameworthiness of individuals in the group. When it can be said that a group without a more or less formalized institutional structure has acted, it must be the case that just about all of its members are personally implicated in its actions. It will be recalled that in our discussion of simple groups, back in chapter 2, the intentions ascribed to the group could, almost

---

[33] *Ibid*, 130–2.

[34] *Ibid*, 121.

without remainder, be ascribed to the members of the group as well. What the group intended and did, its members intended and did. A nation without an institutional structure resembles a simple group; in the oft-quoted words of Ernest Renan, the nation is a 'daily plebiscite'.[35] Like a simple group, membership depends on the interlocking beliefs of members. Like a simple group, the nation without an institution structure makes decisions through unanimity: its members agree, expressly or tacitly, to the action. For a large group, like a nation, these are significant restrictions on its ability to act.

These institutional problems do not disappear when the nation gains statehood. There will still be the question of whether these institutions are actually the institutions of the nation. For instance, it is an open question whether the acts done by the British state were undertaken through that state by a national group. Are the English, the Welsh and the Scottish nations responsible for the wrongs of imperialism, or can any—or all—of those peoples claim that this was the act of a state, the United Kingdom, which was not controlled by their national group? Even when there is a clear correlation between a state and a nation in terms of membership and territory, some within that nation may claim that the state was not 'really' a manifestation of the nation. The more, perhaps, an interlocutor pointed to the wrongs done by the state in the past, the more the nationalist might argue that this, in itself, showed that the vicious state could not have been an emanation of her virtuous nation. The acts of the Nazi regime are, a nationalist might contend, simply too evil to be attributed to the German nation.

The discussion in the previous paragraph sought to show how hard it is for a nation to act, and how easily claims that a nation has acted can be disputed. These arguments do not show that Miller is mistaken in his description of national responsibility, merely that the attribution of such responsibility will be a difficult and contested matter. In some situations the recognition that national groups are entities which can bear responsibility is of considerable importance. After a civil war, for example, the new state may bear no direct moral responsibility for acts during the war; it may be the product of a compromise between the warring parties. The national groups involved in the struggle, in contrast, may bear responsibility for the way they conducted the civil war. The new state may bear remedial responsibility for the injustices of the civil war, and may, consequently, need to recognize and investigate the responsibilities of these national groups.

Miller focuses on nations as bearers of responsibility for a number of reasons. One of these is that he questions the longevity of states[36]—the ability of states to evolve over time whilst maintaining their identity. The following two sections address this concern. It is argued that states are more durable than might at first be supposed and, moreover, that even when their identity changes they can still inherit responsibility for actions done before their creation.

---

[35] E. Renan, 'What is a Nation?' in A. Zimmern (ed), *Modern Political Doctrines* (Oxford: Oxford University Press, 1939), 203.

[36] Miller, note 8 above, 140–1.

THE CONTINUITY OF STATES

In *The Politics* Aristotle touches briefly on the question of the continuity of states. The question of when one state ends and another begins is, he contended, an important one. It is important, in part, because people need to know whether obligations they have incurred in the past are still owed to the current state.[37] Widening Aristotle's argument in the light of the previous sections, we might add that these obligations should be thought of as including those responsibilities which state members are burdened with as a result of their membership. The continuity of the state is important because it relates to the temporal scope of the responsibilities of that state, and, consequently, of the state's members. Debates about whether modern Germany possesses a constitutional continuity with the Nazi regime or whether modern South Africa is a continuation of apartheid South Africa, must be understood in this context. These are not dry academic questions, theoretical puzzles to while away seminars in the late afternoon, but debated political issues, arguments about how people should understand their membership of these states, and what follows from that membership. Having set up the topic so clearly, Aristotle rather disappointingly avoided answering it: the continuity of states, he wrote, did not raise any serious difficulties.[38] Unfortunately, in this claim, at least, he was mistaken. It is far from easy to determine the point at which an old state ends and a new state begins.

In previous chapters a picture of the state was built up which consisted of three ingredients—people, land, and rules—bound together in a complex relationship. Their combination produced at least four elements of the state: state members, a collection of governing institutions, a territory, and a set of rules—the constitution—which establishes and connects the first three. Change to the state can occur—indeed, regularly do occur—by variation of any or all of these four elements. Members come and go, institutions are created, reformed and abolished, territory is acquired and lost, and constitutional rules are formed, evolve and become ineffective.

Faced with this list of distinct but connected features, a person reflecting on the continuity of the state has two strategies. The first is to seek to isolate a single element from within these features and show it to be the core of the identity of the state. If we could identify an essential feature which gave each state its identity, something that remains constant over the life of the state, we could say with confidence when one state came to an end and another begins. It might be hard in practice to discern this golden thread, but it would, at least, be there: there would be an answer to be found. The second strategy is to embrace the diversity of the features of the state and acknowledge that they are all of importance. No one element lies at the core of the state: rather than a single golden thread, the continuity of the state is

---

[37] Aristotle, *The Politics and Constitution of Athens*, ed S. Everson (Cambridge: Cambridge University Press, 1996), III.III, 1276a7–13.

[38] *Ibid*, III.III, 1276a20–24.

to be found in the weaving together of strands of identity provided by members, institutions, territory and rules. No single thread need span the whole length of the rope. This strategy might lead us to doubt that there is always an answer to questions of the continuity of states: sometimes the significance of the connections between the old state and the purported new state might be unclear.

The most attractive advocate of the first strategy was Hans Kelsen. Kelsen, predictably enough, argued that a state retained its identity when its constitution remained constant, or when any changes which had occurred had been empowered by provisions of the constitution.[39] Each legal order—and consequently each state—had a defining *Grundnorm* at the root of its constitution: if all of the present laws of the state could be traced back to the *Grundnorm*, the continuity of the state could be demonstrated.[40] Change to the *Grundnorm* was, in effect, a revolution: the one state came to an end, and a new state was born.[41]

Kelsen's account of the continuity of the state was unsatisfactory in at least two respects. By tying the identity of the state to a single legal rule—even one as odd as the *Grundnorm*—we run the risk that comparatively minor events in the life of the state may be accorded exaggerated significance.[42] It could plausibly be argued, for instance, that the English case of *Factortame*[43] was a 'revolution' in Kelsen's sense—a change to the law made without legal authority[44]—but it would seem strange to claim that the United Kingdom became a new state in 1991. To take a more contentious example, some countries, such as Pakistan, have a long history of military usurpation. On some occasions the usurping army only breaks those constitutional rules necessary to permit it to exercise governing power. The membership of the state, its territory, the bulk of its institutions, and the bulk of its laws may be left unaffected, and sometimes the state's legal system may even contain laws which accommodate and limit such unconstitutional action.[45] Once again, it would seem artificial to say that each time such usurpation occurs a wholly new state emerges. Contrariwise,

---

[39] H. Kelsen, *General Theory of Law and State*, trans A. Wedberg (New York: Russell and Russell, 1946), 368. For a careful critique of this position in the context of the continuity of a legal system, a discussion also relevant to the continuity of the state, see J. Finnis, 'Revolutions and Continuity of Law' in A. W. B. Simpson, *Oxford Essays in Jurisprudence: Second Series* (Oxford: Oxford University Press, 1973) and P. Oliver, *The Constitution of Independence: The Development of Constitutional Theory in Australia, Canada and New Zealand* (Oxford: Oxford University Press, 2005), 11–14.

[40] H. Kelsen, 'Professor Stone and the Pure Theory of Law' (1965) 17 Stanford L Rev 1128, 1148–9.

[41] J. Harris, 'When and Why Does the *Grundnorm* Change?' (1971) 29 Cambridge LJ 103.

[42] See, for example, the discussion of the possible so-called 'disguised revolution' in New Zealand: Oliver, note 39 above, 260–5.

[43] *R v Secretary of State for Transport ex p Factortame (No 2)* [1991] 1 AC 603.

[44] See, for instance, W. Wade, 'Sovereignty—Revolution or Evolution?' (1996) 112 LQR 568, and, further, W. Wade 'The Basis of Legal Sovereignty' [1955] Cambridge LJ 172.

[45] Finnis, note 39 above, 46–7.

Kelsen's account fails to recognize apparently radical changes to the state's identity which can be reconciled with a continuing *Grundnorm*. Some modern Commonwealth countries were given their first constitutions by the British Parliament.[46] Sometimes symbolic acts of 'rebellion' were undertaken to break constitutional continuity[47] but on other occasions—as with Australia and Canada—it is possible to chart a direct connection back to the Imperial Parliament.[48] There is a risk, at least, that a myopic contemporary Kelsenian might conclude that Australia, Canada, and the United Kingdom were still three parts of a single state if no breach in the *Grundnorm* could be identified.

The arguments levelled against Kelsen demonstrate, once more, how far Kelsen's legalistic account of the state is removed from our ordinary understanding of that entity. The importance of the point is, though, reinforced when a connection is drawn between questions of state continuity and state responsibility. Kelsen's restrictive understanding of the continuity of the state has unattractive consequences for the continuity of its responsibility. Paralleling the criticisms of the previous paragraph, two further concerns emerge. First, the relative ease with which the *Grundnorm* can be broken creates the risk that it will be too easy for states to shed responsibility for their past actions. It is hard to believe that a state which has recently completed a vicious and unjust war could escape responsibility and start afresh simply by adopting a new constitution in violation of the provisions of the old. Secondly, it is sometimes implausible to claim that an oppressed region that has been granted independence by an imperial power remains (directly) responsible for the abuses undertaken on its territory by the former regime. Often, the newly liberated country begins with a clean slate. It would be odd to claim, for example, that the Pakistani or Indian states were (directly) responsible for the oppressive acts of the British state undertaken on their territories.[49]

The failure of Kelsen's strategy leads us towards the second option: the claim that the continuity of the state comes from the intertwining of a number of different features: members, institutions, territory, and rules. The state can accommodate some change in any, or all, of these aspects without losing its identity. Sudden fundamental change to any of these features throws the identity of the state into doubt, but, over time, even radical changes can occur. Any state which exists for a significant period of time will, quite naturally, experience a radical change in its membership. Its institutional structure will probably be subject to profound alteration as well. But provided that these changes are gradual, that there is a significant amount of continuity in membership and institutions, the identity of the state will not be challenged. If all of the membership changed overnight, or all of the existing

---

[46] Oliver, note 39 above, 33–53.

[47] K. Wheare, *The Constitutional Structure of the Commonwealth* (Oxford: Oxford University Press, 1960), ch 4.

[48] See the discussion in Finnis, note 39 above, 51–4.

[49] The position may be different where the new state is a colonial off-shoot of the old, a point discussed further below.

institutions were brought to an end and a whole new institutional structure was created, the claim that an old state had died and a new one had been brought into existence would look more attractive.

THE INHERITANCE OF THE STATE

Much of the chapter to this point has been spent discussing the implications of actions of the state for its current members. One aspect of this project has been to explain how current members can plausibly be said to share responsibility for actions of the state which were done before they, and perhaps before their parents, were born. This might be styled the inheritance of membership: the responsibilities which new members accrue from the actions of former members. It is not just new members who can inherit responsibilities, though; new states can also be burdened—or benefited—by the past. States can inherit responsibilities in two ways: through their connection with a parent state or through a remedial obligation to clean up the mess of a predecessor state.

When a territory gains constitutional independence and a new state is born, the story of its creation generally falls into one of two very rough groups. First, there are stories of liberation. In these situations an oppressed people is freed from an imperial power and gains its independence. The constitutional histories of numerous Asian and African countries fall into this category. Second, there are stories of gradual secession, where one part of a state slowly gains increasing autonomy over time until it finally becomes wholly distinct from the parent state. The constitutional histories of Australia and Canada are of this type.

In cases of liberation, the new state marks a sharp constitutional split with the old imperial state; it does not inherit direct responsibility for any of the past actions of its oppressor. In many cases this will be because there has been a radical change in membership at the point of liberation. The old imperial state regarded—more or less explicitly—the people of the liberated state as assets to be exploited, rather than as members whose interests should be supported and advanced. Along with this, new institutions are created—a president, a new supreme court, an army, and so forth—and these institutions are constituted by a new set of rules. In contrast, where a state emerges as a result of the gradual ceding of autonomy, members of the new state were commonly, in some form or other, also members of the old. Furthermore, the institutions of the new state are often continuations of institutions established by the parent state—their Parliaments, Prime Ministers, and court structures have existed for sometime. Finally, in these situations it is often difficult to point to the moment at which the new state broke free from its parent. With regimes which have gained independence through liberation there is normally a specific day when the new state was created. When a state emerges gradually, in contrast, the date at which the state was founded may be unclear: it is obvious that Australia is now a state, but it is not obvious when it gained statehood.[50]

---

[50] Oliver, note 39 above, chs 9 and 10, 269–78.

Deciding which of these categories a new state falls into will often be a tricky matter, and on occasion there may not be an answer to find—it may just be unclear whether the new state should be considered an offshoot of the old or whether it is a completely new polity. The answer does have implications for the responsibilities of the new state, however. Where the new state fits the liberation model, it does not bear responsibility for the actions of the imperial state within what is now its territory. Though there may be many connections between the imperial state and the new state, these are not sufficient to establish constitutional continuity. In contrast, when the new state is an offshoot of a former colonial power, it does inherit responsibility for actions of that power in its territory (and, perhaps, elsewhere too). Practically all of the members of the new state were members of the old, and they brought with them the responsibilities of that state. Both the United Kingdom and Australia are, then, responsible for the mistreatment of the aborigines prior to the turn of the twentieth century. Only Australia is responsible for their mistreatment after the birth of the Australian state.

A second way in which a state can inherit the responsibilities of an older state is when it inherits the responsibility to remedy the mistakes of its predecessor. This type of responsibility connects the outcome of future actions to the state, rather than asserting a connection to past acts. When a state emerges from oppression, from a civil war, or from some other sort of period of strife, the new state is burdened with the responsibility to redress past wrongs. Modern South Africa, for example, should probably not be thought of as a continuation of its apartheid forerunner. There has been a radical change in the nature of membership of the state, and a profound change in the institutions of the state. It is not, therefore, directly responsible for the immoralities of the apartheid era. It is remedially responsible, however, for redressing these wrongs. Contemporary South Africa is responsible for investigating the actions of the old regime, removing benefits which certain people immorally (though perhaps legally) acquired through apartheid, and compensating their victims. South Africa's success as a state should, in part, be judged on how it acquits these tasks, tasks which fall upon it because of the misconduct of its predecessor.

CONCLUSION

This chapter has been concerned with the meaning and implications of claims that the state is 'responsible' for things that occur in the world, in particular, the significance that such claims have for the members of the state. It has not address a further, and very important, issue: what should be done once this type of responsibility has been established. This leads us to questions of punishment, restorative justice, and the public acknowledgment of guilt. To say that, for example, the United Kingdom is responsible for the wrongs committed in its imperial past does not conclude the discussion: rather, it opens up a further debate about what the United Kingdom should now do about these wrongs. This brings forward yet another sense of responsibility, where responsibility relates to the proper reaction of the agent and others to a finding of outcome responsibility. It is this sense of responsibility which is used when people talk of states evading or escaping their responsibilities.

This further question cannot be satisfactorily addressed here. It would require a complete political theory, one which would illuminate the state's obligations in the light of a general model of justice and rights. Such a model would need to explain what people are entitled to—both from the state and from other individuals—and what should be done when things are taken from them. It should not be thought, though, that the answer will lie solely in the realm of corrective justice. We cannot move directly from concluding that the state is responsible for a wrong to the conclusion that it must restore wrongfully acquired benefits or compensate for the harms it has caused. There are at least two further considerations which can qualify the demands of corrective justice.

First, the demands of justice must be tempered with realism. For the state to undertake any activity at all it must maintain some level of stability and control. For example, when a state emerges from a period of civil war, anarchy, or dictatorship, uncomfortable compromises are often made: cruel dictators are granted immunity from prosecution and awarded generous pensions; tacit or express agreements are reached where by the atrocities committed under the previous regime are pardoned or ignored. These negotiated compromises are (morally) justified when, either, they are necessary for the emergence of a decent state, or when the cost—in terms of innocent lives and property—of fighting for a decent state would be excessive. A lesson, perhaps, of the Iraq war is that it is sometimes preferable to secure regime change through bribery and negotiation rather than the exertion of force—even if this means that former dictators escape justice.

Secondly, considerations of corrective justice are sometimes cross-cut by considerations of distributive justice. In some, uncertain, way the claims of those who have been wronged by the state must be balanced against the present needs of the members of that state. Even if it was concluded, for example, that the original occupation of Australia was immoral and that—in corrective terms—the land should be returned to the aborigines, this claim would have to be assessed against the needs of the present non-aboriginal population who currently live on the land.

9

Legal Pluralism

So far this book has focused on the state and has emphasized the interplay between legal and non-legal rules. For the duration of this chapter, both the focus and the emphasis shift: this chapter concentrates on the legal order, and reflects upon the interaction of legal rules. An understanding of law and legal orders is crucial to an understanding of the state. Whilst not all legal orders need be the legal orders of states, all states must possess at least one legal order through which state institutions can communicate with state members. Legal pluralism, as described in this chapter, often, though not invariably, arises as a result of a disagreement about the constitutional ordering of the state or a disagreement over the existence of a state. Legal pluralism may be the product of a dispute between state institutions, where multiple institutions claim to have the final say about the content of the law. It may also be the product of a dispute about the existence of a state, where one political entity claims to be a state, whilst a second political entity claims that the putative state comes under its control.

This chapter seeks to advance a modest account of legal pluralism and its significance for states. It is a modest account because it has so few enemies: many contemporary writers on jurisprudence, such as Joseph Raz and John Finnis, would probably be comfortable with its claims. It is, however, sufficiently controversial to be interesting: Herbert Hart, Hans Kelsen, and Ronald Dworkin would all dissent from its conclusions. This controversy enables the chapter to avoid the central problem that has beset recent work on pluralism: its remarkable popularity. Some recent writers have turned modesty into a vice: 'pluralism' has become so thin a theory that virtually all respectable writers on legal philosophy would endorse their claims. If everyone is a pluralist, legal pluralism ceases to be an interesting theory—it amounts to little more than the application of standard models of legal orders to a new factual situation.

This chapter will argue that a legal order can contain multiple rules of recognition that lead to the order containing multiple, unranked, legal sources. These rules of recognition are inconsistent, and there is the possibility that they will, in turn, identify inconsistent rules addressed to individuals. In addition, pluralist orders lack a legal mechanism able to resolve the inconsistency; there is no higher constitutional body that can resolve this dispute through adjudication or legislation. Consequently, pluralist legal orders contain a risk, which need not be realized, of constitutional crisis; of officials being compelled to choose between their loyalties to different public institutions. There are, then, three claims that must be explained and defended if this pluralist account of a legal order is to appear plausible and interesting. First, the meaning of 'inconsistent' in this context, and whether it is possible for legal rules to be inconsistent. Secondly, whether a legal order can contain legally irreconcilable inconsistent rules of recognition. Thirdly, it must be shown that legal orders with inconsistent rules of recognition are more than rare, brief, aberrations; that the pluralist model of legal orders is helpful in explaining important features of common legal orders. This task will be accomplished by a close examination of the Rhodesian crisis of 1965, which will be presented as a brief but clear example of a pluralist legal order, and then the model will be applied to the more opaque question of the relationships between European and domestic legal orders. Hopefully, the utility of the abstract jurisprudential tools developed in the first half of the chapter will be demonstrated by the practical conundrums resolved in the second.

THE NATURE OF LEGAL PLURALISM

In the 1970s and 1980s a group of academics emerged who described themselves as 'legal pluralists'.[1] They insisted on the significance of rules that were outside the traditional boundaries of 'law' as conventionally understood; norms that were not found in cases or statutes. Early writers were preoccupied with the integration of customary law into the legal system; in particular, the ways in which imperial legal systems had accommodated, incorporated, and limited religious and tribal law.[2] Socio-legal writers paralleled the trend, focusing on the rules that condition people's lives and refusing, or attempting to refuse, to distinguish between 'legal' and 'non-legal' rules.[3] Though providing a healthy antidote to myopic concentration on domestic law as a form of social ordering, the contribution of these 'pluralists' was rather less controversial than they supposed. Though they frequently defined themselves against the work of established writers on jurisprudence—in particular Hart and Kelsen—much of what they asserted was compatible with those they sought to oppose. The suggestion that a legal system can recognize and incorporate rules from other legal orders was hardly revolutionary. Kelsen had already explained how a legal system could incorporate the rules of a separate system in the context of a discussion of conflict of laws cases.[4] In Kelsen's work the apparent conundrum of the

---

[1] See generally, J. Griffiths, 'What is Legal Pluralism?' (1986) 24 Journal of Legal Pluralism 1 and D. J. Galligan, *Law in Modern Society* (Oxford: Oxford University Press, 2006), chs 9 and 10.

[2] For instance, M. B. Hooker, *Legal Pluralism—An Introduction to Colonial and Neo-Colonial Laws* (Oxford: Oxford University Press, 1975).

[3] S. Moore, 'Law and Social Change: the Semi-Autonomous Social Field as an Appropriate Subject of Study' (1973) 7 *Law and Society Review* 719; Griffiths, note 1 above, 38–9; see also E. Ehrlich, *Fundamental Principles of the Sociology of Law,* trans W. L. Moll, (New York: Russell and Russell, 1936).

[4] H. Kelsen, *General Theory of Law and the State*, trans A. Wedberg (Cambridge Mass: Harvard University Press, 1945), 243–8.

courts of one state applying the law of another is quickly resolved: there is a rule of the domestic system that identifies and validates the foreign law, and, in so doing, transforms it into a rule of the domestic system. Exactly the same applies when the legal order recognizes tribal or religious laws: they are recognized by a rule of the national legal system and become part of it. Further, the claim that other normative systems bear on an individual and have a practical impact as great as, or greater than, law is also commonplace. Again, Kelsen had engaged with this objection.[5] Though it is unarguable that the rules that apply to a person will have many sources, law has essential qualities that set it apart from other sets of rules—and much of the rest of Kelsen's work was an attempt to outline these special features. These differences, of course, need not imply that law is more important than other normative systems. It is telling that legal pluralists often felt the need to then distinguish between law, by which they meant all of the norms that bore on a person, and a sub-category of 'state law' or 'legal propositions' which would have been roughly synonymous with law in Kelsen's sense.[6] There is, then, a suspicion that the dispute is rather shallow; that the legal pluralists have used the word 'law' to signify a wider set of things to those identified by Kelsen, but that, under a different label, they share a similar concept with him.

An alternative strand of legal pluralism focused on inconsistency, or contradiction,[7] between rules. Pluralism, on this account, claims that there can be contradictory 'legal mechanisms' that apply to single factual situations.[8] Once again, this form of pluralism might be less controversial that it first appears. As Griffiths points out, many of the supposed contradictions identified by these writers are resolvable.[9] For instance, Vanderlinden presents the legal distinction drawn between the clergy and the laity in the middle ages as an example of a legal contradiction explicable within a pluralist model. In fact, all that the example illustrates is that the clergy enjoyed special privileges within the ordinary legal system. As a consequence of this privilege, different rules applied to the clergy and laity: no contradiction has been shown.

---

[5] *Ibid*, 24–8, discussing Ehrlich, note 3 above.

[6] See, for example, M. Chiba, 'Other Phases of Legal Pluralism in the Contemporary World' (1998) 11 Ratio Juris 228 and A. Hellum, 'Actor Perspectives on Gender and Legal Pluralism in Africa' in H. Petersen and H. Zahle (eds), *Legal Polycentricity: Consequences of Pluralism in Law* (Aldershot: Dartmouth Publishing, 1994), 15.

[7] For reasons explained later I prefer 'inconsistency' to 'contradiction'—though for present purposes they can be used interchangeably.

[8] J. Vanderlinden, 'Le Pluralisme Juridique: Essai de Synthèse' in J. Gilissen (ed), *Le Pluralisme Juridique* (Brussels: Université de Bruxelles, 1971), 19. See also: S. Merry, 'Legal Pluralism' (1988) 22 Law and Society 869, 870; R. de Lange, 'Divergence, Fragmentation and Pluralism', in H. Petersen and H. Zahle (eds), *Legal Polycentricity: Consequences of Pluralism in Law*, (Aldershot: Dartmouth Publishing, 1994); A. Arnaud, 'Legal Pluralism and the Building of Europe' in the same volume; N. MacCormick, 'Juridical Pluralism and the Risk of Constitutional Conflict' in N. MacCormick, *Questioning Sovereignty* (Oxford: Oxford University Press, 1999).

[9] Griffiths, note 1 above, 12–14.

Further, it is equally unremarkable to find contradictions arising between the rules of different normative systems: all sensible accounts of law leave space for conflicts between law and morality. The lesson of these examples is not that contradiction is not central to pluralism, but that it is actually quite hard to find examples of genuine and interesting legal contradictions.

Most recent writing on pluralism in the context of the European Union seems closer to the first strand than to the second; however, elements of both are required if a distinctive pluralist account is to be articulated. In what follows, a pluralist model of a legal order will require both multiple sources of law, and, also, the possibility of inconsistency between legal rules. In the following two sections these claims will be explored further, and contrasted with the work of Hart, Kelsen, and Dworkin.

INCONSISTENT LEGAL RULES

Two arguments have been advanced against the very possibility of inconsistent rules existing within legal orders, both of which have their origins in the work of Hans Kelsen.[10] First, that ranking rules and other legal principles always eliminate apparent inconsistencies. Secondly, that in seeking to understand the law we ought to assume that rules cannot be set in inconsistency: we should, or, perhaps, must, treat the law as a meaningful whole and not as a collection of disparate rules.

(i) The claim that ranking rules always eliminate apparent inconsistencies

Kelsen's first argument against the possibility of inconsistency was that legal systems invariably included principles to resolve such problems. Rules providing for the hierarchical ranking of legal sources, or, when this ran out, the maxim *lex posterior derogate priori,* ensured that valid legal norms could not be set in inconsistency.[11] This assertion can be swiftly disposed of—these ranking rules are as much a matter of positive law as any other rule and law makers are able to alter them.[12] Consequently, whilst it will often be possible to resolve apparent inconsistencies through these rules, this need not always be the case. Sometimes the ranking rules may not provide an answer,

---

[10] Kelsen, note 4 above, 407–8; H. Kelsen, *The Pure Theory of Law,* trans M. Knight, (California: University of California Press, 1967), 205–8. Kelsen abandoned these claims, though he never fully explained the reasons for his change of mind: J. Harris, 'Kelsen and Normative Consistency' in R. Tur and W. Twining (eds), *Essays on Kelsen* (Oxford: Oxford University Press, 1986), S. Munzer, 'Validity and Legal Conflicts' (1973) 82 Yale LJ 1140, 1164.

[11] H. Kelsen, *The Pure Theory of Law,* trans M. Knight (California: University of California Press, 1967), 206.

[12] S. Paulson, 'On the Status of the *Lex Posterior* Derogating Rule', in R. Tur and W. Twining (eds), *Essays on Kelsen* (Oxford: Oxford University Press, 1986). See further, P. Oliver, *The Constitution of Independence: The Development of Constitutional Theory in Australia, Canada and New Zealand* (Oxford: Oxford University Press, 2005), 305–6. For an example of such judicial reflection, see the discussion in *Thoburn v Sunderland District Council* [2003] QB 151 of statutory hierarchy.

or may themselves be inconsistent. Indeed, even the *lex posterior* maxim is not beyond dispute: where two rules in a statute contradict precedence is now given to the later provision, but Lord Ellesmere claimed precedence should be given to the earlier.[13]

(ii) The claim that the logical principle of non-contradiction compels us to conclude the apparent inconsistencies do not exist

Kelsen's second argument was more subtle. In seeking an understanding of law the logical principle of non-contradiction demanded that we not conclude inconsistent rules governed the same situation.[14] There are three ways in which this claim could be fleshed out. The first elaboration would take Kelsen as claiming that principles of logic necessarily form part of the substance of all normative orders; that the principle of non-contradiction is, in some sense, a rule necessarily present in all normative systems. The second elaboration would take Kelsen as claiming that all forms of legal interpretation require certain fundamental assumptions, which include the principle of non-contradiction; on this argument, the principle of non-contradiction is, somehow, inherently part of every legal order. The third elaboration would take Kelsen as claiming that as judges are bound to resolve the case before them only one of the two purportedly inconsistent rules can be held valid. This claim could either be taken as a consequence of either of the first two elaborations, or as a separate claim resting on the rather unKelsenian assertion that the law is what the courts will declare it to be. The second and third arguments are eerily similar to those advanced by Ronald Dworkin, in his claim that legal problems have 'right' answers. If Dworkin is taken as claiming that all, rather than most, legal questions have a right answer, he is also compelled to deny the possibility of inconsistent legal rules.[15]

(a) The first elaboration: that the principle of non-contradiction necessarily forms part of all normative orders

The first elaboration of Kelsen's objection against inconsistent rules arising within legal orders built on the claim that all normative orders must embody the principle of non-contradiction. This might be glossed as a version of the old adage that 'ought implies can'. There are two objections to this claim.

First, it is not immediately obvious why it should be thought that principles of logic, in particular the principle of non-contradiction, should be applied to ethical reasoning. This is a proposition that needs to be argued for rather than just assumed. Those who seek to introduce the principle must either explain how truth values can be attributed to moral imperatives, or explain how questions of the logic of norms

---

[13] Discussed in L. Fuller, *The Morality of Law* (rev edn, New Haven: Yale University Press, 1969), 68.

[14] Kelsen, note 10 above.

[15] R. Dworkin, 'On Gaps in the Law' in P. Amselek and N. MacCormick (eds), *Controversies about Law's Ontology* (Edinburgh: Edinburgh University Press, 1991); R. Dworkin, 'No Right Answer?' in P. M. S. Hacker and J. Raz (eds), *Law, Morality and Society* (Oxford: Oxford University Press, 1978); Munzer, note 10 above, 1156–62.

can be distinguished from questions of their truth.[16] Without wishing to be dragged too deeply into these metaphysical conundrums, the presence of the principle of non-contradiction must depend to a considerable extent on the particular ethical framework adopted. There are certainly some moral systems that lack space for inconsistent obligations. Most obviously, a utilitarian would not accept that a person can be faced with inconsistent moral obligations. Ought always implies can in the strongest sense in this moral universe: ultimately, there is only one obligation—the duty to maximize happiness. However, other ethicists do see a place for inconsistent moral obligations. Most strongly, some have argued that a person may be faced with a direct contradiction: be both obligated to act, and obligated not to act. So, for example, as King, Agamemnon is under an obligation to sacrifice his daughter to save the campaign, whilst as a father he is under an obligation never to harm his children.[17] More weakly, some have argued a person can be faced with moral dilemmas in which it is impossible to fulfil two simultaneous obligations that are empirically contradictory.[18] For example, where a life-guard sees two drowning swimmers, but only has time to save one. To counter the claim that all normative orders must contain the principle of non-contradiction, we can advance these theorists as evidence that moral frameworks can operate without the principle. At the very least, these examples show that the principle is not a necessary part of every plausible normative system. It appears that the hope of establishing a system of deontic logic independent of particular systems of moral philosophy is too ambitious, and that the principle of non-contradiction need not be present in every plausible normative order.

One way around this problem is to recast deontic logic as the logic of propositions of morality. G. A. von Wright experimented with using propositions about norms as the basis of deontic logic.[19] Whilst it might not be possible to talk of the truth or falsity of a norm, it is certainly possible to talk of the truth or falsity of a proposition about a norm. So, the proposition 'drivers are under an obligation not to park on double yellow-lines' cannot stand alongside the proposition 'drivers are not under an obligation not to park on double yellow lines'.[20] Unless these statements describe the

---

[16] J. Jørgensen, 'Imperatives and Logic' (1937–38) 7 *Erkenntnis* 288; S. Coyle, 'The Possibility of Deontic Logic' (2002) 15 *Ratio Juris* 294. For as example of the first strategy, see: G. Volpe, 'A Minimalist Solution to Jørgensen's Dilemma' (1999) 12 *Ratio Juris* 59. For an example of the second, see: G. von Wright, *Logical Studies* (London: Routledge, 1957), vi.

[17] P. Foot, 'Moral Realism and Moral Dilemma' (1983) 80 Journal of Philosophy 379.

[18] T. Nagel, 'The Fragmentation of Value' in T. Nagel, *Mortal Questions* (Cambridge: Cambridge University Press, 1979); B. Williams, 'Ethical Consistency' in B. Williams, *Problems of the Self* (Cambridge: Cambridge University Press, 1973). Neither Nagel nor Williams distinguish between the stronger and weaker forms of moral inconsistency presented here. See Munzer, note 10 above, 1144, applying the distinction to legal inconsistency.

[19] See G. A. von Wright, *Norm and Action* (London: Routledge, 1963), viii; G. A. von Wright, note 16 above, 32.

[20] This also holds for law: the propositions 'there is a rule obligating doing x' and 'there is not a rule obligating doing x' cannot both be true.

products of different normative systems, they are set in contradiction: it cannot both be the case that there exists and that there does not exist such an obligation. In this limited sense, then, the principle of non-contradiction does apply to both ethics and to law. But although the principle of non-contradiction applies to assertions about the existence of norms, this does not show that the principle applies to norms themselves. It could still be the case that 'drivers are under an obligation not to park on double yellow-lines' and also that 'drivers are under an obligation to park on double yellow-lines'.[21] Here, the two obligations conflict, rather than two statements about a single obligation. If deontic logic is confined to propositions about norms rather than applying to norms themselves, it is hard to see how it could help clarify ethical reasoning, beyond the assistance already provided by propositional logic.[22]

Secondly, even if it is the case that the principle of non-contradiction necessarily applies in systems of ethics it does not follow from this that it necessarily applies in systems of law; von Wright expressly excluded legal systems from its reach.[23] Though it may be desirable that rules within a legal order do not contradict each other, this, according to von Wright, is not a logical truth about such orders. Legal systems are artificial normative structures, and, as such, are not constrained to comply with all the dictates of logic.

(b) The second elaboration: that the principle of non-contradiction necessarily forms part of all legal orders

This second objection to the claim that all normative systems must contain the principle of non-contradiction shades into a response to the alternative reading of Kelsen's objection to contradiction. The alternative reading took Kelsen as claiming that there was something special about legal orders that entailed the principle of non-contradiction operated within them. It could be the case that even though the principle is not a necessary part of all normative orders, it is still a necessary part of all legal orders. Indeed, some closure rules do have an unusual place within the legal system. Raz has shown how the closure rule permitting all that is not forbidden by law is inherent in all legal systems.[24] This is a maxim that flows from the practice of identifying legal rules from legal sources: the law-applying institution needs to identify a reason to act, but does not need to identify a reason not to act. Where there is no rule forbidding an action the law-applying institution has no basis for punishing the action, and the action is permitted. Perhaps a similar argument could be made for the principle of non-contradiction, showing it to be rooted in the very practice of law? It seems unlikely: it is hard to imagine how the principle of non-contradiction could be deduced from the practice of legal reasoning. It is not a complete closure

---

[21] So, to transpose into the legal world again, 'there is a rule obligating doing x' and 'there is a rule obligating not doing x' could stand.

[22] Coyle, note 16 above.

[23] G. A. von Wright, 'Deontic Logic' (1999) 12 Ratio Juris 26, 32–3.

[24] J. Raz, 'Legal Reasons, Sources and Gaps', in J. Raz, The Authority of Law (Oxford University Press, 1979), esp. 75–7. Though the point is not beyond dispute: see Aristotle, Nicomachean Ethics, 1138a7.

rule: though it tells us that contradiction is not permitted, it does not tell us which of the two contradictory rules should be preferred. As the answer to this question will depend on the particular system in which the inconsistency has arisen, there is no room for a general legal principle against contradiction. Furthermore, even if the maxim decreeing that all that is not forbidden is permitted is a *prima facie* principle of every legal system, it is certainly not a necessary rule of a legal system. It is possible, if difficult, to imagine a system functioning without such a rule.[25] Similarly, the principle of non-contradiction might not form part of the legal order, or, perhaps, some inconsistencies, in particular over the jurisdiction of constitutional institutions, might lie beyond the power of the courts to resolve.

(c) The third elaboration: inconsistent rules cannot exist because judges are compelled to resolve legal disputes

The final interpretation of Kelsen's objection to contradiction between laws read him as claiming that such situations were impossible because judges are compelled to reach a decision in each case put before them. In essence, the law is what the judges say it is, and as the court must always reach decisions about disputes there is no room for contradictory rules. Setting aside the question of whether it is plausible to imagine Kelsen lapsing into this unsophisticated form of realism, and taking the objection on its own terms, a few arguments can be advanced against the realist position. These points will not show the objection fails: a convinced realist can always evade criticism at the cost of increasing artificiality. The best that can be done is to try to explain why the objection appears attractive, and illustrate some situations where the realist position is less persuasive. A spectrum of positions can be identified. At one extreme, there are those cases in which a superficial contradiction can be resolved through the application of normal principles of interpretation. A citizen faced with a superficial contradiction between an old statute forbidding an act and a new statute permitting it can apply ordinary principles of statutory interpretation and resolve the conflict. In slightly more difficult cases the dispute may reach the court, but this may not show that there was a contradiction within the law: perhaps the dispute is tricky, but a 'right answer' can be found. These situations shade into cases where the contradiction cannot be resolved through the application of principles of interpretation and hierarchy, but the court is competent to resolve the conflict by choosing to prioritize one rule over another. It would be rare for a court to acknowledge that it was exercising its law-making, rather than interpreting, function in these circumstances.[26] The important difference between these cases and those discussed earlier is that when the courts act creatively the citizen cannot know how the dispute will be resolved in advance of the decision: for the citizen, but not for the court, there is an irresolvable conflict. Finally, there are those cases in which the

[25] Perhaps the system could grant a law-making discretion to the judge to decide whether any new action was forbidden or permitted.

[26] J. Finnis, 'The Fairy Tale's Moral' (1999) 115 LQR 170. But see where a court identifies its own earlier contradictory decisions, and claims the right to choose between them: note 29 below.

court is not competent to resolve the inconsistency. This may be because only a higher court is able to resolve the conflict or, more dramatically, because the conflict centres on the relative authority of the court and another body. The example of parliamentary privilege, discussed later in this chapter, is a case where the dispute could be resolved by Parliament, but neither the Commons nor the courts are free to determine the question.[27] In more extreme cases some inconsistencies may not be resolvable by any institution within the constitution.[28]

The realist objection to the possibility of inconsistency is attractive because it captures the frequent possibility of resolving such situations through interpretation and application of the hierarchy of rules. Most legal questions have determinate legal answers. However, the realist position has a number of uncomfortable consequences. First, the realist struggles to distinguish situations where there is a pre-existing legal answer to an apparent contradiction, and those where there is not. Sometimes apparent contradictions do not need the creative intervention of the courts in order to be resolved. Here, the law is not what the courts say it is, but rather may be recognized by citizens, sometimes with the help of lawyers, confident in the knowledge that the courts would reach the identical conclusion. Secondly, the realist objection cannot explain those, rare, situations where the court admits that its earlier decisions were contradictory, or where it declares itself incompetent to resolve the inconsistency. Even assuming that the law is what the courts declare it to be, if they confess that before their decision the rules were set in contradiction it seems odd to be forced to claim that they were mistaken about the relationship of the rules.[29] The objection becomes even stronger if the court then declines to resolve the conflict, and sends it for consideration by another body.[30] Thirdly, and perhaps most strongly, the realist position prevents us from discussing situations where the conflict involves the competency of the court. Here, even if the court purports to resolve the contradiction it may be relying on the very power that lies in dispute. As Peter Oliver has noted, it is a common but regrettable error for constitutional lawyers to assume all hypothetical questions of law are already governed by a rule.[31] It would be ironic if our realist, with her emphasis on the political position of the judge, was unable to discuss these interesting jurisdictional struggles.[32] It will be these conflicts that form the principal focus of the following section.

---

[27] Note that where the court is able, in its law-making capacity, to choose between contradictory rules, the citizen is placed in the same position as the Commons and courts in the privilege example. A resolution is possible, but the law is contradictory pending the creative intervention of another body.

[28] See discussion of Rhodesia and EU below.

[29] The Court of Appeal reserves the right to choose between its own conflicting earlier decisions: *Young v Bristol Aeroplane Co* [1944] KB 718, 726; R. Cross and J. Harris, *Precedent in English Law* (4th edn, Oxford: Oxford University Press, 1991), 144–5.

[30] Fuller, note 13 above, 112.

[31] Oliver, note 12 above, 313.

[32] H. L. A. Hart, *The Concept of Law* (2nd edn, Oxford: Oxford University Press, 1994), 153.

(iii) The truth in Kelsen's claim that legal rules cannot be inconsistent

The meaning of contradiction in the context of legal rules is far from straightforward. Contradiction is a quality of a pair of propositions: its most obvious application is to statements of fact. When two factual propositions are in contradiction one of them must be false: they could not both be correct in any possible world. A person who believed two contradictory factual statements ought to work towards abandoning her belief in one of them.[33] The phenomenon of contradiction is therefore closely tied to the principle of non-contradiction: the presence of contradiction implies a flaw in our reasoning process, or our understanding of the world. Those who believe that legal rules can contradict consequently face a further challenge to those discussed in the previous section. If the principle of non-contradiction does not apply within legal orders, in what sense is it meaningful to talk of legal rules being set in contradiction? A challenger might claim that the advocate of contradiction within legal orders is hoisted by her own petard: that 'contradictions' between legal rules can exist, persist, and need not be evidence of a mistake of reasoning, shows that these are not really 'contradictions' at all. This section of the chapter will attempt to mollify this challenger. Though 'contradiction' does not carry the same implications in law as it does when found in statements of fact, it is still meaningful to talk of contradictory legal rules.

Those who accept the possibility of contradictory moral or legal imperatives face the challenge of explaining what contradiction means in this context.[34] If the concept of contradiction is detached from its meaning in logic, what does it mean to say that two norms are contradictory? Bernard Williams tackled this problem by shifting normative statements into their descriptive equivalents, which might be termed compliance statements.[35] So, the normative statement 'Albert must not kill Alberta' is transposed to 'Albert did not kill Alberta', which is contrary to the rule 'Albert must kill Alberta' transposed to 'Albert did kill Alberta.' This device allows us to talk of contradictory rules without assuming these logical concepts can be directly applied to normative statements. The transposition also makes clear that the contradiction between rules lies not in their inherent truth or falsity, but in their subjects' inability to fully comply with the rules: a claim that both had been fully complied with would necessarily be untrue. Three problems arise from Williams' shift.

First, whilst the compliance statements may be logically contradictory, it should be emphasized that the norms themselves are not set in this logical relationship. This

---

[33] Though as Raz notes, we should not sacrifice truth for consistency: a partially true set of inconsistent propositions is preferable to a consistent set of false propositions. J. Raz, 'The Relevance of Coherence' in J. Raz, *Ethics in the Public Domain* (rev edn, Oxford: Oxford University Press, 1995), 285.

[34] A problem noted by Foot: Foot, note 17 above, 391.

[35] B. Williams, 'Consistency and Realism' in B. Williams, *Problems of the Self* (Cambridge: Cambridge University Press, 1973). Utilized in Hart: H. L. A. Hart, 'Kelsen's Doctrine of the Unity of Law' in H. L. A. Hart, *Essays in Jurisprudence and Philosophy* (Oxford: Oxford University Press, 1983), 324–7.

takes us back to our earlier discussion of deontic logic, and its slippage from the logic of ethics into the logic of ethical propositions. Williams has circumnavigated the question of the possibility of contradictory norms rather than answered the problem.[36] However, this chapter will assume that the connection between the contradictory rules and their compliance statements is sufficient to allow us to talk of contradiction in the context of norms without having to accept the consequences for this relationship that would flow from their existence in propositional logic.

Secondly, and leading on from this, the relationship between the inconsistent rules and their respective inconsistent compliance statements need not be identical. Logicians distinguish between propositions that are contradictory and those that are contrary. Two propositions are contradictory when if one is true the other must be false. Two propositions are contraries where it cannot be the case that both are true, but it could yet be the case that both are false. In the example given earlier the inconsistent rules appeared to be contraries. Though 'Albert *must* kill Alberta' appears to run against the obligation 'Albert *must not* kill Alberta', it could yet be the case that 'Albert *has a permission* to kill Alberta'. In contrast, the compliance statements are contradictories. It is either the case that 'Albert *did kill* Alberta', or it is the case that 'Albert *did not* kill Alberta'. If one of these statements is true the other must be false. So, contrary rules do not generate contrary compliance statements. This might cause doubt as to whether it is useful to talk of contrary and contradictory rules: perhaps in the normative sphere all that can be shown is that joint compliance is impossible, the nuances of the difference between the two forms of inconsistency do not hold. Indeed, neither Hart nor Kelsen chose to make this distinction, preferring just to talk of conflict or solely of contradiction.[37] However, the relationships between normative propositions appear to parallel the relationships found between descriptive propositions.[38]

Thirdly, and perhaps as a consequence of the second difficulty, permissions cause particular problems for Williams' move: though it is easy to transpose mandatory rules into their respective compliance statements, permissions are more complicated. This may explain why it has sometimes been claimed, mistakenly, that two permissions can not be inconsistent.[39] Hart accepted that a mandatory rule and a permissive rule could be inconsistent. So, 'Derek *must not* eat the sweet' and 'Derek *has permission* to eat the sweet' are contraries. Transposed into their relative compliance statements, we find: 'Derek *did not* eat the sweet' set against 'Derek *either did or did not* eat the sweet', which are in contradiction.[40] Though the mandatory rule and the permissive rule could be complied with in a compatible fashion, full compliance

---

[36] As he recognizes: Williams, note 35 above, 193–5.

[37] Though Foot assumes that there is room for the two sorts of conflict between normative statements: Foot, note 17 above, 390.

[38] G. H. Von Wright, 'Deontic Logic: A Personal View' (1999) Ratio Juris 26, 28. Von Wright notes that 'possible', 'impossible', and 'necessary', seem to parallel 'some', 'no' and 'all'—as do, for our purposes, 'permission', 'must' and 'must not'.

[39] Hart makes this claim: note 35 above, 327. Munzer, note 10 above, 1146.

[40] Assuming, of course, that the second compliance statement is indivisible.

with each is impossible. If this is accepted, then two permissive rules may be inconsistent in a similar sense. So, 'Derek *has permission* to eat the sweet' and 'George *has permission* to eat the sweet' are contraries. Transformed into compliance statements, we find: 'Derek *either did or did not* eat the sweet' and 'George *either did or did not* eat the sweet'. Again, whilst there are ways in which, if divided, these statements are compatible, if they are taken in their entirety they are set in contradiction.

Following Williams, then, when I assert that two rules are inconsistent, I mean that complete joint compliance with each rule is logically impossible. This can be tested by transposing the rule into its equivalent compliance statement. Whilst it is appropriate to judge assertions of the possibility of joint compliance as being true or false, I do not assume that the norms themselves that generate these compliance statements are susceptible to attributions of truth-value. Consequently, I will describe the relationship between pairs of contrary or contradictory rules as one of inconsistency, which is not intended to imply that one of the imperatives must be invalid or untrue.

(iv) A note on Lon Fuller's doubts about the desirability of inconsistent rules

Though these points tackle the particular arguments advanced by Kelsen, they may still leave advocates of the principle of non-contradiction unsatisfied. They may feel that though it is possible for inconsistent rules to arise, their presence is a standing criticism of the order that contains them, a blow against the rule of law.[41] Any pairing of rules that puts the citizen in a position where she cannot help but fall foul of one of their demands seems problematic; running against law's aspiration to guide conduct. Even if the principle of non-contradiction is not a necessary feature of a legal order, the advocate might retaliate, it is such an attractive principle that just about every sane legal order should embrace it. In the remainder of this chapter two responses will be made to this charge. First, that sometimes it is possible to have inconsistent legal rules without forcing people or institutions to act unlawfully or, necessarily, compelling them to choose between the rules. Secondly, that there are sometimes political reasons for embracing inconsistent rules. Inconsistent rules may reflect a compromise at the political level, and the institutions of the constitution ought to preserve this ambiguity, and the underlying compromise, rather than attempting to resolve it.

THE POSSIBILITY OF MULTIPLE RULES OF RECOGNITION

Herbert Hart's account of legal systems turned, in part, on the existence and operation of a single rule: the rule of recognition.[42] One of the many tasks of the rule of recognition was to provide an answer to the tricky question of identity: the manner

[41] Fuller, note 13 above, 65–70.

[42] Austin also provided a much less persuasive non-pluralist account of legal orders. See N. W. Barber, 'Sovereignty Re-Examined: The Courts, Parliament and Statutes' (2000) 20 Oxford J Legal Studies 131, 132–3; J. Austin, *The Province of Jurisprudence Determined* (London: University of London Press, 1954), Lecture vi.

in which the boundaries of legal systems are drawn.[43] The identity question can be split into two parts.[44] First, the drawing of the boundaries of a legal system at a given point in time: how are we to distinguish between the laws of different legal systems? This question asks about the criteria for membership of what has been termed a 'momentary' legal system, criteria that will isolate the rules of the system at a point in time. The second part of the question addresses the continuity of legal systems: how do we know that two momentary legal orders form part of one continuing legal order? The rules of the English legal system in 1960 and in 2000 are profoundly different, and yet both momentary systems are part of the same, continuing, entity. Hart's answer to both of these questions came in the form of the rule of recognition.[45]

The rule of recognition served to unite the rules of a legal system, providing a test by which the other rules could be shown to form part of the legal order.[46] Each legal system therefore possessed its own unique rule of recognition.[47] The rule of recognition answered the question of which rules belonged to a given momentary legal system.[48] All the rules that could be identified through the application of the rule of recognition constituted a single legal system. The rule of recognition also provided an answer to the question raised by the continuity of legal systems.[49] Two momentary legal systems formed aspects of one continuing legal system when the changes that had occurred between the two sets of rules occurred in conformity to the rules of change identified by the rule of recognition. Obviously, each rule of recognition would, ordinarily, be enormously complicated, with a large number of different criteria identifying the rules of the system.[50] Supporters of Hart could either present the rule of recognition as a single rule with lots of sub-elements, or as a collection of rules that are set in a relationship with each other.[51] It is possible

[43] J. Raz, *The Concept of a Legal System* (2nd edn, Oxford: Oxford University Press, 1980), 2–4.

[44] J. Raz, 'The Identity of Legal Systems' in J. Raz, *The Authority of Law* (Oxford: Oxford University Press, 1979), Raz, note 43 above, chapter 8; J. Finnis, 'Revolutions and Continuity of Law' in A. Simpson (ed), *Oxford Essays in Jurisprudence (Second Series)* (Oxford: Oxford University Press, 1973).

[45] The distinction between these two questions is alluded to by Hart: Hart, note 32 above, 116.

[46] Hart, note 32 above, 113–15.

[47] H. L. A. Hart, 'Legal Duty and Obligation' in H. L. A. Hart, *Essays on Bentham* (Oxford: Oxford University Press, 1982), 155, ftn. 77. See also: N. MacCormick, 'The Concept of Law and "The Concept of Law"' (1994) 14 Oxford J Legal Studies 1, 13–15; N. MacCormick, 'A Very British Revolution' in N. MacCormick, *Questioning Sovereignty* (Oxford: Oxford University Press, 1999).

[48] Raz, note 43 above, 198–9.

[49] Though Hart does not make this point explicitly: Finnis, note 44 above, 54–7.

[50] On the troublesome task of pinning down the content of the rule of recognition, see: M. Bayles, *Hart's Legal Philosophy* (London: Kluwer, 1992), 79–81; K. Greenwalt, 'Hart's Rule of Recognition and the United States' (1988) 1 *Ratio Juris* 40; R. Sartorius, 'Hart's Concept of Law' in R. Summers, ed., *More Essays in Legal Philosophy* (Oxford: Blackwell, 1971).

[51] T. Honoré, 'How is Law Possible?' in T. Honoré, *Making Law Bind* (Oxford: Oxford University Press, 1987), 23.

that some of these sub-rules might be inconsistent, in the sense used in this chapter, but it is essential for the success of Hart's project that the inconsistency is resolvable within the legal system. So, there might be two courts within a system, both of which claimed supremacy over a particular topic. These claims would be inconsistent, but if both courts recognized Parliament as a higher source of law this agreement would be sufficient to allow the inconsistency to be contained within a single rule, or set of rules.[52] Whilst these rules are inconsistent they are set in a relationship: mutual recognition of the legal superiority of statute. However, if the two rules are not set in a hierarchical relationship, if those advancing the rules do not both acknowledge a higher source of law, it is far harder to see how they can be considered parts of a single rule, or part of a distinct group of rules. Here, the rule of recognition would no longer play its part as the unique identifier of legal systems. In such a situation how could we distinguish between two separate legal systems and one legal system with two inconsistent rules of recognition at its core? If it is possible to conceive of inconsistency operating at this level of the legal order, the rule of recognition will not be able to identify and unite the disparate rules of the system by itself.[53]

Hart was not unaware of the problems that disputes over the rule of recognition caused his theory. In the context of revolutions and invasion he acknowledged the possibility of such a state of affairs: it was conceivable that two rival rules of recognition might operate within a territory, and yet only one legal system was in operation. This was, though, a 'substandard, abnormal case containing with it the threat that the legal system will dissolve'.[54] Such cases needed to be marginalized because if they were a common occurrence they would throw doubt on the success of the rule of recognition as the answer to the identity questions posed earlier.

Hart's account of a legal system was non-pluralist. The central case of a legal system contained a single rule of recognition, directing the law-applying institutions to the sources of law. Whilst Hart envisaged the possibility of pluralist systems, where there were inconsistent rules of recognition, he understood these as deviant cases. They constituted legal systems because of their similarity to the central case he presented, and were inherently unstable. If pluralist systems are more common, or more lasting, than Hart believed, the centrality of his non-pluralist account would have to be reconsidered. Reflection on these, and other, problems with the rule of recognition led Hart's students away from the rule of recognition as the answer to the questions of the identity of legal systems. Both Joseph Raz and John Finnis have advanced more flexible understandings of legal systems, which moved away from Hart's rule-focused account and have made room for the possibility of pluralist legal orders.[55]

---

[52] See the discussion of parliamentary privilege later in this chapter.

[53] See also the discussion of this issue MacCormick, note 47 above, esp 81–6.

[54] Hart, note 32 above, 123.

[55] Finnis, note 44 above; Raz, note 44 above.

THE RHODESIAN CRISIS AS A TEST CASE FOR LEGAL PLURALISM

The task of the first half of the chapter was to explain what was entailed by inconsistent rules of recognition, and to explain why they were controversial and interesting. It is now time to see whether these abstractions can help us understand the functioning of real legal orders. Is it conceivable that a legal order could exist with a pair of inconsistent rules of recognition at its core? The first test-case for legal pluralism examines the constitutional crisis surrounding the Unilateral Declaration of Independence by the government of Rhodesia in 1965.[56] This will provide a relatively clear example of inconsistent rules of recognition operating within a legal order— though only for a brief period of time. Following this discussion, the chapter will turn to the harder problems presented by the relationships between the legal orders of the European Union. It will be argued that there are important points of similarity between the European and Rhodesian cases.[57]

(i) The implications of UDI for the Rhodesian legal order

Prior to 1965 the Rhodesian Constitution took the form of an Order in Council,[58] made under a power conferred by a British statute.[59] The Rhodesian Parliament was given considerable independence, but was not given the power to alter entrenched provisions of the Constitution.[60] On 11 November 1965 the Rhodesian Prime Minister announced the independence of Rhodesia, and the introduction of a new constitution, the 'Constitution of Rhodesia, 1965'.[61] This document purported to replace the previous Constitution, and provided that no Act of the United Kingdom Parliament would apply to Rhodesia unless extended to Rhodesia by the Rhodesian Parliament.[62] It also removed the right of appeal to the Privy Council on matters arising out of the Declaration of Rights. The United Kingdom Parliament responded with the Southern Rhodesian Act 1965 which reasserted Westminster's control over Rhodesia, and, in an Order in Council made under the Act, emphasized that constitutional change could only occur through an Act of the Westminster Parliament.[63] In *Madzimbamuto v Lardner-Burke*[64] the legality of the 1965 Constitution was considered by the Privy

---

[56] T. Mahmud, 'Jurisprudence of Successful Treason' (1994) 27 Cornell Int LJ 49, 60–5.

[57] See Oliver, note 12 above, especially chapters 11 and 12, for a wider discussion of the constitutional foundations of former territories of the British Empire. A number of these might fit our model of a pluralist legal order—at least for a period of their existence.

[58] Southern Rhodesia (Constitution) Order in Council 1961, SI 1961/2314.

[59] Southern Rhodesia (Constitution) Act 1961.

[60] G. Marshall, *Constitutional Theory* (Oxford: Oxford University Press, 1971), 64–72; J. Eekelaar, 'Splitting the *Grundnorm*' (1967) 30 MLR 156.

[61] Rhodesian Proclamation 53, 1965: RG Notice 737N, 1965.

[62] ss 3–5.

[63] SI 1965/1952.

[64] [1969] 1 AC 645.

Council. The Privy Council held that the usurpation was unlawful and that the purported 1965 Constitution was of no legal effect. In contrast, the Rhodesian courts, after some vacillation,[65] endorsed the 1965 Constitution[66] and declined to accept the Privy Council's continued position as final court of appeal for Rhodesia.[67]

Here, there were two separate pairs of inconsistent rules, both of which turned on the inclusion of institutions within the order.[68]

(a) First pair: inconsistent rules relating to the status of Westminster statutes
There was a dispute about the role of the Westminster Parliament as a future source of Rhodesian law. According to the Westminster Parliament, and the Privy Council, statutes from Westminster continued to have effect in Rhodesia after UDI, and were the highest source for Rhodesian law. According to the Rhodesian Constitution 1965, and, subsequently, the Rhodesian High Court, Westminster statutes passed after 1965 did not have effect in Rhodesia. There are several dimensions to this inconsistency. First, there was a dispute as to whether the Westminster Parliament had a power to alter the law applying in Rhodesia. One rule stated that the Westminster Parliament may make any changes it wished to Rhodesian law. This rule was presented as a rule of common law, an aspect of sovereignty, and is reflected in the pronouncements of the Westminster Parliament. Set against this was a rule stating that the Westminster Parliament was disabled from making changes to the Rhodesian law. Such a disability is quite unusual: it is rare to see a rule asserting that something *is not* a source of law. This disability is found in the 1965 Constitution. Secondly, the power entailed a duty. One rule stated that people generally, and the courts in particular, were under a legal obligation to comply with statutes of the Westminster Parliament. Again, this duty constitutes an aspect of sovereignty, and is found in the common law. This rule is countered by that contained in the 1965 Constitution, which stated that individuals and courts were not under a legal duty to comply with statutes of the Westminster Parliament and, indeed, were under a duty not to comply with such statutes where they were inconsistent with Rhodesian law. Both of these pairs of inconsistent rules were foundational: neither was created by virtue of a power conferred by some higher rule of law, though both depend for their legal status on their inclusion within a purported source of law. Each sought to define part of the boundaries of Rhodesia's legal system.

(b) Second pair: inconsistency relating to the position of the Privy Council
Secondly, there was a dispute about the Privy Council's position as the final arbiter of the content of Rhodesian law. One rule, contained in the old Constitution

---

[65] Eekelaar, note 60 above; J. Eekelaar, 'Rhodesia: Abdication of Constitutionalism' (1969) 32 MLR 19; Mahmud, note 56 above, 60–5.

[66] *R v Ndhlovu* 1968 (4) SA 515. See C. Munro, *Studies in Constitutional Law* (2nd edn, London: Butterworths, 1999), 152.

[67] *Dhlamini v Carter* (1968) (2) SA 464.

[68] See more generally, K. Wheare, *The Constitutional Structure of the Commonwealth* (Oxford: Oxford University Press, 1960), ch 4.

appointed the Privy Council the final court of appeal. The other rule, contained in the 1965 Constitution, dramatically limited the Privy Council's role in the Rhodesian system. As with the other pair of inconsistent rules, the inconsistency had two aspects. First, there was an inconsistent pair of duties: in some areas both the Privy Council and the Rhodesian High Court were presented as under a duty to make final determinations of the content of Rhodesian law. Second, there were corresponding duties directed to the subjects of the law and the lower courts, directing them to apply the determinations of these bodies.

(ii) Two interpretations of the conundrums of the Rhodesian crisis

There are many different ways in which the legal dilemmas caused by the Rhodesian crisis might be presented. Two accounts at two different points in time will be suggested below: first, the period after the Rhodesian courts accepted the legal validity of the 1965 Constitution; secondly, the period immediately prior to this when it was unclear whether the Rhodesian courts would follow the 1965 Constitution or the pronouncements of the Privy Council.

(a) The period following the acceptance of the 1965 Constitution

After it had become clear that local Rhodesian courts no longer accepted the authority of the Privy Council, a split existed between the local Rhodesian legal system and the Privy Council's version of the Rhodesian legal system. These two accounts differed in some key respects. On the Privy Council's account, it, the Privy Council, was the highest court of appeal in Rhodesia, and competent to produce definitive ruling on the inclusion of rules within the system. In contrast, the Rhodesian High Court asserted that it was the highest court in the order, with the Privy Council treated only as a persuasive source, and that it was competent to produce definitive rulings on the inclusion of rules within the system. On the Privy Council's account of the Rhodesian legal system the 1965 Emergency Powers Regulation was not legally valid. In contrast, the Rhodesian High Court found that the Emergency Powers Regulation was valid. According to the Privy Council, Madizambuto's detention, based on the ineffective Regulation, was unlawful and officials were under a legal duty to release him. According to the Rhodesian High Court, Madizambuto's detention was lawful, and the officials were under no duty to release him.

From the perspective of the Privy Council there was only one legal system operating in Rhodesia; a legal order with the Privy Council as final adjudicator, and with Madizambuto entitled to freedom. Similarly, from the perspective of the Rhodesian High Court there was only one legal system operating in Rhodesia, but with it as the final court and with Madizambuto validly detained. The High Court of Rhodesia, in contrast to the Privy Council, recognized that a second, separate, legal system existed: some of the pronouncements of the Privy Council might be incorporated into the Rhodesian system, but only because of an incorporating rule of the local Rhodesian system.

This stage of the Rhodesian crisis is compatible with Hart's account of the rule of recognition. Though there are inconsistent rules of recognition they lie within different legal systems. The position is identical to the conflict of laws example discussed earlier, in which a dominant legal order recognizes the rules of a subservient legal system to a limited extent.

A problem with this interpretation is that, aside from the rule empowering the Privy Council, the Privy Council and the Rhodesian courts agreed on just about every other law within the Rhodesian system. This might appear to make the dual system characterization of the position artificial: after all, the two purportedly different systems are virtually identical. The attraction of the dual system interpretation in the Rhodesian case is especially strong because of the Rhodesian courts' outright rejection of the Privy Council as a future legal source for Rhodesian law. After the crisis it was irrelevant how close the Privy Council's view of the content of the Rhodesian system was to that of the Rhodesian courts: future pronouncements of the Privy Council were no more part of the law of Rhodesia than, say, pronouncements of the Australian High Court. It would therefore be odd to continue to assert that within the Rhodesian order inconsistent rules of recognition operated after the crisis simply because the Privy Council did not acknowledge the shift in power. Perhaps we should distinguish between the Rhodesian legal order proper, with the Appellate Division of the Rhodesian High Court as the supreme court of the order, and the Privy Council's (ineffective) version of the Rhodesian legal system. Both of these purported legal orders claimed to operate over the same territory.

(b) The period prior to the acceptance of the 1965 Constitution by the Rhodesian courts

In this period prior to the acceptance of the 1965 Constitution, when it was unclear which body was the supreme legislator for Rhodesia, there were inconsistent rules of recognition operating within the system; the split outlined in the previous section had yet to occur. One rule of recognition identified the Westminster Parliament as the highest source of law in the system, and the Privy Council as the highest adjudicative body. The second identified the Rhodesian Parliament as the highest source of law, and the Rhodesian High Court as the supreme adjudicative body. This period of the Rhodesian crisis poses problems for Hart's understanding of the rule of recognition, and may give us a glimpse of what a 'pluralist' model of a legal system might look like. Supporters of Hart's account of the rule of recognition might make one of two replies.

First, though Hart insisted that there was a single rule of recognition in each system, it is quite possible that within the rule there are areas of ambiguity or conflict. A brief reflection on parliamentary privilege provides an example of a conflict within a rule of recognition that does not challenge Hart's account.

Both the House of Commons and the courts assert that they are under a duty to determine whether a matter falls within the scope of parliamentary privilege. The judges have consistently asserted that it is only once they have concluded a matter is subject to privilege that the issue falls within the exclusive jurisdiction of the Commons.[69] In contrast, the Commons asserts that the breadth of privilege is a

[69] *Stockdale v Hansard* (1839) 9 Ad & E 1, esp 165; *Bradlaugh v Gosset* (1884) 12 QBD 271, esp 278–80; S. A. de Smith, 'Parliamentary Privilege and the Bill of Rights' (1958) 21 MLR 465; A. Denning, 'Memorandum on The Strauss Case' (1985) Public Law 80.

matter for it to determine.[70] These two rules are duty-imposing: neither institution regards itself as having a choice about the resolution of the jurisdictional question. They are compelled to reach a decision on the issue, even if that decision amounts to an endorsement of the other body's interpretations. These jurisdictional rules also embody a power: once the institution has reached a decision, officials within the order are obliged to accept and act upon that judgment. The two rules have different sources.[71] The source of the Commons' jurisdictional rule lies in the law of the Commons: both Houses of Parliament are bodies of inherent jurisdiction, and their customary practices, as expressed principally in the rulings of Speakers and resolutions, have the status of law.[72] The source of the courts' jurisdictional rule, in contrast, is the common law. The Commons and the courts agree that Parliament is entitled to resolve disputes about the scope of privilege. So, when these inconsistent jurisdictional rules generated an actual dispute in *Stockdale v Hansard* the Parliamentary Papers Act 1840 succeeded in ending the conflict.[73]

The mutual acceptance of Parliament as a higher legal source allows this conflict to be contained within a single rule of recognition: it is one rule, or one set of rules, with conflicting elements. In contrast, in the Rhodesian example there was no agreed higher source; the question of competence turned on the issue of supremacy. It was unclear whether the 1965 Constitution was the highest legal instrument, or whether statutes of the Westminster Parliament took precedence. It was unclear whether the Rhodesian High Court or the Privy Council had legal authority to resolve the dispute.

Secondly, supporters of Hart could argue that though there appeared to be two inconsistent rules of recognition operating in this period, in fact only one was the 'true' rule of recognition; the other was an impostor, a legal mistake. The conduct of the Rhodesian courts following *Madizambuto* revealed a split that already existed. The difficulty with adopting this argument is that the rule of recognition is deduced from the conduct and understanding of officials—in particular, from that of the judges.[74] If the conduct of the judges, as shown in their decisions and reasoning, at a given point in time is divided between inconsistent rules of recognition, then there is no single 'true' rule of recognition to be found.[75] The judges agree that

---

[70] E. May, *Parliamentary Practice* (22nd edn, London: Sweet and Maxwell, 1997), ch 10; CJ (1702–04) 308; CJ (1837) 418–20; M. L. Gwyer, *Anson's Law and Custom of the Constitution* (5th edn, Oxford: Oxford University Press, 1922), 192–3; C. R. Munro, *Studies in Constitutional Law* (London: Butterworths, 1987), 148–50.

[71] This distinction has traditionally been presented as a contrast between *lex parliamenti* and *lex terrae*. See C. Wittke, *The History of English Parliamentary Privilege* (Ohio: Ohio University Press, 1921) and J. Chaftez, *Democracy's Privileged Few* (New Haven: Yale University Press, 2007).

[72] Munro, note 66 above, 216–18.

[73] On which, see Wittke, note 71 above, and Chaftez, note 71 above, ch 3. A more colourful description of the crisis can be found in J. Dean, *Hatred, Ridicule or Contempt* (London: Constable, 1953), ch 19.

[74] Hart, note 32 above, 101–2.

[75] J. Raz, 'The Identity of Legal Systems' in J. Raz, *The Authority of Law* (Oxford: Oxford University Press, 1979), 95–6.

there is a single legal order, but disagree about the content of the rule of recognition.[76] As the Rhodesian example shows, the inconsistency may be resolved, but this does not mean that the inconsistency was not present in the system for a period of time.

The Rhodesian crisis is sufficient to show that a pluralist legal system could exist for a brief period of time. Hart could reply that this was just the sort of substandard, abnormal, case he had in mind when he spoke of unstable systems containing multiple rules of recognition. The inconsistency was swiftly resolved. However, the ambiguities raised by the legal systems of the European Union may provide a more durable collection of examples of pluralism. With the Rhodesian crisis as our model, it is time to approach Europe's troubled legal orders.

LEGAL PLURALISM AND THE EUROPEAN UNION

The Court of Justice of the European Union (ECJ) makes three, interconnected, claims of supremacy.[77] First, that the ECJ is entitled to definitively answer all questions of European Law.[78] Secondly, that the ECJ is entitled to determine what constitutes an issue of European Law.[79] Thirdly, that European Law has supremacy over all conflicting rules of national law.[80] These claims are distinct: making any one of the claims does not entail making the other two. National supreme courts have sometimes proved unwilling to accept these assertions.[81] Most famously, the German courts have refused to cede their role as guardians of the German Constitution.[82] As the pronouncements of the German constitutional court provide the clearest, and most widely discussed, challenge to Europe's supremacy claims, it is the German example that will be used in the following paragraphs.

[76] As Coleman notes, the rule of recognition is defined not merely by the practice of officials, but also by their shared grasp of what the rule entails: J. Coleman, *The Practice of Principle* (Oxford: Oxford University Press, 2001), 80–1.

[77] K. Alter, *Establishing the Supremacy of European Law* (Oxford: Oxford University Press, 2001), ch 1; J. Weiler, 'The Autonomy of the Community Legal Order' in J. Weiler, *The Constitution of Europe* (Cambridge: Cambridge University Press, 1999).

[78] Art. 267 of the Treaty on the Functioning of the European Union (TFEU) (previously Art. 234 EC and, before that, Art. 177).

[79] J. Weiler, 'The Transformation of Europe' in J. Weiler, *The Constitution of Europe* (Cambridge: Cambridge University Press, 1999), 21. Case 314/85, *Foto-Frost v Hauptzollamt Lübeck-Ost* [1987] ECR 4199.

[80] Case 6/64 *Costa v ENEL* [1964] ECR 585.

[81] J. Baquero Cruz, 'The Legacy of the Maastricht-Urteil Decision and the Pluralist Movement' (2008) 14 European LJ 389, W. Sadurski, 'Solange Chapter 3: Constitutional Courts in Central Europe' (2008) 14 European LJ 1, 6–24.

[82] For discussion, see Alter, note 77 above, ch 3. Other national courts have expressed similar doubts. France: Nicolo [1990] 1 CMLR 173; Italy: *Frontini v Ministero delle Finanze* [1974] 2 CMLR 372; Denmark: *Carlsen v Prime Minister* [1999] 3 CMLR 854.

At various times the German courts have adopted a different view of the impact of European Law to that articulated by the ECJ.[83] In *Solange I*[84] the German Constitutional Court rejected the supremacy of European Law: rules of Community Law that conflicted with fundamental constitutional rights would not be applied in the German order. This was a challenge to the third of the three assertions of supremacy. More recently, in the *Maastricht*[85] decision, the German Court rejected the ECJ's claim to have the final say as to the meaning and scope of European Law. The German Court stated that it would not accept surprising readings of the Treaty that had the effect of extending the Union's powers.[86] This challenges both the first and the third of the ECJ's supremacy claims. As with the Rhodesian example, two groups of inconsistent rules can be determined. These two groups, a rich mixture of duties and powers, together constitute a pair of inconsistent rules of recognition.

(i) Inconsistent rules giving supremacy to different sets of legal rules

According to the German Constitutional Court the German Constitution is the highest source of law within Germany. European Law takes effect through the German Constitution, and, consequently, can be constrained by constitutional rules. This supremacy doctrine is presented as implicit within the framework of the German Constitution. In contrast, the ECJ regards European Law as the highest source of law within the European Union, which, of course, encompasses Germany. This supremacy doctrine is presented as a consequence of the signing of the Treaties establishing the Union, and does not depend on the validation of the German Constitution. Each supremacy claim contains an implicit negation of the other. In both cases these rules are presented as duties resting on the courts: each court claims that it is compelled to give precedence to the different sources of law.

(ii) Inconsistent rules giving adjudicative supremacy to different courts

The dispute over the priority of sets of rules is coupled with a dispute about the hierarchy of courts within Germany. Again, this inconsistency takes the form of a combination of duties and powers. In some situations both courts regard themselves as under a duty to make the final determination about the content of law

---

[83] For recent tensions produced by the European Arrest Warrant, see M. Fichera, 'The European Arrest Warrant and the Sovereign State: A Marriage of Convenience?' (2009) 15 European LJ 70.

[84] *Internationale HandelsgesellschaftmbH v Einfuhr-und Vorratsstelle für Getreide und Futtermittel*, [1974] CMLR 540.

[85] *Brunner v The European Treaty* [1994] CMLR 57. See M. Zuleeg, 'The European Constitution Under Constitutional Constraints: The German Scenario' (1997) 22 European L Rev 19 for energetic criticism of the decision, and M. Kumm, 'Who is the Final Arbiter of Constitutionality in Europe?' (1999) 36 Common Market L Rev 351.

[86] Brunner, note 85 above, paragraphs 33, 48–9.

in Germany. The rules are asymmetrical: whilst the German Constitutional Court regards itself as under a duty to have the final say about the content of all the laws operative in Germany, the ECJ only claims to be obliged to have the final say about those laws with a European element that are operative in Germany. As with the example drawn from parliamentary privilege, these duties could be acquitted by merely endorsing the decision of the other body—but the duties prohibit the acceptance of the other body's claim to authority. A simple pair of duties to express a view about the law within a territory would not be inconsistent. What makes these rival claims to adjudicative supremacy inconsistent is their assertion of finality: a duty to state authoritatively for those affected by the law what the law requires of them. Adjudicative supremacy is a duty coupled with a power to bind people, courts and other institutions. It is these powers, inextricably mixed with the duties, which create the potential for inconsistency. This inconsistency need not be realized—perhaps the rival bodies will agree—but there is the unavoidable potential for actual inconsistency; that individuals will be placed in a position where they cannot fully comply with the directives produced by each court.

Two further aspects of European law combine to make these inconsistencies even more piquant.

First, and most obviously, people and institutions are sometimes under a duty to comply with European Law even when its demands run contrary to the apparent requirements of national law. Such a duty is imposed on all parties, public and private, when rules of European Law are directly effective, and, in addition, applies to public bodies when the conditions for vertical direct effect are satisfied. The supremacy of European Law does not, therefore, entirely depend on the support of the national courts: in some situations people and institutions are required to set aside conflicting national law.

Secondly, in the recent case of *Köbler*[87] the ECJ extended *Francovich*[88] liability to decisions of national courts. An action in damages lies when a final court of appeal makes a sufficiently serious error in its application of European Law. *Francovich* required domestic courts to create a national remedy: the obligation to have such liability comes from Europe, but the right itself must be grounded in the law of each of the Member States. Consequently, after *Köbler*, national courts of first instance will occasionally be compelled to pass judgment on decisions of higher courts in their system.

If a national constitutional court were to reject a judgment of the ECJ a number of interesting legal problems within the domestic system would arise. First, there would be the position of people and institutions within the Member State. Should they follow the ECJ's assertion of their legal duties, or the demands of their national constitutional court? Secondly, compounding this, what of the lower courts in the

---

[87] C-224/01 *Köbler v Austria* [2003] ECR I-10239; H. Scott and N. W. Barber 'State Liability Under *Francovich* for Decisions of National Courts' (2004) 120 LQR 403.

[88] Cases 6/90 & 9/90 *Francovich v Italy* [1991] ECR I-5357.

national legal hierarchy? The ECJ does not regard lower courts' obligation to apply European Law as mediated through the national legal order; lower courts should not follow incorrect decisions of higher courts.[89] Each judge of first instance must therefore decide whether to accept the supremacy claims of the ECJ, or the rival supremacy claims of her national court. Thirdly, after *Köbler* the dissenting decision can be challenged immediately and directly. The first instance judge will be in a very difficult situation: what is to be done about the plaintiff's claim for damages, a claim certain to be supported by the ECJ if a reference is made? This scenario begins to look very like the Rhodesian case examined earlier; the devices used to protect the supremacy claims of the ECJ have the potential to fragment the national legal order in the event of a dispute, subverting existing judicial hierarchies.

There are lots of ways of interpreting the relationship of the German legal order and the European Union,[90] but only two will be considered here: a non-pluralist and a pluralist reading.

It is possible to hold rigidly to the view that there is one European legal order which has a separate relationship with each legal order of each Member State. Each Member State has a legal device, contained within a constitution or statute, which allows national courts to recognize and apply rules of European Law—even to the extent of setting aside some contrary rules of national law. This is very like the conflict of laws example considered right at the start of the chapter. The European legal order is the subservient legal order, dependent for its force on recognition by the national, dominant, legal orders. This interpretation fits with the account given in the *Maastricht* decision by the German Constitutional Court. On this reading, some of the European supremacy claims are ineffective: they are legally correct within the European legal order, but cannot be recognized and incorporated within national orders. Broadly, this is the 'pluralist' account advanced by Neil MacCormick in his valuable book, *Questioning Sovereignty*.[91]

MacCormick provides two versions of this interpretation: radical pluralism, and pluralism under international law. Both of these forms of pluralism begin by identifying a variety of distinct, but connected, legal orders within Europe. Radical pluralism then asserts that this is the end of the matter: there are multiple systems, and the answer given to a particular legal question will depend on which system the lawyer chooses to reason within.[92] Pluralism under international law, in contrast, claims

---

[89] Case 106/77 *Amministrazione delle Finanze dello Stato v Simmenthal* [1978] ECR 629.

[90] See C. Richmond, 'Preserving the Identity Crisis: Autonomy, System and Sovereignty in European Law' (1997) 16 Law and Philosophy 377.

[91] See especially, 'Juridical Pluralism and the Risk of Constitutional Conflict' in N. MacCormick, *Questioning Sovereignty* (Oxford: Oxford University Press, 1999). See also the discussion in P. Oliver, 'Sovereignty in the Twenty-First Century' (2003) 14 King's College LJ 137, 157–78.

[92] Intriguingly, MacCormick talks of legal systems 'overlapping' in these pluralist models: MacCormick, note 91 above, 119. It is unclear what he means by this. Mere recognition of the rules of one legal order by another is not an 'overlap'. In what follows below, I try to develop an account of overlapping legal orders that goes beyond mutual recognition.

that international law may provide rules which can help resolve conflicts between these different systems. This reduces the chances of a legally irresolvable conflict arising between the orders. MacCormick's interpretation is sophisticated, but it may not be sufficiently controversial to be described as 'pluralist'. Once again, Hart and Kelsen could, without too great a stretch, endorse either of these two interpretations. Radical pluralism posits a number of distinct legal systems, each with its own rule of recognition or *Grundnorm*. Pluralism under international law posits, effectively, a single legal system (international law) with domestic legal orders as subsets contained within it. These models bring to mind Kelsen's famous claim that international law and domestic law were parts of a single entity.[93] As with MacCormick's 'pluralisms', Kelsen's unified model turned on the point of view adopted.[94] From the view point of a national system, there was only one legal order, with elements of international law identified by rules of domestic law. From the view point of international law, there was only one legal order, with elements of domestic law identified by rules of international law.

The danger of sticking with these readings is that they may oversimplify the split between the German and European orders. They assume that the judges within Germany would unquestioningly follow the ruling of the Constitutional Court, regardless of their apparent European obligations. If the judiciary were divided, or undecided, it might be more accurate to say that both of these inconsistent rules of recognition exist in the German legal system at the present time. The situation might resemble the Rhodesian crisis in reverse. To begin with, there were two, clearly distinct, legal systems: the German and the European. Over time they have moved together, the boundaries of each becoming blurred. It would be a mistake to say that they have become, or will become, a single legal order. The German system differs from the European in a number of important respects, none of which are challenged by the inconsistency between the rules of recognition. An enormous number of rules are untouched by Europe, operating only within the German system. The institutions—courts and legislatures—in Germany are created by, and largely defined by, domestic rules. On the other hand, the ECJ claims a jurisdiction that reaches beyond Germany; it applies to the territories of other Member States, too. The ECJ has never claimed that national legal orders are mere subsets of the European. Rather than moving towards a single system, it might be better to say that the two systems overlapped, with the duties and loyalties of those within the German order becoming increasingly ambiguous.[95] It is likely that this ambiguity will increase if and when citizens and judges come to see the European Union as a permanent feature of their constitutional framework. Both the European and the German legal orders are, and will

[93] Kelsen, note 11 above, 328–44.

[94] See further, Richmond, note 90 above, who presents a collection of internally coherent models in Kelsenian terms, asserting that these provide a plurality of viewpoints from which to look on the European legal order.

[95] N. Walker, 'The Idea of Pluralism' (2002) 65 MLR 317, 337–8.

remain, distinct, and yet overlap in significant ways. This overlap means that both systems might be termed 'pluralist' in that the judges, officials and citizens within them may be faced with inconsistent rules of recognition.[96]

If it is accepted that there are inconsistent rules of recognition within the German system, the result may be a combination of elements from the examples set out earlier. Like Rhodesia, there are inconsistent rules of recognition operating within a given territory. Like Rhodesia, the inconsistency cannot be resolved by an appeal to a higher body, because the dispute turns on the question of supremacy. Like Rhodesia, the ultimate resolution of the debate would depend on the loyalty of officials—in particular, but not exclusively, the loyalty of the judges. Like the parliamentary privilege example, though, and unlike Rhodesia, this inconsistency is sustainable if each side shows institutional restraint. Though the German Constitution Court and the ECJ make inconsistent claims these need not produce actual constitutional dilemmas. Much as the courts and Commons have accommodated each others' rival claim to precedence by carefully avoiding pushing the issue to a crisis such as that seen in *Stockdale*, the ECJ and German Constitutional Court could avoid a crisis by adopting compatible decisions about the impact of European Law.[97]

I have used the *Maastricht* decision to illustrate what a pluralist system might look like, but a pluralist model might also be applied to the legal orders of other Member States. In the United Kingdom, for example, the simple certainties of sovereignty appear increasingly implausible.[98] In *Factortame (No 2)*[99] Lord Bridge claimed that after the European Communities Act 1972 the English courts would 'accord...supremacy to rules of Community law in areas to which they apply...'[100] Even this apparently wide acceptance of the claims to supremacy made by the ECJ is not without its ambiguities. First, it is not clear how the courts would respond to a ruling of the ECJ that was perceived as falling outside of the sphere of European Law—would they give effect to such jurisdictional mistakes? Secondly, Lord Bridge may be wrong in asserting that supremacy will *always* be accorded to directly effective European Law: if Parliament were to pass a statute purporting to withdraw from the Union the courts would probably follow the statute, even though it would conflict with the

---

[96] The European Union legal system includes the judges and courts of the national legal orders, as well as the judges of the Court of Justice of the European Union. Whilst there is disagreement between the judges of the European Union legal system about the supremacy of EU law, the European legal order will be a pluralist legal order—though still distinct from the pluralist legal orders at the level of the Member States.

[97] Which seems to have been the case: F. Mayer, 'The European Constitution in the Courts' in A. Von Bogdandy and J. Blast (eds), *Principles of European Constitutional Law* (Oxford: Hart Publishing, 2006); Baquero Cruz, note 81 above, 395–7.

[98] N. W. Barber, 'Sovereignty Re-examined: The Courts, Parliament and Statutes' (2000) 21 Oxford J Legal Studies 130 and see Oliver, note 91 above.

[99] *R v Secretary of State for Transport ex p Factortame Ltd* (No 2) [1991] 1 AC 603.

[100] *Ibid*, at 659.

United Kingdom's treaty obligations.[101] The English legal order may therefore also contain inconsistent rules of recognition.

CONCLUSION

The question remains: even if a pluralist model of a legal system is plausible, is it attractive? It may be that whilst a pluralist model provides a good basis for a description of the relationship between the European legal order and the national legal orders, this description is regrettable; the inconsistencies within the model are unattractive. Perhaps we should push towards a legal system in which these disputes are resolved, one in which the hierarchy of legal sources is more clearly defined. There are at least two reasons why we should welcome, rather than regret, inconsistency.

First, as Maduro has argued, the sort of inconsistency described here may amount to a political compromise; a tacit agreement to disagree.[102] It allows supporters of ECJ supremacy and supporters of national supremacy to both claim victory; conversely, and perhaps even more importantly, it avoids either constituency having to admit defeat. As we have seen, inconsistent laws need not demand inconsistent action; the constitutional dilemma can remain unresolved, provided that each side exercises restraint. *Stockdale* and *Madizambuto* are examples of where these disagreements did generate constitutional crisis—but as the peaceful history of privilege since *Stockdale* shows, these crisis could have been avoided. The emergence of pluralist legal systems within the European Union may provide a desirable compromise between the old models of sovereignty and constitutional supremacy, and the new claims to supremacy made by Europe. Whilst these positions cannot reach a compromise through the adoption of an agreed middle course, the pluralist model provides a compromise framework within which these inconsistent claims can co-exist. Provided that the practical conflict within this model remains potential, and actual disputes are avoided, this can provide a stable, even a long-lasting, form of settlement. The advantage of such a settlement is that it avoids unnecessary and potentially destructive conflict, and allows the protagonists to work together on beneficial projects where agreement exists.

Secondly, these competing supremacy claims could provide a form of what Alison Young and I have elsewhere described as 'constitutional self-defence'.[103] A rule of

[101] *Macarthys Ltd v Smith* [1979] 3 All ER 325, 329; *Thoburn v. Sunderland District Council* [2003] QB 151, 184–5.

[102] Richmond, note 90 above. M. Maduro, 'Europe and the Constitution: What If This Is As Good As It Gets?' in J. Weiler and M. Wind (eds), *European Constitutionalism Beyond The State* (Cambridge: Cambridge University Press, 2003). See also N. Krisch, 'The Open Architecture of European Human Rights Law' (2008) 71 MLR 183.

[103] N. W. Barber and A. L. Young, 'Prospective Henry VIII Clauses and their Implications for Sovereignty' (2003) Public Law 112. Similar points are discussed by Weiler and by Walker: see J. Weiler, 'The Reformation of European Constitutionalism' (1997) 35 J Common Market Studies 97 and N. Walker, 'Sovereignty and Differentiated Integration in the European Union' (1998) 4 European LJ 355, 375–9.

constitutional self-defence empowers an institution to protect itself against other constitutional bodies. For instance, legislatures are given judicial powers in the area of privilege to stop the encroachment of the courts, judges often run the administrative side of the court process. Sometimes these measures are more aggressive, giving one institution a weapon it can use against another: for instance, giving one legislature the power to strike down the acts of another legislative body. Competing claims to supremacy arm national and European courts with weapons that may help ensure mutual respect and restraint. If the potential conflicts caused by inconsistent rules of recognition were realized, with inconsistent rules addressed to individuals, all sides in the dispute would pay a price. As Fuller commented, non-contradiction is one of the requirements of the rule of law: if the courts face the citizen with irreconcilably inconsistent rules they have failed to live up to its aspirations. Further, in the event of actual conflict, one side will, probably, emerge from the crisis as a victor: whilst it is unclear who will win, each side has an interest in avoiding the contest. The risks of actual conflict provide incentives on each party to strive towards harmonious interpretation of the law. It encourages the ECJ to interpret European law in a manner that will be palatable to national courts,[104] and, at the same time, discourages national courts from blindly insisting on the primacy of national rules. In short, the competing supremacy claims may serve to create an atmosphere of co-operation between the courts, where each side has an incentive to strive to respect the position and tradition of the other.

We have travelled such a long way from the origins of legal pluralism that some might argue the label should be abandoned: does an account of the relationship between the various legal orders of Europe really have anything in common with the work of the legal anthropologists of the 1970s and 1980s? There are two threads that bind these very different approaches together. First, legal pluralism most often arises where two legal orders are bound together, and interact in interesting and important ways. Secondly, to be interesting, this interaction must present the risk of contradiction: inconsistent rules of recognition are at the heart of the pluralist model.

---

[104] As evidence of this see, perhaps, J. Coppel and A. O'Neill, 'The European Court of Justice: Taking Rights Seriously?' (1992) 12 Legal Studies 227, though their claims are challenged in J. Weiler and N. Lockhart, '"Taking Rights Seriously" Seriously: The European Court and its Fundamental Rights Jurisprudence' (1995) 32 Common Market L Rev 51 and 579.

❧ 10 ❧

Constitutional Pluralism

The previous chapter argued that it was possible for a form of legal pluralism to arise within a legal order and, furthermore, that this was, or may become, a characteristic of a number of the legal orders that are connected to the European Union. This chapter reflects on a second type of pluralism, constitutional pluralism. It contends that this is distinguishable from legal pluralism, and that, additionally, constitutional pluralism also casts some light upon the nature of the European Union. This requires us to address a question which has often been raised in European scholarship: that is, whether the European Union is, or may become, a state, and what the implications would be for its citizens and Member States if the Union were to gain statehood. This chapter starts by considering two forms of constitutional ordering—the federation and the confederation—and comparing those with the model of the state provided in earlier chapters. It then turns to the European Union, and contrasts that polity against these orderings, concluding that the Union stands somewhere between a federation and a confederation. It is the location of the Union in this conceptual borderland which generates a special, perhaps unique, form of constitutional pluralism.

FEDERATIONS AND CONFEDERATIONS

In a federation a single constitution allocates powers between the centre and the regions: all of the institutions of government, both at the federal and local levels, are exercising delegated powers.[1] These are powers conferred by a constitution[2] which frequently claims to derive its legitimacy directly from the people as a whole.[3] Sir Kenneth Wheare expressed the same point slightly differently: a political entity is a federation whenever power in the state is divided in such a way that each level of government has the final

---

[1] D. Elazar, *Exploring Federalism* (Tuscaloosa: University of Alabama Press, 1992), 39–41. See also R. L. Watts, 'Comparing Forms of Federal Partnerships' in D. Karmis and W. Norman (eds), *Theories of Federalism: A Reader* (Basingstoke: Palgrave Macmillan, 2005).

[2] Watts, note 1 above, 240.

[3] J Weiler, 'Federalism without Constitutionalism: Europe's *Sonderweg*' in K. Nicolaidis and R. Howse (eds), *The Federal Vision* (Oxford: Oxford University Press, 2001), 56.

decision about some matters.[4] The possibility of finality requires the existence of a single, unifying, constitution to allocate competences. Building on this definition, Arend Lijphart has identified a number of secondary characteristics of a federal state.[5] Federal states normally have written constitutions that are difficult to amend, constitutional courts which can police the boundaries between the regions and the centre, and bicameral legislatures, one chamber of which represents the regions.

These accounts of federation fall comfortably within the account of the state developed earlier in this book. There is a territory, a membership and a set of institutions. Furthermore, these institutions make the type of claims over individuals that were central to Max Weber and Leslie Green's understandings of the state. In Weber's account, in a federation the constitution divides the ability to exercise legitimate force between state institutions. The state as a whole, therefore, continues to claim the monopoly of the legitimate use of force, though each institution within the state is only given the capacity to exert such force in limited situations. Green's account of the state permits a very similar analysis: the state as a whole claims to regulate all exercises of power within the territory, though, once again, the execution of this regulation may be divided between state institutions.

Citizenship, the paradigmatic form of state membership, can also arise within federal structures. Members of federations can be citizens of those federations. The attitude of loyalty towards the state, an attitude that is characteristic of citizenship, need not be threatened by the competing demands of the centre and the regions. In a federation the loyalty of the citizen is owed to the state as a whole. This does not mean that in a dispute between the federal level and the regional level citizens are required, or expected, to side with the federal level. Federal constitutions normally create mechanisms—most obviously and ordinarily the state's supreme court—that are empowered to resolve such disputes. In a well-functioning federation, each of these three levels of state institution—the federal level, the regional level, and the citizen—should accept the decision of such adjudicative institutions as determinative of the division of powers within the system.

In contrast to the federation there has been little systematic effort to illuminate the nature of the confederation.[6] Most writers understand confederations as political entities in which the central government is subordinate to the regional governments.[7] In a confederation the centre and the regions lack the unifying constitution

[4] K. C. Wheare, *Federal Government* (4th edn, Oxford: Oxford University Press, 1963), 33; see generally, A. Lijphart, *Patterns of Democracy* (New Haven: Yale University Press, 1999), ch 10; D. MacKay, *Federalism and the European Union: A Political Economy Perspective* (Oxford: Oxford University Press, 1999), ch 2.

[5] Lijphart, note 4 above, 186–91.

[6] Though see M. Forsyth, *Unions of States: The Theory and Practice of Confederations* (Leicester: Leicester University Press, 1981) and D. Elazar, *Constitutionalizing Globalization: The Post Modern Revival of Confederal Arrangements* (Maryland: Rowman & Littlefield Publishers, 1998).

[7] Wheare, note 4 above, 33; C. Hughes, 'Cantonalism: Federation and Confederacy in the Golden Epoch of Switzerland' in M. Burgess and A. Gagnon, *Comparative Federalism and Federation* (Toronto: University of Toronto Press, 1993), 155.

of a federation: the centre has its own constitution, and each of the constituent states has its own, distinct, underived, constitution. In Daniel Elazar's phrase, confederations are 'communities of polities'.[8] It is sometimes argued that a further division between federations and confederations lies in their manner of addressing people: government at a federal level addresses its people directly, whereas government at a confederal level communicates to its people through its constituent states.[9] On this understanding of a confederation many international associations are drawn within its compass: the North Atlantic Treaty Organization and the signatories to the European Convention on Human Rights would amount to confederations in this sense. Others have asserted that a confederation may be distinguished from a strictly international association by a limited capacity to directly affect the legal position of individuals.[10] Even if the power of the confederation is dependent on the support of the states, it still possesses limited, contingent, authority over the people within its territory.

Confederations do not possess statehood. Whilst they have a territory, a membership and a set of institutions, the institutions at the confederal level do not make the type of claims over their people which have been identified as characteristic of states. The authority of the central government of a confederation depends on the continued support of the states. The confederation, in contrast to its constituent states, does not claim the monopoly of the legitimization of force, in Weber's terms, nor does it claim to possess supreme authority over people within its territory, in Green's language. The confederation's authority is derivative, and the states may limit or remove the powers that it possesses. It is the constituent states of the confederation that make the authority claims identified by Weber and Green; the authority of the centre is parasitic. If members of the confederation are labelled 'citizens' this title is used in an analogous sense: their membership resembles that which state-members have with their states. The loyalty of members of a confederation is, primarily, owed to their state and only secondarily to the confederation.

The line between federations and confederations is blurred in much of the political science literature, an elision that is probably not accidental. Whilst the existence of a single constitution in a federation in contrast to the multiple constitutions of confederations provides a sharp theoretical division, this may not be of great practical significance.[11] As we have seen, a constitution is not merely a legal document; it is the whole assemblage of rules that define the structure of the state. Some of these rules are legal, some are not. Sometimes the legal rules of the constitution fossilize, leaving an impression in the constitution even once the effective rule has disappeared. The fossilization of legal rules coupled with the emergence of new

---

[8] Elazar, note 1 above, 93, 50–4.

[9] Wheare, note 4 above, 13; J. Bryce, 'The Australian Commonwealth' in J. Bryce *Studies in History and Jurisprudence* (Oxford: Oxford University Press, 1901), vol 1, 489–91; Watts, note 1 above, 240.

[10] Forsyth, note 6 above, 15; M. Burgess, *Federalism and the European Union: The Building of Europe, 1950–2000* (London: Routledge, 2000), 264.

[11] Elazar, note 1 above, 11.

conventions may allow a state to move from one form of polity to another, without explicit constitutional amendment.[12] Whilst Wheare identified a federation as a state in which different levels of government have the final say in defined areas, he did not specify that this finality must be guaranteed through law. A confederation might grow into a federation as the boundaries between the competences of the centre and the states became more rigid. The relationships between the confederation's separate constitutions could become regulated by conventions—and, through these conventions, the distinct constitutions could combine into a single constitutional entity. The possibility of this shift entails that the question of whether a given political entity is a confederacy of states or a federated state may be impossible to answer in some instances.[13]

THE STATEHOOD OF THE EUROPEAN UNION

The European Union clearly possesses a territory, a membership, and a set of institutions. The question of its statehood centres on the relationship these institutions have with these people; whether the Union makes the type of authority claims identified by Weber and Green as characteristic of the state.

European law, like all law, is couched in the language of authority: law does not advise, suggest, or recommend, it commands. There is relationship of claimed authority between the law, expressed through the law-making and law-applying institutions, and those whom the law addresses.[14] Further, if the legal system is to be more than a mere abstraction its rules and institutions must be generally efficacious.[15] Two of the elements of the authority-based accounts of the state are, of necessity, present in all operative legal systems: the legal system issues commands that embody a claim to authority, and, ordinarily, these commands are effective.

As well as asserting authority, European law also claims to have a direct, unmediated, relationship with the peoples of Europe. The case of *Van Gend en Loos*[16] resolved that provisions of European law could be relied upon by individuals within their national courts: European law bound the Member States of the Union and, additionally, their nationals. European law, according to the ECJ, has effect within the Member States because these States are part of the Union; the Community's effectiveness is not dependent on incorporating rules of national law.[17] Furthermore,

---

[12] See Wheare's discussion of various constitutions which have shifted in nature over time: Wheare, note 4 above, ch 2.

[13] On which see M. Kumm, 'Why Europeans will not Embrace Constitutional Patriotism' (2008) 6 Int J Constitutional Law 117.

[14] J. Raz, 'The Claims of Law' in J. Raz, *The Authority of Law* (Oxford: Clarendon Press, 1983).

[15] J. Raz, *The Concept of a Legal System* (2nd edn, Oxford: Oxford University Press, 1980), 93, 201–2.

[16] Case 26/62 *Van Gend en Loos* [1963] ECR 1.

[17] Case 11/70 *Internationale Handelsgesellschaft* [1970] ECR 1125, para 3; Case 106/77 *Simmenthal* [1978] ECR 629, paras 17, 22.

not only does the European Union speak directly to individuals and institutions within its territory, it also claims primacy over conflicting rules of national legal systems. The Court has repeatedly asserted that European law takes precedence over contrary provisions of national law. In *Costa v ENEL* the Court derived the primacy of European law from the very nature of the European legal order:[18] one of the fundamental objectives of European law, the Court claimed, was to ensure legal consistency throughout the territory of the Community, and this objective could not be achieved unless European law was given priority over national law.[19] This assertion of legal primacy even encompasses the fundamental constitutional rules of the Member States. In *Internationale Handelsgesellschaft* the Court asserted that the validity of a Community measure could not be affected by fundamental rights contained within a national constitution,[20] and in *Grogan* the Court held that Ireland's constitutional provision restricting abortion was justiciable under European law.[21] In addition to asserting the priority of European law, the Court makes two further, distinct, claims to supremacy: that it is entitled to definitively answer all questions of European law,[22] and, additionally, that it is entitled to determine what constitutes an issue of European law.[23] There are, therefore, three distinct but connected supremacy claims advanced by the Court: the claim that European law is supreme over national law; that the Court is the supreme adjudicative body in this area; and that the Court is entitled to determine the limits of its own jurisdiction.

Not only does the Union advance a claim of authority over its members, it also characterizes those members as citizens.[24] One of the motivations behind the introduction of citizenship was to bolster the apparent legitimacy of the Union, to persuade the people of Europe that the commands of Community institutions ought to be obeyed.[25] Advocates of citizenship hoped that when citizenship was transposed into the European system it would retain some of the lustre it displayed within national constitutions, perhaps hoping that European citizens would, because of their new-found citizenship, develop loyalty towards the institutions of the Union.

---

[18] Case 6/64 *Costa v ENEL* [1964] ECR 585.

[19] Ibid., 594.

[20] Case 11/70 *Internationale Handelsgesellschaft* [1970] ECR 1125.

[21] Case C–159/90 *SPUC v Grogan* [1991] ECR I–4685.

[22] Art. 267 TFEU (previously Art. 234 EC and, before that, Art. 177).

[23] J. Weiler, 'The Transformation of Europe' in J. Weiler, *The Constitution of Europe* (Cambridge: Cambridge University Press, 1999) 21. Case 314/85, *Foto-Frost v Hauptzollamt Lübeck-Ost* [1987] ECR 4199.

[24] See generally, N. W. Barber 'Citizenship, Nationalism and the European Union' (2002) European L Rev 241, and S. Douglas-Scott, *Constitutional Law of the European Union* (London: Longman, 2002), ch 14.

[25] Barber, note 24 above; S. O'Leary, *The Evolving Concept of Community Citizenship* (London: Kluwer, 1996), ch 1.

Several writers have noted that the Union stands between a federation and a confederation, possessing elements of each form of ordering.[26] The consensus appears to be that the Union is more like a confederation than a federation[27]—but the claims made by the Union extend far beyond those we would expect a confederal entity to make. The ECJ does not acknowledge that its authority is dependent upon the continued consent of the individual Member States: Member States have 'limited their sovereign rights, albeit within limited fields. . .'[28] In contrast, in a confederation the constituent parts retain sovereignty. In some respects the self-understanding of the Union is much closer to that of a federation than to that of a confederation. Its institutions claim to have the final say about matters within their sphere of competence—Wheare's hallmark of a federal state. Recalling Lijphart's secondary characteristics of a federal state, many of them are present in the Union. There is a court which claims to police the boundaries between the centre and the regions. At a push, it could be argued that the Council resembles a second chamber of the Union's legislature, a body constructed to represent the Member States.[29] And, finally, the Treaties resemble a written constitution: a set of documents which define the respective powers of the centre and the regions, documents which are resistant to easy amendment.

Though the self-understanding of the Union comes close to the classic model of a federation, it departs from it in at least three significant respects.

First, and most importantly, the Union does not claim that there exists a unifying constitution that empowers, or purports to empower, both the Community institutions and the institutions of Member States; there is no single constitution that delegates power to both European and national institutions.[30] Whilst the Treaties may

---

[26] For example, D. Elazar, 'The United States and the European Union: Models for Their Epochs', 55; J. Weiler, 'Federalism Without Constitutionalism: Europe's *Sonderweg*', 55–8; A. Morvacsik, 'Federalism in the European Union: Rhetoric and Reality', 176, 186. All of which are to be found in K. Nicolaidis and R. Howse (eds), *The Federal Vision* (Oxford: Oxford University Press, 2001). See also M. Burgess, note 10 above, ch 9.

[27] Elazar, Weiler, and Burgess, note 26 above, see also N. MacCormick, *Who's Afraid of A European Constitution?* (London: Imprint Academic, 2005), ch 7. Supporting the opposite view: Morvacsik, note 26 above, V. Schmidt, 'Federalism and State Governance in the European Union and the United States: An Institutional Perspective' in K. Nicolaidis and R. Howse (eds), *The Federal Vision* (Oxford: Oxford University Press, 2001) 336–8; D. McKay, *Federalism and European Union: A Political Economy Perspective* (Oxford: Oxford University Press, 1999), 21–2.

[28] *Costa*, note 18 above, 597.

[29] A point noted by Giscard d'Estaing and Amato: V. Giscard d'Estaing, 'The Convention and the Future of Europe: Issues and Goals' (2003) 1 Int J Constitutional Law 346, 349; G. Amato, 'The European Convention: First Achievements and Open Dilemmas' (2003) 1 Int Journal Constitutional Law 355, 362.

[30] It is worth noting that Giscard d'Estaing advocated that the Draft Constitution delineate the competences of the Union *and* the Member States—this suggestion was not ultimately adopted. Giscard d'Estaing, note 29 above, 348.

seek to define the boundary between the competence of the Member States and the Union, they only empower one half of the equation: the Union consequently lacks the constitution that Elazar and others identified as fundamental to a federal state. However, as the relationship between the Union institutions and the Member States becomes more rigid this point may become of less significance. As we have already seen, confederal systems can solidify into federations without experiencing a defining 'constitutional moment', a specific point in time when this shift can be identified as having occurred.[31] Over time, the mesh of rules that regulate the interaction of the states and Europe may tie national constitutions and the European constitution together ever more tightly; it may become increasingly hard to determine whether these are separate constitutions which interconnect, or a single, but exceptionally complex, constitution.

Secondly, the Union does not claim to exercise control over the extent of its territory.[32] Though the political science literature does not pick out control over territory as one of the features that distinguishes federal states from confederal entities, it would appear a plausible characteristic of a federal state that expansion or contraction of its territory would require a decision at the federal level, whereas in a confederation the constituent states would have control over their, and indirectly the confederation's, territorial reach. It seems that when a Member State expands its territory, this new territory automatically comes within the reach of European Law.[33] On the other hand, when an existing part of a Member State becomes independent, European Law ceases to apply to this new state.[34]

Thirdly, the Union does not claim to exercise control over the acquisition of citizenship of the Union. It is relatively common to see dual citizenship in federal states, people are citizens both of the state and of their region, but ordinarily the conferral of citizenship is a federal matter.[35] In contrast, citizenship of the Union is dependent upon citizenship of one of the Member States.[36] Once again, this would seem more

---

[31] The allusion is to Bruce Ackerman: B. Ackerman, *We The People: Foundations* (Cambridge Mass: Harvard University Press, 1991). See also Forsyth, note 6 above, 60–72.

[32] See generally, K. Lenaerts and P. van Nuffel, *Constitutional Law of the European Union* (2nd edn, trans and ed R. Bray, London: Sweet and Maxwell, 2005), ch 8.

[33] As with, for example, the reunification of Germany: see Lenaerts and van Nuffel, note 32 above, 8–003.

[34] See, for example, the position of Sainte-Pierre-et-Miquelon, discussed in Lenaerts and van Nuffel, note 32 above.

[35] R. Koslowski 'A Constructivist Approach to Understanding The European Union as a Federal Polity' (1999) J European Public Policy 561, 572; P. H. Schuck, 'Citizenship in Federal Systems' (2000) 48 Am J Comparative Law 195, 216–17. See, for example, the jurisdiction to change naturalization law in Canada and America: P. Hogg, *The Constitutional Law of Canada* (4th edn, Toronto: Thomson Press, 1997), §34.1(d); L. Tribe, *American Constitutional Law* (3rd edn, New York: Foundation Press, 2000), vol 1, 967–8.

[36] Art 17(1) EC.

characteristic of a confederal entity than a federal state.[37] However, European Law has reduced the significance of Member States' regulation of citizenship. Member States retain control over national citizenship, but they are obliged to accept as a European citizen anyone accorded citizenship by another Member State. Once a person is a European citizen, they enjoy significant legal and political rights within all the Member States of the Union. For most practical purposes, a French citizen working in Germany enjoys legal rights virtually equivalent to her German co-workers.

The conclusion that the Union has some of the characteristics of a federal state and some of a confederation is unremarkable. Dispute over which of the two forms it more closely resembles will turn on questions of degree, and, for this reason, may prove unanswerable. But do these limited authority claims advanced by the Union institutions entail that the Union perceives itself to be a state? As we saw earlier, Weber and Green would have both concluded that a federation was a state, whereas a confederation was a collection of states. When we turn to the intermediate position which the European Union purports to occupy, an interesting division emerges between Weber and Green's accounts.[38]

Turning to Green's account first, the claim of the Union to exercise supreme authority in certain areas, coupled with its claim to determine the boundaries of those areas, might suffice. The Union does claim to be the supreme authority within its territory; no other body can question or deny its commands. At the very least, these are, for Green, state-like authority claims, even though he might conclude that the Union was not a state for other reasons. These claims consequently challenge the statehood of the Member States. Do they remain 'supreme' authorities, in Green's sense? The Court claims to be entitled to determine the area of power left to the Member States; every exercise of authority by the Member States is, in principle, reviewable by an institution of the Union. Even within their continued areas of power, the Member State's authority is contingent upon Union restraint. If the claims of the European Union were effective, Member States would no longer exercise supreme authority within their territories—and, on Green's account, their identity as states would be lost.

For Weber, in contrast, the limited authority claims advanced by the Union would not suffice to characterize the Union as a state. The Union does not claim that all exercises of legitimate power within its territory are legitimated by it, or by a broader constitution of which it is a part. The Union is clearly not a Weberian state: but what would Weber make of the position of Member States, if the Union's claims are assumed to be correct? If there has been a division of authority, if both the Union and

---

[37] A point made by Sujit Choudhry: S. Choudhry, 'Citizenship and Federations: Some Preliminary Reflections' in K. Nicolaidis and R. Howse (eds), *The Federal Vision* (Oxford: Oxford University Press, 2001), 388. In Switzerland the Cantons and Municipalities still exercise significant control over naturalization law: T. Fleiner, A. Misic and N. Töpperwien, *Swiss Constitutional Law* (London: Kluwer, 2005), 146–8.

[38] See also N. MacCormick, 'On Sovereignty and Post-Sovereignty' in N. MacCormick, *Questioning Sovereignty* (Oxford: Oxford University Press, 1999), 127–31.

its constituent Member States are supreme in their respective areas of competence, it seems that neither of these two entities claims the monopoly of legitimate force within their territories. Whilst the limited authority claims of the Union would not be enough to cause the Union to resemble a state, they are sufficient to challenge the statehood of the Member States.

The claims made by the Union consequently present a fundamental challenge to the identity of the Member States. But there is a vital element of Weber and Green's accounts of the state that has been deliberately left to one side so far. The state does not merely make a claim to exercise authority; it is also able, to a significant extent, to make good on its claim. Either it must succeed in persuading its citizenry of its legitimacy, on Weber's account, or it must succeed in guiding conduct, on Green's account.

It might be assumed that the paucity of the Union's executive branch in itself demonstrates that the Union lacks the capacity to take effective action to back its claim to exert authority. The institutions of the Union are almost entirely reliant on the support of the Member States to execute their commands; the Union lacks a developed, autonomous, set of coercive institutions and the majority of its executive work is undertaken by officials of its Member States.[39] It could be claimed that the virtual absence of European enforcement officials entails that the Union is not a state. However, neither Weber nor Green specify *how* the state must be effective; it is enough that it is able, generally, to guide conduct successfully. That it makes use of mechanisms established by another state or institution does not, necessarily, show that it is ineffective. The problem faced by those reflecting on the nature of the Union is more subtle: even if officials and private individuals are doing as the Union commands, are they acting because of the Union's command, or because the Union's command has been endorsed by their domestic state?[40] The Union will not be effective on Weber and Green's accounts if its commands are effective because they are subsequently endorsed by another state: people will be doing what the Union requires, but not because the Union requires it. If the Union's effectiveness actually depends on the incorporating rules of national constitutions, the Union will not be a state on either Weber or Green's accounts. It may understand itself to be a state, but this understanding will not square with reality.

The unwillingness of the supreme courts of Europe to endorse the claims to legal supremacy advanced by the ECJ was discussed in the previous chapter. A number of constitutional courts have asserted that European Law takes effect within their territories because of a rule of their state constitutions, and have, furthermore, indicated that they possess the capacity to review the jurisdiction of European institutions—at

---

[39] A. Moravcsik, 'The European Constitutional Compromise and the Neofunctionalist Legacy' (2005) 12 J European Public Policy 349, 370.

[40] As Tierney notes, the constitutional nature of the polity cannot be completely deduced from its formal structures: S. Tierney, ' "We the Peoples": Constituent Power and Constitutionalism in Plurinational States' in M. Loughlin and N. Walker, *The Paradox of Constitutionalism* (Oxford: Oxford University Press, 2007), 236–7. See also N. Walker, 'European Constitutionalism in the State Constitutional Tradition' (2006) 59 Current Legal Problems 51, 72–5.

least so far as their domestic legal order is concerned. The account of the Union's authority presented by many domestic constitutional courts is clearly confederal: the authority of the Union is subordinate to that of the Member States, and it has only a limited, contingent, authority to act.

Consideration of Weber and Green's efficacy criterion is not exhausted by an examination of the legal relationship between the Union and its Member States. Even if there was complete acceptance by the courts of the Member States of the supremacy of the ECJ, it need not follow that the people within those states accepted the jurisdiction asserted by the Court on behalf of the Union. People might still comply with European law because of their relationship with their nation state, and not because of their relationship with the Union. It is this consideration, perhaps, that Walter van Gerven is referring to when he asserts that the most important reason the Union is not a state is that its peoples do not wish it to gain statehood.[41] The Union will only have become a state when the people of Europe obey the commands of the Union because the Union wills it, and not because of their allegiance to their national constitutional order. It is this lack of effectiveness that sets the Union apart from a state: it may make the claims of a state, but it has little hope of making good on these claims.

The relationship between the Union and its people is not unchangeable. It may become harder to tell whether European law is obeyed because people regard themselves as citizens of Europe or because of the mediation of their nation state; indeed, different people may obey for different reasons. The authority claims of the Union may look more plausible over time. It should be recalled that neither Green nor Weber required that the state's commands be *completely* successful; both acknowledged that the success required was a matter of degree. This permits, on Green's account at least, the possibility of what could be termed 'constitutional pluralism'.[42] Unless the Member States are prepared to abandon statehood, the authority claims of the States and the Union will always be in conflict, but, eventually, each of the rival claims may be sufficiently plausible to allow both entities to constitute a state.[43] We may reach a stage when Europe presents itself as a federal state, with power divided between the regions and the centre, whilst some of the Member States continue to view the Union as a confederation, with the centre's authority subordinate to that of the states. As the lines of authority between people, Member States and the Union become yet more ambiguous, with the basis of the effectiveness of the Union's commands either fragmented within its population or just so unclear as to be indeterminate, both claims might become plausible enough to satisfy Green's test. There is no need to suppose that there is, in some sort of Schmittian

---

[41] W. van Gerven, *The European Union: A Polity of States and Peoples* (Oxford: Hart Publishing, 2005), 37–9.

[42] See generally, N. Walker 'The Idea of Constitutional Pluralism' (2002) 65 MLR 317, 336–9.

[43] It is arguable that the relationship between Quebec and Canada might also fit this model. See S. Tierney, *Constitutional and National Pluralism* (Oxford: Oxford University Press, 2004), 104–9.

sense, a single person or body who would be able to end this indeterminacy in a moment of crisis. It is possible that we may come to experience an overlap of states in Europe, with two states asserting authority over the same group of people.

LEGAL AND CONSTITUTIONAL PLURALISM CONTRASTED

In the previous chapter it was argued that the legal systems of the European Union may be characterized, or may come to be characterized, by a form of legal pluralism. A system is characterized by legal pluralism when it contains inconsistent rules of recognition and no institution within the system is legally empowered to resolve the inconsistency. This most commonly occurs when two legal systems overlap—or collide—and make rival demands on state officials. A number of the legal systems of the European Union, indeed, the legal system of the Union itself, may be touched by legal pluralism, containing inconsistent rules of recognition giving supremacy to different sources of law. This account of legal pluralism is similar to the account of constitutional pluralism set out above: in both the rival supremacy claims of national and European law are of significance. Though legal and constitutional pluralism are closely related, there are important differences between the two.

Constitutional pluralism is concerned with the overlap of states and not legal systems. Whilst every state must have its own legal system—in order to allow it to interact with its people—not every legal system need have a state. There are legal systems which span states, such as the European Convention on Human Rights, and systems which exist independently of states, such as religious legal systems or mercantile law. States can also contain multiple legal systems—as with the United Kingdom, which contains both the English and the Scottish legal systems. Legal pluralism can arise within a state without posing a challenge to its statehood, or outside the state within these international systems. A judge could be faced with a conflict generated by legally irreconcilable rules of recognition, and yet this crisis might contain no threat to the identity of the state, as both of the rival sources of law identified are contained within a single constitution. As constitutions are not merely legal documents—they contain non-legal rules as well—the constitution can contain legally inconsistent rules of recognition without compelling these inconsistent rules to become aspects of a single, if internally contradictory, legal rule. It is this capacity of constitutions to embrace multiple rules of recognition without combining them into a single legal rule that enables a state to contain multiple legal systems; the connections between the systems lie in convention, as well as in law. On the other hand, constitutional pluralism can arise without incurring legal pluralism. Two states may each advance plausible claims over a territory and a people, and yet may have completely separate legal systems through which these rival claims are advanced. It is hard to imagine such a situation continuing for a long period of time, but, perhaps, at points in history divisions caused by rivalry between secular and ecclesiastical powers might have fitted this model.[44]

---

[44] See the discussion in D. J. Galligan, *Law in Modern Society* (Oxford: Oxford University Press, 2006), 163–7.

Bibliography

Ackerman, B., *We The People: Foundations* (Cambridge Mass, 1991)

Allen, T. R. S., 'Law, Conventions, Prerogative: Reflections Prompted By the Canadian Constitution Case' (1986) 46 Cambridge LJ 305

——*Law, Liberty and Justice* (Oxford, 1993)

—— 'Parliamentary Sovereignty: Law, Politics and Revolution' (1997) 113 LQR 443

Allport, F. H., *Social Psychology* (Boston, 1923)

Alter, K., *Establishing the Supremacy of European Law* (Oxford, 2001)

Amato, G., 'The European Convention: First Achievements and Open Dilemmas' (2003) 1 Int J Constitutional Law 355

Anderson, G., *Constitutional Rights After Globalisation* (Oxford, 2005)

Arendt, H., *The Origins of Totalitarianism* (London, 1968)

——*Eichmann in Jerusalem: A Report on the Banality of Evil* (London, 2006)

Argyle, M., *The Psychology of Interpersonal Behaviour* (London, 1994)

Ariely, D., *Predictably Irrational*, (London, 2008)

Aristotle, *The Politics and Constitution of Athens*, ed S. Everson, trans J. Barnes (Cambridge, 1996)

——*The Nicomachean Ethics*, trans J. Thomson (London, 1976)

Arnaud, A., 'Legal Pluralism and the Building of Europe' in H. Petersen and H. Zahle (eds), *Legal Polycentricity: The Consequences of Pluralism in Law*, (Aldershot, 1994)

Aronson, E., *The Social Animal* (10th edn, New York, 2007)

Austin, J., *The Province of Jurisprudence Determined*, ed H. L. A. Hart (London, 1954)

Bagehot, Walter, *Physics and Politics* (2nd edn, London, 1872)

Baldwin, T., 'The Territorial State' in H. Gross and R. Harrison (eds), *Jurisprudence: Cambridge Essays* (Oxford, 1992)

Barber, N. W., 'Sovereignty Re-examined: The Courts, Parliament and Statutes' (2000) 20 Oxford J Legal Studies 131

—— 'The Doctrine of State Necessity in Pakistan' (2000) 116 LQR 569

—— 'Prelude to the Separation of Powers' (2001) 60 Cambridge LJ 59

—— 'The Doctrine of State Necessity and Revolutionary Legality in Fiji' (2001) 117 LQR 370

—— 'Citizenship, Nationalism and the European Union' (2002) 27 European L Rev 241

Barber, N. W., 'Must Legalistic Conceptions of the Rule of Law Have a Social Dimension?' (2004) 17 Ratio Juris 474

——and Young, A. L., 'Prospective Henry VIII Clauses and their Implications for Sovereignty' (2003) Public Law 112

Barker, E., 'The Discredited State' in E. Barker, *Church, State and Study* (London, 1930)

Baron, R., and Crawley, K., and Paulina, D., 'Aberrations of Power: Leadership in Totalist Groups' in M. Hogg and D. van Knippenberg (eds), *Leadership and Power* (London, 2003)

Barry, B., 'Political Accommodation and Consociational Democracy' (1975) *British J Political Science* 477

—— 'The Consociational Model and its Dangers' (1975) *European J Political Research* 393

Bayles, M., *Hart's Legal Philosophy* (London, 1992)

Bellamy, R., *Political Constitutionalism* (Oxford, 2007)

Bion, W., *Experiences in Groups,* (London, 1989)

Bix, B., 'Conceptual Questions and Jurisprudence' (1995) 1 Legal Theory 465

—— 'H. L. A. Hart and the Hermeneutic Turn in Legal Theory' (1999) 52 SMU Law Rev 167

Blackstone, W., *Commentaries on the Laws of England* (1st edn, Oxford, 1795)

Böckenförde, E., 'The Concept of the Political: A Key to Understanding Carl Schmitt's Constitutional Theory' in D. Dyzenhaus (ed), *Law as Politics: Carl Schmitt's Critique of Liberalism* (Durham, 1998)

Boudreau, C., McCubbins, M. D., and Rodriguez, D. B., 'Statutory Interpretation and the Intentional(ist) Stance' (2004–2005) 38 Loyola of Los Angeles L Rev 2131

Bratman, M., 'Shared Cooperative Activity' in M. Bratman, *Faces of Intention* (Cambridge, 1999)

—— 'Shared Intention' in M. Bratman, *Faces of Intention* (Cambridge, 1999)

Braybrooke, D., *Philosophy of Social Science* (New Jersey, 1987)

Brazier, R., 'The Non-Legal Constitution: Thoughts on Convention, Practice and Principle' (1992) 42 NILQ 262

Brazier, R., and Robilliard, St. J., 'Constitutional Conventions: The Canadian Supreme Court's Views Revisited' (1982) Public Law 28

Brookfield, F. M., *The Treaty of Waitangi and Indigenous Rights* (Auckland, 1999)

Brown, R., *Group Processes* (2nd edn, Oxford, 2002)

Bryce, J., 'The Australian Commonwealth' in J. Bryce, *Studies in History and Jurisprudence,* vol 1 (Oxford, 1901)

—— *The American Commonwealth,* vol 2 (Indiana, 1995)

Burgess, M., *Federalism and the European Union: The Building of Europe, 1950–2000* (London, 2000)

Cane, P., *Responsibility in Law and Morality* (Oxford, 2003)

Canovan, M., *Nationhood and Political Theory* (Cheltenham, 1996)

Carens, J., *Culture, Citizenship and Community* (Oxford, 2000)

Chafetz, J., *Democracy's Privileged Few* (New Haven, 2007)

Chiba, M., 'Other Phases of Legal Pluralism in the Contemporary World' (1998) 11 Ratio Juris 228

Choudhry, S., 'Citizenship and Federations: Some Preliminary Reflections' in K. Nicolaidis and R. Howse, *The Federal Vision* (Oxford, 2001)

Christie, G., *Law, Norms and Authority* (London, 1982)

Coleman, J., *The Practice of Principle* (Oxford, 2003)

Cooper, J., and Kelly, K., and Weaver, K., 'Attitudes, Norms and Social Groups' in M. Hogg and S. Tindale (eds), *Blackwell Handbook of Social Psychology: Group Processes*, (London, 2003)

Coppel, J., and O'Neill, A., 'The European Court of Justice: Taking Rights Seriously?' (1992) 12 Legal Studies 227

Coyle, S., 'The Possibility of Deontic Logic' (2002) 15 Ratio Juris 294

Craig, P. P., *Public Law and Democracy in the United Kingdom and the United States of America* (Oxford, 1990)

Cristi, R., 'Carl Schmitt on Sovereignty and Constituent Power' in D. Dyzenhaus (ed), *Law as Politics: Carl Schmitt's Critique of Liberalism* (Durham, 1998)

Crone, P., 'The Tribe and the State' in J. Hall (ed), *States in History* (Oxford, 1986)

Cross, R., and Harris, J., *Precedent in English Law* (4th edn, Oxford, 1991)

Cruz, J. Baquero, 'The Legacy of the Maastricht-Urteil Decision and the Pluralist Movement' (2008) 14 European LJ 389

D'Estaing, V. Giscard, 'The Convention and the Future of Europe: Issues and Goals' (2003) 1 Int J Constitutional Law 346

De Board, R., *The Psychoanalysis of Organisations* (London, 1990)

De Lange, R., 'Divergence, Fragmentation and Legal Pluralism' in H. Petersen and H. Zahle (eds), *Legal Polycentricity: The Consequences of Pluralism in Law* (Aldershot, 1994)

De Lolme, J. L., *The Constitution of England* (1st edn, London, 1784)

De Smith, S. A., 'Parliamentary Privilege and the Bill of Rights' (1958) 21 MLR 465

De Sousa Santos, B., *Towards a New Common Sense: Law Science and Politics in Paradigmatic Transition* (2nd edn, London, 2002)

Dean, J., *Hatred, Ridicule or Contempt* (London, 1953)

Denning, Lord A., 'Memorandum on the Strauss Case' (1985) Public Law 80

Dicey, A. V., *An Introduction to the Study of the Law of the Constitution* (10th edn, London, 1959)

Dickson, Julie, *Evaluation and Legal Theory* (Oxford, 2000)

—— 'Methodology in Jurisprudence' (2004) 10 Legal Theory 117

—— 'Is the Rule of Recognition Really a Convention?' (2007) 27 Oxford J Legal Studies 373

Douglas-Scott, S., *Constitutional Law of the European Union* (London, 2002)

Dummett, A., and Nicol, A., *Subjects, Citizens, Aliens and Others* (London, 1990)

Durkheim, E., *Suicide*, trans J. A. Spaudling and G. Simpson (London, 2002)

Dworkin, R., 'Model of Rules 1' in R. Dworkin, *Taking Rights Seriously* (London, 1977)

——'No Right Answer?' in P. Hacker, and J. Raz (eds), *Law Morality and Society* (Oxford, 1978)

——*Law's Empire* (Cambridge Mass, 1986)

——'On Gaps in the Law' in P. Amselek and N. MacCormick (eds), *Controversies About Law's Ontology* (Edinburgh, 1991)

——'Thirty Years On' (2002) 115 Harvard L Rev 1655

Dyson, K., *The State Tradition in Western Europe: A Study of an Idea and Institution* (Oxford, 1979)

Dyzenhaus, David, *The Constitution of Law: Legality in a Time of Emergency* (Cambridge, 2006)

Eekelaar, J., 'Splitting the *Grundnorm*' (1967) 30 MLR 156

——'Rhodesia: Abdication of Constitutionalism' (1969) 32 MLR 19

Ehrlich, E., *Fundamental Principles of the Sociology of Law*, trans W. L. Moll (New York, 1936)

Ekins, Richard, *The Nature of Legislative Intent*, D.Phil submitted to Oxford University, 2009

Elazar, D., *Exploring Federalism* (Tuscaloosa, 1992)

——*Constituting Globalization: The Post Modern Revival of Confederal Arrangements* (Maryland, 1998)

——'The United States and the European Union: Models for their Epochs' in K. Nicolaidis and R. Howse (eds), *The Federal Vision* (Oxford, 2001)

Elliott, M., 'Parliamentary Sovereignty and the New Constitutional Order', (2002) 19 Legal Studies 340

Endicott, T., 'Herbert Hart and the Semantic Sting' in J. Coleman (ed), *Hart's Postscript: Essays on the Postscript to* The Concept of Law (Oxford, 2001)

——'Interpretation, Jurisdiction and the Authority of Law' (2007) 6(2) *American Philosophical Association Newsletter on Law and Philosophy* 14

——'The Logic of Freedom and Power' in J. Tasioulas and S. Besson (eds), *Philosophy of International Law* (Oxford, 2010)

Etzioni, A., 'Social Norms: Internalization, Persuasion and History' (2000) 34 Law and Society Rev 157

Fichera, M., 'The European Arrest Warrant and the Sovereign State: A Marriage of Convenience?' (2009) 15 European LJ 70

Filmer, R., *Patriarcha*, ed J. Sommerville (Cambridge, 1991)

Finer, S., 'The Individual Responsibility of Ministers' (1956) 34 Public Administration 377

——*History of Government Volume 1: Ancient Monarchies and Empires* (Oxford, 1997)

Finnis, J., 'Revolutions and the Continuity of Law' in A. W. B. Simpson (ed), *Oxford Essays in Jurisprudence: Second Series* (Oxford, 1973)

——*Natural Law and Natural Rights* (Oxford, 1980)

——'Persons and Their Associations' (1989) 63 *Aristotelian Society Supplementary Volumes* 267

——*Aquinas* (Oxford, 1998)

——'The Fairy Tale's Moral' (1999) 115 LQR 170

——'Law and What I Truly Should Decide' (2003) 48 Am J Jurisprudence 108

——'H. L. A. Hart: A Twentieth Century Oxford Political Philosopher' available at <http://ssrn.com/abstract=1477276>

Fleiner, T., Misic, A., and Töpperwien, N., *Swiss Constitutional Law* (London, 2005)

Foot, P., 'Moral Realism and Moral Dilemma' (1983) 80 *Journal of Philosophy* 379

Forsyth, D., *Group Dynamics* (4th edn, Belmont, 2006)

Forsyth, M., *Unions of States: The Theory and Practice of Confederations* (Leicester, 1981)

Freeman, E., *The Growth of the English Constitution* (3rd edn, London, 1876)

French, P., *Collective and Corporate Responsibility* (Columbia, 1984)

Fried, M. H., 'The State, The Chicken, and the Egg; Or, What Came First?' in R. Cohen and E. R. Service (eds), *Origins of the State: The Anthropology of Political Evolution* (Philadelphia, 1978)

Fuller, L., 'Positivism and Fidelity to Law—A Reply to Professor Hart' (1958) 71 Harvard L Rev 630

——*The Morality of Law* (New Haven, 1969)

Galligan, D., *Law in Modern Society* (Oxford, 2007)

Gardner, J., 'Law's Aims in *Law's Empire*' in S. Hershovitz, *Exploring Law's Empire: The Jurisprudence of Ronald Dworkin* (Oxford, 2006)

——'The Mark of Responsibility' in J. Gardner, *Offences and Defences*, (Oxford, 2007)

——'How Law Claims, What Law Claims' (2008) Oxford Legal Studies Research Paper No 44/2008

Geertz, C., 'The Integrative Revolution' in C. Geertz, *Old Societies and New States* (London, 1963)

Gibney, E., and Roxstom, E., 'The Status of State Apologies' (2001) 23 HRQ 119

Gilbert, M., *On Social Facts* (New York, 1989)

Green, Leslie, *The Authority of the State* (Oxford, 1990)

——'The Functions of Law' (1998) 12 Cogito 117

——'Positivism and Conventionalism' (1999) 12 Canadian J Law and Jurisprudence 35

Greenwalt, K., 'Hart's Rule of Recognition and the United States' (1988) 1 Ratio Juris 40

Griffith, J., 'The Political Constitution' (1979) 42 MLR 1

Griffiths, J., 'What is Legal Pluralism?' (1986) 24 J Legal Pluralism 1

Gwyer, M. L., *Anson's Law and Custom of the Constitution* (5th edn, Oxford, 1922)

Hall, J. A., and Ikenberry, G. J., *The State* (Buckingham, 1989)

Halton, W., 'Some Unconscious Aspects of Organizational Life: Contributions From Psychoanalysis' in A. Obholzer and J. Stokes (eds), *The Unconscious At Work*, (Abingdon, 1994)

Harden, I., 'The Constitution and its Discontents' (1991) 21 British J Political Science 489

Harlow, C., and Rawlings, R., *Law and Administration* (2nd edn, London, 1997)

Harré, R., and Secord, P. F., *The Explanation of Social Behaviour* (London, 1972)

Harris, J., 'When and Why Does the *Grundnorm* Change?' (1971) 29 Cambridge LJ 103

—— 'Kelsen and Normative Consistency' in R. Tur and W. Twining (eds), *Essays on Kelsen*, (Oxford, 1986)

Hart, H. L. A., 'Legal Duty and Obligation' in H. L. A. Hart, *Essays on Bentham* (Oxford, 1982)

—— 'Kelsen's Doctrine of the Unity of Law' in H. L. A. Hart, *Essays in Jurisprudence and Philosophy* (Oxford, 1983)

—— *The Concept of Law* (2nd edn, Oxford, 1994)

—— 'Postscript: Responsibility and Retribution' in H. L. A. Hart, *Punishment and Responsibility* (2nd edn, Oxford, 2008)

Harvey, C. J., 'The New Beginning: Reconstructing Constitutional Law and Democracy in Northern Ireland' in C. J. Harvey (ed), *Human Rights, Equality and Democratic Renewal in Northern Ireland* (Oxford, 2001)

Heard, A., *Canadian Constitutional Conventions* (Oxford, 1991)

Hellum, A., 'Actor Perspectives on Gender and Legal Pluralism in Africa' in H. Petersen and H. Zahle (eds), *Legal Polycentricity: Consequences of Pluralism in Law* (Aldershot, 1994)

Hemple, C. G., *Philosophy of Natural Science* (New Jersey, 1966)

Hobbes, T., *Leviathan,* ed R. Tuck (Cambridge, 1991)

Hobsbawn, E., *Nations and Nationalism Since 1780* (Cambridge, 1990)

Hoffman, J., *Beyond the State* (Cambridge, 1995)

Hogg, P., 'Necessity in a Constitutional Crisis' (1989) 15 *Monash University L Rev* 253

—— *The Constitutional Law of Canada* (4th edn, Toronto, 1997)

Honoré, T., 'Real Laws' in P. Hacker and J. Raz, *Law, Morality and Society* (Oxford, 1977)

—— 'Groups, Laws and Obedience' in T. Honoré, *Making Law Bind* (Oxford, 1987)

—— 'How is Law Possible?' in T. Honoré, *Making Law Bind* (Oxford, 1987)

—— 'What is a Group?' in T. Honoré, *Making Law Bind* (Oxford, 1987)

—— 'Introduction' in T. Honoré, *Responsibility and Fault* (Oxford, 1999)

—— 'Responsibility and Luck' in T. Honoré, *Responsibility and Fault* (Oxford, 1999)

—— 'Being Responsible and Being a Victim of Circumstance' in T. Honoré, *Responsibility and Fault* (Oxford, 1999)

Hooker, M. B., *Legal Pluralism—An Introduction to Colonial and Neo-Colonial Laws* (Oxford, 1975)

Hughes, C., 'Cantonalism: Federation and Confederacy in the Golden Epoch of Switzerland' in M. Burgess and A. Gagnon, *Comparative Federalism and Federation* (Toronto, 1993)

Hunt, M., *Using Human Rights Law in English Courts* (Oxford, 1997)

Jackson, P., and Leopold, P., *O. Hood Phillips and Jackson: Constitutional and Administrative Law* (London, 2001)

Jaconelli, J., 'The Nature of Constitutional Conventions' (1999) 19 Legal Studies 24

—— 'Do Constitutional Conventions Bind?' (2005) 64 Cambridge LJ 149

Janis, I. J., *Groupthink* (2nd edn, Boston, 1982)

Janoski, T., *Citizenship and Civil Society* (Cambridge, 1998)

Janowitz, M., *The Reconstruction of Patriotism: Education for Civic Consciousness* (Chicago, 1983)

Jennings, I., 'The Institutional Theory' in I. Jennings (ed), *Modern Theories of Law* (Oxford, 1933)

—— *The Law and the Constitution* (5th edn, London, 1959)

Johnson, C., *Aristotle's Theory of the State* (London, 1990)

Jørgensen, J., 'Imperatives and Logic' (1937–1938) 7 *Erkenntnis* 288

Kelsen, Hans, 'Professor Stone and the Pure Theory of Law' (1965) 17 Stanford L Rev 1128

—— *The Pure Theory of Law*, trans M. Knight (Berkley, 1967)

—— *General Theory of Law and State*, trans A. Wedberg (New York, 1961)

King, J. A., 'Institutional Approaches to Judicial Restraint' (2008) 28 Oxford J Legal Studies 409

Krisch, N., 'The Open Architecture of European Human Rights Law' (2008) 71 MLR 183

Koslowski, R., 'A Constructivist Approach to Understanding the European Union as a Federal Polity' (1999) J European Public Policy 561

Kramer, M., *In Defense of Legal Positivism* (Oxford, 1999)

Kumm, M., 'Who is the Final Arbiter of Constitutionality in Europe?' (1999) 36 *Common Market L Rev* 351

—— 'Why Europeans Will Not Embrace Constitutional Patriotism' (2008) 6 Int J Constitutional Law 117

Lagerspetz, E., *The Opposite Mirrors: A Conventionalist Theory of Institutions* (London, 1995)

Lamond, G., 'Coercion and the Nature of Law' (2001) 7 Legal Theory 35

Laski, H., *Authority in the Modern State* (New Haven, 1919)

—— *Foundations of Sovereignty* (London, 1921)

Le Bon, G., *The Crowd* (New Jersey, 1995)

Leiter, B., 'Naturalism and Naturalized Jurisprudence' in B. Bix (ed), *Analyzing Law: New Essays in Legal Theory* (Oxford, 1998)

——'Legal Realism, Hard Positivism and the Limits of Conceptual Analysis' in J. Coleman (ed), *Hart's Postscript: Essays on the Postscript to* The Concept of Law, (Oxford, 2001)

——'Beyond the Hart/Dworkin Debate: The Methodology Problem in Jurisprudence' (2003) 48 Am J Jurisprudence 17

Lenaerts, K., and van Nuffel, P., *Constitutional Law of the European Union* (2nd edn), ed R. Bray (London, 2005)

Lenin, V., *The State and Revolution*, trans R. Service (London, 1992)

Leopold, P., 'Standards of Conduct in Public Life' in J. Jowell and D. Oliver (eds), *The Changing Constitution* (6th edn, Oxford, 2007)

Lewis, D., *Convention* (London, 2002)

Lijphart, A., *Democracy in Plural Societies* (New Haven, 1977)

——*Patterns of Democracy* (New Haven, 1999)

Lipset, S. M., 'The Indispensability of Political Parties' (2000) 11 J Democracy 48

Loughlin, M., *The Idea of Public Law* (Oxford, 2003)

MacCormick, N., 'Law as an Institutional Fact' in N. MacCormick and O. Weinberger, *An Institutional Theory of Law: New Approaches to Positivism* (London, 1986)

——'The Concept of Law and "The Concept of Law"' (1994) 14 Oxford J Legal Studies 1

——'A Very British Revolution' in N. MacCormick, *Questioning Sovereignty* (Oxford, 1999)

——'The United Kingdom: What State? What Constitution?' in N. MacCormick, *Questioning Sovereignty* (Oxford, 1999)

——'The State and the Law' in N. MacCormick, *Questioning Sovereignty* (Oxford, 1999)

——'A Kind of Nationalism' in N. MacCormick, *Questioning Sovereignty* (Oxford, 1999)

——'Juridical Pluralism and the Risk of Constitutional Conflict' in N. MacCormick, *Questioning Sovereignty* (Oxford, 1999)

——'On Sovereignty and Post-Sovereignty' in N. MacCormick, *Questioning Sovereignty* (Oxford, 1999)

——'Is There a Constitutional Path to Scottish Independence?' (2000) 53 *Parliamentary Affairs* 721

——*Who's Afraid of A European Constitution?* (London, 2005)

——*Institutions of Law* (Oxford, 2007)

MacDermott, Lord, 'The Decline of the Rule of Law' (1972) 23 NILQ 474

Macedo, S., *Liberal Virtues* (Oxford, 1990)

MacKay, D., *Federalism and the European Union: A Political Economy Perspective* (Oxford, 1999)

Maduro, M., 'Europe and the Constitution: What If This Is as Good as it Gets?' in J. Weiler and M. Wind (eds), *European Constitutionalism Beyond the State* (Cambridge, 2003)

Mahmud, T., 'The Jurisprudence of Successful Treason' (1994) 27 Cornell Int LJ 49

Manin, B., *The Principles of Representative Government* (Cambridge, 1997)

Marmor, A., 'On Convention' (1996) 107 *Synthese* 349

Martin, A., 'The Accession of the United Kingdom to the European Communities: Jurisdictional Problems' (1968–1969) 6 Common Market L Rev 7

Martin, M., 'Taylor on Interpretation and the Sciences of Man' in M. Martin and L. McIntyre (eds), *Readings in the Philosophy of Social Science* (London, 1994)

Marshall, G., *Constitutional Theory* (Oxford 1971)

——*Constitutional Conventions* (Oxford, 1984)

Marshall, G., and Moodie, G., *Some Problems of the Constitution* (5th edn, London, 1971)

Marshall, T. and Bottomore, T., *Citizenship and Social Class* (London, 1992)

May, E., *Parliamentary Practice* (22nd edn, London, 1997)

May, L., *Sharing Responsibility* (Chicago, 1992)

Mayer, F., 'The European Constitution in the Courts' in A. von Bogdandy and J. Blast (eds), *Principles of European Constitutional Law* (Oxford, 2006)

McCrudden, C., 'Institutional Discrimination' (1982) 2 Oxford Journal of Legal Studies 303

——'Northern Ireland and the British Constitution' in J. Jowell and D. Oliver (eds), *The Changing Constitution* (6th edn, Oxford, 2007)

McIlwain, C. H., *Constitutionalism: Ancient and Modern* (rev edn, New York, 1947)

Megarry, R., 'Lay Peers in Appeals to the House of Lords' (1949) 65 LQR 22

Merry, S., 'Legal Pluralism' (1988) 22 Law and Society Rev 869

Miliband, R., *The State in Capitalist Society* (London, 1969)

Mill, J. S., 'Considerations on Representative Government' in J. S. Mill, *On Liberty and Other Essays* (Oxford, 1991)

Miller, David, *On Nationality* (Oxford, 1995)

——*National Responsibility and Global Justice* (Oxford, 2007)

Mithen, S., *The Prehistory of the Mind* (London, 1996)

Moore, M., 'Law as a Functional Kind' in R. P. George (ed), *Natural Law Theory: Contemporary Issues* (Oxford, 1992)

Moore, S., 'Law and Social Change: the Semi-Autonomous Social Field as an Appropriate Subject of Study' (1973) 7 Law and Society Rev 719

Morgan, E., *Inventing the People: The Rise of Popular Sovereignty in England and America* (London, 1988)

Morrall, J. B., *Political Thought in Medieval Times* (Toronto, 1980)

Morvacsik, A, 'Federalism in the European Union: Rhetoric and Reality' in K. Nicolaidis and R. Howse (eds), *The Federal Vision* (Oxford, 2001)

—— 'The European Constitutional Compromise and the Neofunctionalist Legacy' (2005) 12 Eur J Public Policy 349

Munro, C., 'Laws and Conventions Distinguished' (1975) LQR 218

—— 'Dicey on Constitutional Conventions' (1985) Public Law 637

—— *Studies in Constitutional Law* (London, 1987)

—— *Studies in Constitutional Law* (2nd edn, London, 1999)

Munzer, S., 'Validity and Legal Conflicts' (1973) 82 Yale LJ 1140

Nagel, T., 'The Fragmentation of Value' in T. Nagel, *Mortal Questions* (Cambridge, 1979)

Nicholls, D., *The Pluralist State* (Basingstoke, 1994)

Nicol, D., *EC Membership and the Judicialization of British Politics* (Oxford, 2001)

O'Leary, S., *The Evolving Concept of Community Citizenship* (London, 1996)

Oliver, D., *Common Values and the Public-Private Divide* (London, 1999)

Oliver, P., 'Sovereignty in the Twenty-First Century' (2003) 14 King's College LJ 137

—— *The Constitution of Independence: The Development of Constitutional Theory in Australia, Canada and New Zealand* (Oxford, 2005)

Orizio, R., *Talk of the Devil: Encounters With Seven Dictators* (New York, 2003)

Park, J. J., *The Dogmas of the Constitution* (London, 1832)

Paulson, S., 'On the Status of the *Lex Posterior* Derogating Rule' in R. Tur and W. Twining, *Essays on Kelsen*, (Oxford, 1986)

—— 'On the Background and Significance of Gustav Radbruch's Post-War Papers' (2006) 26 Oxford J Legal Studies 17

Pettit, P., *Republicanism: A Theory of Freedom and Government* (Oxford, 1997)

—— *A Theory of Freedom: From the Psychology to the Politics of Agency* (Cambridge, 2001)

—— 'Collective Persons and Powers' (2002) 8 Legal Theory 443

—— 'Responsibility Incorporated' (2007) 117 Ethics 171

—— 'Rationality, Reasoning and Group Agency' (2007) 61 Dialectica 495

—— and Schweikard, D., 'Joint Actions and Group Agents' (2006) 36 *Philosophy of the Social Sciences* 18

Phillips, O. Hood, 'Constitutional Conventions: Dicey's Predecessors' (1966) 29 MLR 137

Pierson, C., *The Modern State* (2nd edn, Abingdon, 2004)

Popper, K., *The Poverty of Historicism* (2nd edn, London, 1960)

Posner, E., *Law and Social Norms* (Cambridge Mass, 2000)

Pratkanis, A., and Aronson, E., *Age of Propaganda: The Everyday Use and Abuse of Persuasion* (rev edn, New York, 2001)

Quinton, A., 'Social Objects' (1975) Proceedings of the Aristotelian Society 75

Rawlings, R., 'Concordats of the Constitution' (2000) 116 LQR 257

Rawls, J., 'Two Concepts of Rules' (1955) 64 Philosophical Review 3

Raz, J., 'Legal Principles and the Limits of the Law' (1972) 81 Yale LJ 823

—— 'The Rule of Law and its Virtue' in J. Raz, *The Authority of Law* (Oxford, 1979)

—— 'The Institutional Nature of Law' in J. Raz, *The Authority of Law* (Oxford, 1979)

—— 'Legal Reasons, Sources and Gaps' in J. Raz, *The Authority of Law* (Oxford, 1979)

—— 'The Identity of Legal Systems' in J. Raz, *The Authority of Law* (Oxford, 1979)

—— 'The Claims of Law' in J. Raz, *The Authority of Law* (Oxford, 1979)

—— *The Concept of a Legal System* (2nd edn, Oxford, 1980)

—— *The Morality of Freedom* (Oxford, 1986)

—— *Practical Reason and Norms* (2nd edn, New Jersey, 1990)

—— 'The Problem About the Nature of Law' in J. Raz, *Ethics in the Public Domain* (rev ed, Oxford, 1995)

—— 'Authority, Law and Morality' in J. Raz, *Ethics in the Public Domain* (rev edn, Oxford, 1995)

—— 'The Relevance of Coherence' in J. Raz, *Ethics in the Public Domain* (rev edn, Oxford, 1995)

—— 'On the Authority and Interpretation of Constitutions: Some Preliminaries' in L. Alexander (ed), *Constitutionalism: Philosophical Foundations* (Cambridge, 1998)

—— 'Two Views About the Nature of Law: A Partial Comparison' in J. Coleman (ed), *Hart's Postscript: Essays on the Postscript to* The Concept of Law (Oxford, 2001)

Reicher, S., 'The Psychology of Crowd Dynamics' in M. Hogg and S. Tindale, *Blackwell Handbook of Social Psychology: Group Processes* (Oxford, 2001)

Reicher, S., and Hopkins, N., 'On the Science of the Art of Leadership' in M. Hogg and D. van Knippenberg (eds), *Leadership and Power* (London, 2003)

Renan, E., 'What is a Nation?' in A. Zimmern (ed), *Modern Political Doctrines* (Oxford, 1939)

Richmond, C., 'Preserving the Identity Crisis: Autonomy, System and Sovereignty in European Law' (1997) 16 Law and Philosophy 377

Ridley, F., 'There is No British Constitution: A Dangerous Case of the Emperor's Clothes' (1988) 41 Parliamentary Affairs 340

Ridley, M., *The Origins of Virtue* (London, 1996)

Rosenblum, N. L., *On the Side of the Angels: An Appreciation of Parties and Partisanship*, (Princeton, 2008)

Rossiter, C., *Constitutional Dictatorship* (Princeton, 1948)

Sadurski, W., 'Solange Chapter 3: Constitutional Courts in Central Europe' (2008) 14 *European Law Journal* 1

Sartorius, R., 'Hart's Concept of Law' in R. Summers (ed), *More Essays in Legal Philosophy* (Oxford, 1971)

Schauer, F., *Playing By the Rules* (Oxford, 1991)

—— 'The Social Construction of the Concept of Law: A Reply to Julie Dickson' (2005) 25 Oxford Journal of Legal Studies 493

Schelling, T., 'The Intimate Contest for Self Command' in T. Schelling, *Choice and Consequence* (Cambridge Mass., 1984)

Schmidt, V., 'Federalism and State Governance in the European Union and the United States' in K. Nicolaidis and R. Howse (eds), *The Federal Vision*, (Oxford, 2001)

Schmitt, C., *The Concept of the Political*, trans G. Schwab (Chicago, 1996)

——*Political Theology: Four Chapters on the Concept of Sovereignty*, trans G. Schwab, (Chicago, 2006)

Scott, H., and Barber, N. W., 'State Liability Under *Francovich* for Decisions of National Courts' (2004) 120 Law Quarterly Review 403

Schuck, P. H., 'Citizenship in Federal Systems' (2000) 48 Am J Comparative Law 195

Searle, J. R., *Speech Acts: An Essay in the Philosophy of Language* (Cambridge, 1969)

——'Collective Intentions and Actions' in P. R. Cohen, J. Morgan and M. E Pollack (eds), *Intentions in Communication*, (Cambridge, 1990)

——*The Construction of Social Reality* (London, 1996)

——*Mind: A Brief Introduction* (Oxford, 2004)

Seidenfeld, M., 'A Civic Republican Justification for the Bureaucratic State' (1992) 105 Harvard L Rev 1511

Service, E. R., 'Classical and Modern Theories of the Origins of Government', in R. Cohen and E. R. Service (eds), *Origins of the State: The Anthropology of Political Evolution*, (Philadelphia, 1978)

Sighele, S., *La Folle Delinquente* (Italy, 1891)

Skinner, B. F., 'The Operational Analysis of Psychological Terms' (1945) 52 *Psychological Rev* 270

Smith, T. B., 'The Union of 1707 as Fundamental Law' (1957) Public Law 99

Snyder, F., 'The Unfinished Constitution of the European Union', in J. H. H. Weiler and M. Wind (eds), *European Constitutionalism Beyond the State* (Cambridge, 2003)

Somers, M. R., 'Citizenship and the Place of the Public Sphere' (1993) 58 *Am Sociological Rev* 587

Spencer, H., *Principles of Sociology* (London, 1898)

Stevens, R., 'The Final Appeal: Reform of the House of Lords and Privy Council 1867–1876' (1964) 80 LQR 354

Stokes, J., 'The Unconscious at Work in Groups and Teams: Contributions From the Work of Wilfred Bion' in A. Obholzer and J. Stokes (eds), *The Unconscious At Work* (Abingdon, 1994)

Stokes, S. C., 'Political Parties and Democracy' (1999) Annual Review of Political Science 243

Sunstein, C., *Why Societies Need Dissent* (Cambridge Mass, 2003)

Surowiecki, J., *The Wisdom of Crowds* (London, 2004)

Tamanaha, B., *A General Jurisprudence of Law and Society* (Oxford, 2001)

Taylor, C., 'Interpretation and the Sciences of Man' in C. Taylor, *Philosophy and the Human Sciences: Philosophical Papers Vol 2* (Cambridge, 1985)

—— 'Understanding and Ethnocentricity' in C. Taylor, *Philosophy and the Human Sciences: Philosophical Papers Vol 2* (Cambridge, 1985)

—— 'Social Theory as Practice' in C. Taylor, *Philosophy and the Human Sciences: Philosophical Papers Vol 2* (Cambridge, 1985)

—— 'Neutrality in Political Science' in C. Taylor, *Philosophy and the Human Sciences: Philosophical Papers Vol 2* (Cambridge, 1985)

Thomas, G. M. and Meyer, J. W., 'The Expansion of the State' (1984) 10 Annual Review of Sociology 461

Tierney, S., *Constitutional Law and National Pluralism* (Oxford, 2004)

—— ' "We the Peoples": Constituent Power in Plurinational Societies' in M. Loughlin and N. Walker, *The Paradox of Constitutionalism* (Oxford, 2007)

Tinturé, M. Köpcke, *Some Main Questions Concerning Legal Validity*, D.Phil Submitted to Oxford University, 2009

Titus, C. H., 'A Nomenclature in Political Science' (1931) 25 Am Polit Sci Rev 45

Todd, A., *Parliamentary Government in England*, vol 2 (London, 1892)

Tomkins, A., *Our Republican Constitution* (Oxford, 2005)

Travis, C., and Aronson, E., *Mistakes Were Made (But Not By Me)* (London, 2007)

Tribe, L., *American Constitutional Law* (3rd edn, New York, 2000)

Trinidade, F. A., 'Parliamentary Sovereignty and the Primacy of European Community Law' (1972) 35 MLR 375

Tyler, T. R., *Why People Obey the Law* (Princeton, 2006)

Usman, J., 'Non-Justiciable Directive Principles: A Constitutional Design Defect', (2007) 15 Michigan State J Int L 643

Vanderlinden, J., 'Le Pluralism Juridique: Essai de Synthése' in J. Gilissen (ed), *Le Pluralisme Juridique* (Brussels, 1971)

Van Gerven, W., *The European Union: A Polity of States and Peoples* (Oxford, 2005)

Van Ginneken, *Crowds, Psychology and Politics, 1871–1899,* (Cambridge, 1992)

Veitch, S., *Law and Irresponsibility* (London, 2007)

Vincent, A., *Theories of the State* (Oxford, 1987)

Volpe, G., 'A Minimalist Solution to Jørgensen's Dilemma' (1999) 12 Ratio Juris 59

Von Wright, G., *Logical Studies* (London, 1957)

—— *Norm and Action* (London, 1963)

—— 'Deontic Logic: A personal view' (1999) 12 Ratio Juris 26

Wade, W., 'The Basis of Legal Sovereignty' (1955) Cambridge LJ 172

—— 'Sovereignty—Revolution or Evolution?' (1996) 113 LQR 568

Walker, N., 'Sovereignty and Differentiated Integration in the European Union' (1998) 4 European LJ 355

Walker, N., 'The Idea of Constitutional Pluralism' (2002) 65 MLR 317

—— 'European Constitutionalism in the State Constitutional Tradition' (2006) 59 Current Legal Problems 51

Walzer, M., 'The Civil Society Argument' in R. Beiner (ed), *Theorising Citizenship* (Albany, 1995)

Watts, R. L., 'Comparing Forms of Federal Partnerships' in D. Karmis and W. Norman (eds), *Theories of Federalism: A Reader* (Basingstoke, 2005)

Weber, Max, *Economy and Society*, ed G. Roth and C. Wittich, (California, 1978)

—— *From Max Weber: Essays in Sociology*, trans and ed, H. H. Gerth and C. Wright Mills (Abingdon, 2004)

Weiler, J., 'The Reformation of European Constitutionalism' (1997) 35 J Common Market Studies 97

—— 'The Autonomy of the Community Legal Order' in J. Weiler, *The Constitution of Europe* (Cambridge, 1999)

—— 'The Transformation of Europe' in J. Weiler, *The Constitution of Europe* (Cambridge, 1999)

—— 'Federalism Without Constitutionalism: Europe's *Sonderweg*' in K. Nicolaidis and R. Howse (eds), *The Federal Vision* (Oxford 2001)

Weiler, J. and Lockhart, N., ' "Taking Rights Seriously" Seriously: The European Court and its Fundamental Rights Jurisprudence' 32 Common Market L Rev 51 and 579

Wheare, K., *The Statute of Westminster and Dominion Status* (5th edn, London, 1953)

—— *The Constitutional Structure of the Commonwealth* (Oxford, 1960)

—— *Federal Government* (4th edn, Oxford, 1963)

—— *Modern Constitutions* (2nd edn, Oxford, 1966)

Whittington, K. E., *Constitutional Construction: Divided Powers and Constitutional Meaning* (Cambridge Mass., 1999)

Williams, B., 'Ethical Consistency' in B. Williams, *Problems of the Self* (Cambridge, 1973)

—— 'Consistency and Realism' in B. Williams, *Problems of the Self* (Cambridge, 1973)

Williams, M. S., 'The Uneasy Alliance of Group Representation and Deliberative Democracy', in W. Kymlicka and W. Norman (eds), *Citizenship in Diverse Societies* (Oxford, 2000)

Wilson, Lord, 'The Robustness of Conventions in a Time of Modernisation and Change' (2004) Public Law 407

Wittke, C., *The History of Parliamentary Privilege* (Ohio, 1921)

Zimbardo, P., *The Lucifer Effect: How Good People Turn Evil* (London, 2007)

Zuleeg, M., 'The European Constitution Under Constitutional Constraints: The German Scenario' (1997) European L Rev 19

Index